# HORSEPLAYERS

## Life at the Track

Ted McClelland

CHICAGO
REVIEW
PRESS

Library of Congress Cataloging-in-Publication Data

McClelland, Ted.
    Horseplayers: Life at the track / Ted McClelland.— 1st ed.
      p.  cm.
    ISBN 1-55652-567-2
     1. Horse racing—Betting—United States—Anecdotes.
    2. Horseplayers—United States—Anecdotes.    I. Title.
    SF331.M149  2005
    798.4019 0973—dc22

                                  2004028251

Some of the material in this book was originally published in the *Chicago Reader* under the name Ted Kleine. Ted Kleine is the former name of Ted McClelland.

Cover images: (top photo) Dennis O'Clair/Stone; (main photo) The Image Bank/ Archive Holdings Inc.
Cover design: Emily Brackett/Visible Logic
Interior design: Pamela Juárez

Published by Chicago Review Press, Incorporated
814 North Franklin Street
Chicago, Illinois 60610
ISBN 1-55652-567-2
Printed in the United States of America
5 4 3 2 1

# How Gambling Saved My Life

Getting hooked on gambling was the best thing that ever happened to me. No racetrack or casino would be brazen enough to print that testimonial, but there it is.

It happened in the summer of 1996, when I was twenty-nine years old. I had been living in Chicago for a year, working part-time for a publication that billed itself as the World's Greatest Newspaper, sleeping alone in a stuffy studio apartment, and writing a novel about a rock band called Rumpledforeskin.

It was late June, a few weeks after the Belmont Stakes, when my father called. His wife was coming to town for a conference, and he needed to kill an afternoon. He suggested we do it at the track.

At the time, I followed horse racing as closely as I followed the rodeo circuit—I didn't know who'd won that year's Kentucky Derby, I'd never heard of the Breeders' Cup, and I'd skipped over all the gambling poems in Charles Bukowski chapbooks—but going to the track seemed like a guy thing to do. We'd done it before. When I was growing up, my father took me, once a year, to a little harness track in Jackson, Michigan, forty miles south of our home in Lansing. It was the sleaziest place I'd ever been. The bar sold shots of bourbon in paper cups. There was a pawnshop 200 feet from the entrance. All the patrons chain-smoked and complained about the attitudes of the local police. I figured Arlington Park would have the same biker bar/bingo hall ambience. That's one reason I agreed to go.

I was mistaken. Arlington was absolutely pastoral. From the Northwest Highway, the pre-Interstate pike that links it to Chicago, the track resembled a grand resort hotel. Its roof, a cowl painted the green of ancient copper, floated above the summer trees. We walked through a stadium-sized parking lot to the east gate, where a garden spelled out A-R-L-I-N-G-T-O-N in red begonias.

It was a Monday afternoon, so the grandstand had the empty, aimless feeling of a shopping mall. I spread out my program on a table and ran my eyes across lines of statistics as dense and tiny as box scores.

I had learned to handicap—to dope out the winner of a horse race—when I was just a small child. In our family photo album, there is a picture of me holding a racing sheet as if it were a choir book. My great-uncle, Johnny Peralta, was a Wall Street short-order cook and harness racing nut who vacated his Bronx apartment every summer and checked into a motel near Monticello Raceway, in the Catskill Mountains of New York State. My Aunt Peggy always came along for the trip. She didn't seem to mind his horse fever. They had no children, and Johnny had made a lot of money in the stock market by reading *Business Week* and trading on tips from customers, so he was allowed to gamble all he wanted. I was seven in 1974, the year we visited Peggy and Johnny in their motel. He was a tall man with wavy white hair and a deep complexion (a black man from Arkansas posing as a Puerto Rican, we discovered after his death, which explained why he didn't speak with a Spanish accent). The pockets of his guayabera shirts were always filled with cellophane-wrapped cigarillos, which he puffed by the pool and in the smog-alert atmosphere of the track. Uncle Johnny guided me through the program, and when I'd learned enough to pick a horse, he ran two-dollar bets for me. My first winner was Ratsatam, a name I still remembered.

But twenty-two years had passed since then, and I didn't remember how to read the program. So I handicapped at Arlington by looking for horses who had finished second or third in their last race, figuring they were due for a win.

"I'm going to bet five dollars to win on Flash Light," I told my father, as "Call to Post" blatted through the loudspeakers and eight horses cantered out of the tunnel for the second race. "And I'm going to bet a two-dollar exacta: Flash Light first and A Sunny Delight second." (An exacta requires a gambler to pick the top two finishers, in order. They're more popular than win bets, because they pay more.)

We carried our tickets out to a bench on the apron, the concrete terrace that stair-stepped from the grandstand down to the track. The afternoon was so dazzlingly bright that the sky looked overexposed, and the white sun cast a glow on the infield willows blocking the view of the backstretch. I watched the race on the Diamond Vision screen posted across from the bleachers, but I only remember the last 200 yards, when the horses were charging past my seat. Flash Light took the lead and hurtled down the stretch like a running back headed for the end zone. I was a single guy, and this was the biggest thrill I'd had in months. Leaping from the bench, I fanned the air with my tickets, two flimsy squares of paper.

"He's gonna win!" I shouted, jumping up and down as I anticipated the finish. "He's . . . gonna . . . win!"

He won, by two-and-a-half lengths. I was so excited I didn't notice A Sunny Delight galloping in behind him, fulfilling my exacta. When I cashed my tickets, I collected forty-eight dollars. After that, I felt confident enough to attempt a trifecta, which raises the exacta's degree of difficulty by demanding the top three finishers. I used the favorites, Dreamy and Jukebox Dance, for first and third. Between them I set an eccentrically named long shot, Salukis Corazon. It was a turf race, run on a ring of grass set within the dirt track.

A beginning horseplayer picking a cold trifecta is like a guy who's never held a dart shooting three straight bull's-eyes, but my horses ran 1-2-3. The finish is still fixed in my mind, like one of those 3-D freeze-frame commercials. As Dreamy crossed the wire, the horses were perfectly spaced on the fairway-smooth course, so I could watch the numbers on their saddlecloths—my winning numbers—rush past like lottery balls whooshing from a chute.

The trifecta paid "an even hundred dollars," according to Arlington's nasal Australian race caller. This, I later learned, wasn't a lot of money, but I was now up nearly $150—three times as much as the

World's Greatest Newspaper paid me for an article. My father shook his head as I walked away from the window, stuffing twenties into my pants.

That Friday, I was supposed to meet some friends on the steps of the Art Institute for the Fourth of July fireworks. I left home early, so I could stop at the offtrack betting parlor on State Street, a gambling joint favored by film critic Gene Siskel and baseball manager Don Zimmer. The races went on past our meeting hour, but I could not drag myself from the OTB. "Maybe they'll be late," I said to myself, as I placed losing bets on the seventh, then the eighth, then the ninth. By the time I got to the museum, my friends were gone. I turned around and headed for a dingy Waldenbooks under the El tracks, where I bought the only horse racing book on the shelf: *Commonsense Handicapping* by Dick Mitchell, a computer programmer-turned-gambler. The system that had worked so well on Monday busted me out on Friday, so I figured I'd better learn to handicap.

By the end of July, I was at the track four days a week. That $150 score had ignited an immediate romance. I had always loved games—dice baseball games, war games, the puzzles in *Games* magazine—but horse racing was the most magnificent game I had ever experienced, because it was *real*. It was played with real money, bet on real animals. And it wasn't a game of chance, like the slots or the lottery or *Let's Make a Deal*. It was a game of skill and judgment, the *Jeopardy!* of gambling. At the track, the odds are not set by the house, as they are in a casino. They're set by the amount of money bet on each horse. The more money bet, the lower the odds. This is known as pari-mutuel wagering, from a French term meaning "among ourselves." Over the long haul, you can't beat a slot machine, but you can beat the races if you're smarter than all the other bettors. I learned what that felt like when I discovered Bonnie Rob running in a turf race at Arlington. He was undefeated at the track, but the crowd was letting him go at 5–1. I bet him to win, bet him in the exacta, and went home with a wad that caused an awed friend to exclaim, "You won *two hundred dollars*?"

*For Johnny Peralta, 1909–1982*

# Contents

# Acknowledgments

First of all, I have to thank my father, for getting me hooked on horse racing. And I have to thank Bonnie Rob, for keeping me hooked.

I'd also like to thank my editors at the *Chicago Reader*: Benjamin Ortiz, J. R. Jones, Patrick Arden, Kitry Krause, Holly Greenhagen, Cliff Doerksen, and Alison True. Alison kept me on the payroll, even though I was at the track every day. You can't ask for a better boss than that. She also allowed me to write a column about horseplayers. Many of those articles have become part of this book.

The public relations pros at the Chicago tracks—Jim Miller at Hawthorne, Dan Leary and Dave Zenner at Arlington—made sure I got in free every day and set up the interviews I needed.

Susan Lersch typed up the manuscript from my penciled scribblings. Susan is a playwright, and she offered encouragement and suggestions as she turned in the pages.

Cynthia Sherry convinced her bosses at Chicago Review Press to take a chance on a book about gamblers, and Lisa Rosenthal guided the manuscript to its final form. I hope to see them both out at the track again someday.

I also have to thank Kate, for tolerating first my gambling obsession, then my writing obsession. Thanks for betting on me, Kate. I'm finished now.

Most men wander in their twenties—the Germans call that age the *Wanderjahren*—but mine had been especially rootless. I'd drifted through three colleges, lived in seven cities, and never earned more than $24,000 a year. But now, finally, I had found my passion.

That August, my editor offered me a promotion to police reporter. I turned him down. The job would have doubled my salary, but it was an afternoon gig, and what good is money if you can't gamble with it? He was disappointed, but he got used to hearing a bugle in the background when I called to talk about the evening's assignments.

When an old friend asked if I was interested in a job in Seattle, I told him I was tied to Chicago.

"Ahhh," he said. "You meet a woman there?"

"No," I responded vehemently. "*Horse racing!*"

In the fall, the Thoroughbreds moved to Hawthorne Race Course, in the polluted suburb of Stickney, Illinois. At Hawthorne, I began keeping a racing log, copying the results from the newspaper into a loose-leaf binder that I carried around the track. After two-and-a-half months, I showed a balance of minus thirteen dollars. Not a bloodbath, but I had to ask myself whether it was worth spending all my afternoons at Hawthorne—a cesspool of cigarette smoke, surly ticket clerks, horse manure, shredded tickets, hot dogs vile enough to burn an inch off your stomach lining, and losing gamblers screaming rabid obscenities at horses and jockeys—if I was just going to lose money. Some days I would devote two or three hours to searching the *Daily Racing Form* for winners and still leave the track with an empty wallet. I was beginning to question the horseplayer's maxim that "the best thing in the world is to win money at the track, and the second best thing is to lose money at the track."

If I was going to win, I decided, I would need a mentor, someone who treated the track as his own personal automatic teller machine. In the winter of 1997, my second year as a horseplayer, I met John Goritz on the second floor of Sportsman's Park, which was right next door to Hawthorne. After the ninth race, most horseplayers chuck their programs into the trash and slump out to the parking lot. But John was dismembering a *Daily Racing Form* with a pair of scissors, clipping results charts from tracks all over the country. He worked like a tailor at a bolt of cloth, paring away the edges of each page and placing them atop a neatly trimmed stack. He had emptied his backpack, setting out cellophane bags filled with years of *Chicago Sun-Times* racing pages. Half the horseplayers at Sportsman's couldn't even read the *Form*, which was the *Wall Street Journal* of horse racing, with pages of agate-type statistics on every race. They relied on dollar-fifty tip sheets or newspaper touts. But this man was a scholar.

"You've got a ton of stuff here," I said.

"I've been making my living out here for eight years," he told me, working his scissors. "I hit the twin trifecta at Hawthorne for $24,000 last year. That's the only thing keeping me going. I don't make a lot of money at this. A lot of times I starve."

The scholar was thirtyish, short and pudgy with thinning red hair and the mug of an extra from *On the Waterfront*. He wore a grubby Raiders jacket, an old purple T-shirt, and jeans as baggy as a rhino's skin.

"Come out here tomorrow and I'll teach you how to look at the horses," he said, as he loaded papers into his backpack. "That's the key to this whole game. I used to work with horses, and if you know how to look at them, you'll own this fucking place."

I couldn't meet John at the track that Sunday; the cops towed my car and I had to go downtown to bail it out. But I found him the next day, after the second race, making notations on his *Form* with a red pen. He looked exhausted.

"I was up until five in the morning handicapping the Fair Grounds," he said, referring to a racetrack in New Orleans. I looked down at his newspaper. Every horse's record had been marked up with a private code of ovals, lines, numerals, and letters. "I got home at six o'clock last night, and I spent eleven hours on this."

Sportsman's broadcasted races from tracks all over the country, and John was beating up on three at once: the Fair Grounds in New

Orleans, Gulfstream Park in Hallandale, Florida, and the home track. I, meanwhile, had just lost thirty dollars on Sally's Hero, a bum colt who'd run out of the money in the second.

As the bugle sounded, heralding the horses' arrival on the track for the third race, John yanked on his Raiders jacket and we hustled outside to watch the post parade. My father had given me a pair of Bushnell 15x binoculars for Christmas, and I trained them on the cavalcade of horseflesh.

"Do you see any horses that look really straight, that their legs are lined up really straight?" John asked.

"The 2 looks good."

The horse I was looking at, Danzig's Design, walked as though his spine were an iron rod. No Civil War general's horse had ever looked so controlled, I thought.

"Are you going to bet him?"

"I'm not going to bet this race."

"How come?" John asked, seeming offended that I'd waste his lesson.

"I like Fast Phone, but he's only even money, so he's not worth betting on."

"So bet on the 2," John insisted.

"Look at his record." I spread out my *Form*. "He hasn't been close in his last three races."

I ran out to the bleachers to watch the race. Danzig's Design leapt from the starting gate, led all the way around the track, and won by a head, paying $9.80 for every two dollars bet to win.

Back in the grandstand, I found John sitting with his head in his arms.

"You were right about that 2," he moaned. "Jesus, we should have bet that 2 horse. If we had just bet twenty dollars, we could have won ninety-eight bucks."

For a horseplayer, the only thing worse than losing money is not winning money you should have won, since the sums involved are much larger. John whipped open his *Form* to Danzig's Design's record.

The horse had won a third of his races at Sportsman's. Fast Phone was 1-for-16.

"Look at that. It was obvious. Look how good he does at Sportsman's. He loves Sportsman's."

In the eighth race, I bet thirty dollars on Don't Waste Time, who had won in his first race of the year at Sportsman's.

"See, he loves this track," I insisted, trying to apply the lesson I'd learned earlier in the day.

John disagreed. He liked Notamomentosoon, who figured to take the early lead, and who was running on the drug Lasix for the first time. (Lasix is a diuretic that prevents internal bleeding caused by exertion.) Notamomentosoon jumped to the front of the pack and won by a length.

Now I was out $142, my worst one-day ass-whipping ever. John tallied up his booty. He'd beaten all three tracks, for $272, but he seemed more exhausted than excited. He then had to drive twenty-five miles to Balmoral Park in Crete, Illinois, for an evening of harness racing. By the time Balmoral completed its card, he would have spent twenty-nine of the last thirty-four hours either gambling or handicapping.

"I'm starting to get burned out on this," he admitted, as he packed away his charts and notebooks. "I've been doing it for eight years. I don't have a life. I don't even have a girlfriend. All I do is handicap and go to the track. I feel like a bond trader."

That was in February. By March, after a month of John's tutelage, his horseplaying skills began to rub off on me. I was examining horses with a veterinarian's eye. I was taking notes on races. I was cutting out charts and storing them in the satchel I took to the track. My studiousness was rewarded when I hit a spectacular winning streak.

It started on a Friday afternoon in the fourth race. All the touts were pushing A New Way of Life, who had finished second in several recent races but hadn't actually won in two years. You might as well have bet on the Cubs. I liked the number 7 horse, Bold Jonathan, who had won his last race while weaving through traffic like Jeff Gordon at Daytona.

When the odds came up on the tote board, I swear to God I thought it was my birthday. A New Way of Life was 1–2. This was an underlay of stupendous proportions. (An underlay is a horse whose chances of winning are less than its odds. It's similar to the Wall Street concept of an overvalued stock. Imagine someone tried to sell you stock in Hyundai for $500 a share. Would you buy it? I don't think so. That's how out of proportion A New Way of Life's chances were to his odds.) Meanwhile, Bold Jonathan was 11–1, while Oconto, another horse with a strong chance to win, was 6–1. I panted after those odds the way the hart panteth after the water brooks in the psalm. I ran to a window, where I bet twenty-five dollars on number 7, Bold Jonathan, and fifteen dollars on number 6, Oconto.

I have saved the chart of this race for inclusion in my posthumous papers. Here's what it says: "BOLD JONATHAN raced in good position from the start, was beginning his rally when he shied away from A NEW WAY OF LIFE in the stretch, exchanged bumps with that rival and was offstrided while coming in a bit late, then prevailed by a narrow margin."

As Bold Jonathan crossed the finish line, I practically dissolved with ecstasy. My skull filled with helium. Then the red neon Inquiry sign on the tote board lit up. Mark Guidry, A New Way of Life's jockey, had complained about the bumping and demanded that Bold Jonathan be disqualified. I ran inside to watch a replay of the stretch run. It was hard to tell who'd started the shoving match, but since Guidry was the winningest rider at Sportsman's, I figured the stewards would take his side. The veteran gambler next to me agreed.

"Looks like that 7's coming down," he said.

The stewards rewound the tape and played it again. And again. The numbers 7 and 4 blinked on the tote board. If the 7 came down, I vowed to leave the track and never again play this rigged game. Then a fire bell rang, signaling that the result was official. I looked at the tote board: Bold Jonathan's number was still on top, and he was paying off at twenty-seven dollars for every two dollars invested. When I presented my twenty-five-dollar ticket to the teller, he gave me back $337, my biggest score ever. Yes yes yes oh yes. Say it over and over again, like the last sentence of *Ulysses*. Never had I felt so blessed. I thanked God for creating this world and thanked Him again for putting racetracks in it.

For the next week, I thought I was the hottest prospect in American handicapping. I imagined I could be like Martin Ritt, the film director who made his living at the New York tracks when he was blacklisted during the 1950s. Betting on horses was going to be a part-time job, a sideline to my writing. Every afternoon as I shouldered my satchel for the trip to the track, I thought, "It's time to go to work." My obsession with horses reached unnatural levels: when the *Sports Illustrated* swimsuit issue came out, I flipped past the bikini shots, looking for articles about racing. At gas stations, when I asked for "ten dollars on number five," my tongue wanted to add "to win." I called my father to tell him, "I'm coming home the weekend of the twenty-ninth. That's when they're having the Dubai World Cup," a lucrative international horse race.

"That's also Easter weekend," he reminded me.

"Is it? I didn't see anything about that in the *Racing Form*."

I conceived a system that was sure to bring me a profit: bet fifty dollars on horses who look like cinches and are going off at odds of 7–5 or better. At first it worked beautifully. That Wednesday, I hit a horse named L'Eric who paid off at 2–1, and on Friday I scored with a pair of 2–1 shots, Laugh Alot and She's Just Winking, putting me up over $700 since the beginning of the streak.

But then, just as night follows day, just as vultures follow lions, I began losing. Badly. It started in Michigan, during the Dubai World Cup weekend. I wanted to show off my brilliant handicapping to my father, so we drove to a small harness track near Flint that simulcasted races from around the country. Before the fourth at Sportsman's, I announced that Fortunate Wish was a lock and went to the window to bet fifty dollars. I also bet ten dollars for my father, who believed my stories of horse racing triumphs and trusted me to invest his cash.

Fortunate Wish finished third. My other surefire bet, Pappa Lee, came in sixth, so I was out $100 for the day. After that it got worse. Much worse.

The losing streak lasted two weeks. After going that long without cashing a ticket, I was nearly deranged. I lost all confidence in my ability to pick winners and was beginning to wonder whether I could make a correct decision about anything. One morning, I stood in front of my closet, unable to choose a shirt. Why get dressed? I thought. I'll screw that up, too.

I was getting tension headaches every time I went to Sportsman's Park. Yet I never left the track without buying the next day's *Form* and searching it for the horse who would get me off the schneid (a losing streak). I wanted a magic insight, like the feverish boy in D. H. Lawrence's short story "The Rocking-Horse Winner," who changes his family's fortunes when he picks the winner of the Epsom Derby. "It's Malabar!" he cries, just before dropping dead.

Eventually I found my Malabar. Allens Alley had stumbled out of the starting gate and then rallied to finish second by a nose. If he got a decent start in his next race, he was sure to win. And, indeed, Allens Alley won by two lengths, at odds of 7–2. A handsome payoff—or it would have been, if I'd been at the track. But Allens Alley won on a day I had decided to stay home and take a break from this game that was tearing down the wall that separated me from madness.

The next morning, when I read the Sportsman's results in the paper, I screamed in anguish. "Mother fuck! The one day I don't go to the track, my horse wins! I haven't had a winner in a week and a fucking half, and now that I finally pick one, I'm not there to bet him. How do you beat this game? How, how, how? Do you have to be there every day of your fucking life?"

The answer to that question, I realized, was yes.

Writing is an isolated, self-absorbed lifestyle, but gambling is on an entirely different plane of selfishness. No wonder everyone I'd met at the track was single or divorced. Charles Bukowski, the legendary poet/soak/horseplayer, once wrote that any man who can beat the horses should be painting or writing symphonies or making some woman happy. I want to ask, when would he find the time? A career in gambling is worth it only if you are so free-spirited and/or asocial that you can never endure the confinements of marriage or employment. Horseplayers make sacrifices that would horrify the most driven starving artist in his third-floor walk-up, because their goal isn't money or fame, but rather simply to keep playing the horses. John felt he'd pissed away his youth pursuing the skills that netted him ten grand a year.

"The old-timers, the horses ruined 'em, and they're ruining me, too," he said. "I see myself gettin' older and my life gettin' wasted away, even though I make money at it. For $10,000 a year you could be a gas station attendant or something. This ain't easy. This is hard work what I do."

After Allens Alley won, I stopped trying to gamble for a living. Once I realized that a part-timer couldn't turn a profit, it was an easy decision to go to the track only on Saturdays, never taking more than forty bucks. But I found another way to make money off horse racing. I wrote an article about John and sold it to the *Chicago Reader*, a weekly newspaper that loved stories about esoteric subjects such as bee stings, archaeology, and, as it turned out, handicapping. They ran it on the cover and paid me $1,200, which I split with John. I had always justified my trips to the track by telling myself, "Hey, if you wanna be a writer, you gotta have something to write about." Now I was vindicated. I continued to write for the *Reader*, covering other seedy male obsessions—fishing, playing with military miniatures, politics—and, eventually, they hired me as a full-time reporter. John drifted away from the track, too. The last time I saw him, he was smoking a joint outside the Hawthorne clubhouse. Later on, I heard a rumor that he'd gotten on the wrong side of a judge in Wisconsin.

The more energy I devoted to journalism, the less remained for gambling. By the turn of the century, four years after I'd first caught horse fever, I was going to the track just a few days a year, mostly for

Feast Days: the Kentucky Derby, the Arlington Million, the Breeders' Cup. Playing the horses had to be an all-consuming passion or it had to be a hobby, pursued with two- and five-dollar bets. My schooling with John had taught me that dilettantes are doomed to lose their money to racetrack lifers. I always wondered, though, whether I could beat the races if I made it a full-time job. Andrew Beyer, the *Washington Post* columnist and high priest of American handicapping, once wrote, "As difficult as it is, anyone who loves handicapping ought to make at least one attempt in his life to do it seriously. Although handicapping can be wonderfully entertaining as a casual hobby, there is nothing quite so satisfying for a horseplayer as the knowledge that he can make a profit from the game."

Most of us have a Life List. Or maybe we have a single ambition, which we have to achieve to feel fulfilled on our deathbeds. Some people have to climb the highest mountain on every continent. Some people have to run an ultramarathon. Some people have to own every James Brown LP on vinyl or decorate their houses entirely in Coca-Cola memorabilia. I had to go back to the track. It may sound like a frivolous way to spend one of the forty or fifty years I had left, but finding out whether I could beat the races was one of the great unanswered questions of my life. I had to settle it while I was still young and single, not when I was retired, beyond ambition, and, God forbid, living on a fixed income that might cramp my betting.

As it happens, writing a book was my other unrealized ambition. I figured out a way to satisfy both: I would write about the year I spent trying to beat the races and all the odd characters I met along the way. The publisher of this volume liked the idea and gave me a $4,000 advance on royalties. That was my bankroll. If you mean to gamble seriously, you must have a bankroll, a fund set aside for betting. It prevents you from choking on a hot $100 wager, because you're thinking, "I don't get paid for another week, and I need gas money."

My living expenses were covered because the *Reader*, bless them, agreed to let me spend the year writing a column about the track. It was just the sort of eccentric project they love, or at least tolerate. On the first Saturday in March, New Year's Day on the Chicago racing calendar, I stepped off the Cicero Avenue bus and walked toward Hawthorne Race Course, my gait quickened by a sharp, unbroken wind and by the delicious anticipation of gambling nonstop for the next ten months.

# 1

# The Blind Man and the Hustler

Hawthorne Race Course is a smoky urban racetrack on the western fringe of Chicago. It was laid out in pastureland over a century ago, but the city has overwhelmed it and suburbia leapt past it, so its highest seats look beyond the dirt oval onto an industrial skyline of round-bellied oil tanks and cigarette-slim chimneys, a vista that has earned it the nickname Refinery Downs. Hawthorne's three-tiered brick grandstand, as imposing as an old ironworks, replaced a sleeker model that was burned to the ground in 1978, supposedly by a pair of grifters who'd fixed a race and were trying to destroy the evidence. The air over the neighborhood is scented with a chemical tang from the world's largest sewage treatment plant, located a few blocks from the horse barns.

The blind man had been begging outside Hawthorne for decades. The track was open in the chilly months of spring and fall, and he sat outside the doors in the hour before post time, clattering his tin cup like a Salvation Army bell, crying, "Please help the bliiiiind" in a wood-wind alto. In his paint-black sunglasses, he looked like a Maxwell Street bluesman. His cane was wrapped in rags and carpet strips, with an American flag bobbing from the handle. Hanging from his neck was an AM/FM radio, nested in a tangle of chains and trinkets.

Most horseplayers ignored the blind man as they lurched toward the doors. But I was hoping to see him squatting on his plastic chair. As I hurried across the parking lot, I felt in the pocket of my parka for a twenty-dollar bill to drop in his cup. I owed him.

A year and a half before, on an idle November afternoon during what Nelson Algren, another Chicago horseplayer, once called "that smoke-colored season between Indian summer and December's first true snow," I'd dropped a twenty in the blind man's cup. I wasn't trying to buy luck. I was writing a color piece on the racetrack for the *Reader*, and I wanted an interview. The bill was a terrific icebreaker. ("Twenty dollars?" he sang, his voice rising to the pitch of a penny-whistle. "Is this really a twenty? Oooh, a twenty-dollar bill. You're gonna make me get up and dance. You're gonna see an old blind man dance. Twenty dollars! You can ask me whatever you want.") We talked for half an hour in the cold, then I went inside and hit a $660 exacta. There was some serious juju in that cup.

The blind man was straddling a chair at the foot of the concrete ramp that leads to the two-dollar gate. As soon as the old beggar heard my boots scuffling up the ramp, he rattled his cup to arrest them. I stopped and called out to him.

"Who's that?" he asked, tilting his blank eyes in my direction.

"It's Ted. Remember me?"

"Taaaid," he drawled excitedly. "Sure, I remember. You got another twenty for me?"

"I've got another twenty for you."

The blind man extended a hand as worn as an old golf glove. I fed the bill to its hunting fingertips.

"I need some luck this year," I said. "You've always brought me good luck."

"You have good luck when you help the blind," he assured me. "It's in the Bible. When you help the blind, you have good luck. I don't know where it's in the Bible, but I heard it's in the Bible."

The blind man's name was Lewis. He never revealed his last name, because he feared that "Soc' Security" would cut off his check if they discovered he was making money at the track. He claimed to be eighty—"I done made eighty, young man," he'd once told me—but in his timeless, lightless mind he could not estimate how many years he had been sitting outside Hawthorne. It started sometime after he went blind. His sight began to dim when he was in his twenties, due to a condition "generated down through the family." He moved to Chicago to see a doctor, who sent him to a hospital for "fever therapy," raising his temperature to save his eyes. It didn't help. During those sunset years, Lewis worked as a shoveler in a coal yard, paying a friend to drive him to work.

Once the shades closed completely, Lewis started begging outside the track. He had never seen a horse race, even though he'd grown up in Louisville, home of the Kentucky Derby. But horse racing, it seemed to him, was about numbers—a horse's number in the betting program, the dollars and cents of the payoffs—and numbers were something he could still apprehend.

"I didn't know anything about playing the horses until I went blind," he said. "I figured I had to do something to make money. I bet a 1-2-3 trifecta, and it won. It paid $270."

Lewis began each day by betting the Daily Double, trying to pick the winners of the first two races. He used numerology to make his selections. But in this, he needed help. Lingering behind him was a wall-eyed man in a green army jacket. Glenn was with the blind man most afternoons, ready to fetch his coffee and run his bets in exchange for a few of the bills that landed in the cup.

"Glenn, you got the paper?" he asked. Glenn slid the *Chicago Sun-Times* from under his arm and opened it to the "Hawthorne Line," in which the newspaper's handicapper ranked the horses in each race, listing them by name and program number. Lewis was only interested in the numbers.

"Add up the numbers of the top three horses in the first race and the last horse in the first three races," Lewis told Glenn. "What that add up to?"

"Twenty-four," Glenn responded.

"Now, count down twenty-four horses."

Glenn's index finger tapped down the page.

"What number you come up with?"

"Five."

"Number 5 horse in the first race," Lewis declared. "You bet that 5 horse, you'll win some money. Daily Double's going to be 5-6."

Lewis pulled a pair of origami-folded singles from his pocket and asked Glenn to run inside and bet the Daily Double, using number 5, Limit Up, in the first race, and number 6, Light As a Cat, in the second.

There is a large school of horseplayers that treats the races as a lottery, rather than as a competition between animals. I know a man named 1-2-3 Don who's so devoted to the first three cardinal numbers that he always plays them in the exacta, and he drives a car with the license plate "DON D 123." He claims this system produces bigger profits than handicapping, or "logic," as he calls it. These gamblers never cheer horses by name, only by the numbers on their saddlecloths. "Come on with that 8!" they shout during a stretch run, or "Get that 2 up there!" After the race is over, they blame themselves for getting the numbers wrong. "Damn!" they curse. "It came 1-3-5 and I had it 1-5-3." The horses change every race, but the numbers don't, so the superstitious believe they form recurring patterns. If an old woman's lucky numbers are 6 and 3, and her 6-3 exacta came in for $250 (the payoffs on numbers bets are often large, since there's no handicapping logic behind them), it's bound to come in again someday, isn't it?

Numbers players never buy the *Form*. They can't be bothered with all that information. They tear out the tip sheet from the *Chicago Sun-Times* or buy the *Green Sheet* ("Illinois Sports News Finest Little Newspaper"), which offers exacta, trifecta, and superfecta (a wager requiring bettors to pick the top four finishers in a race), combinations that hit about as often as the figures in lottery dream books.

I asked Lewis how long it had been since he'd picked a winner.

"Oh, I don't know," he said. "'Bout a year ago."

But he seemed extremely confident about his 5 horse, and I hadn't had time to handicap, so I bet two dollars on the 5-6 Daily Double.

It didn't come in. In fact, Lewis's 5 horse finished last. After the race, Glenn hurried outside to report the results.

"How much we get?" Lewis asked excitedly.

"Hold out your hand," Glenn teased, dangling the losing ticket.

"No. Don't make me guess."

"Come on. Hold out your hand."

Lewis's scaly palm peeked out from a nylon cuff. Glenn set the wrinkled ticket in its hollow.

"We didn't get nothin'," he said. "That 5 horse ran last."

Lewis counted out eight quarters and handed them to Glenn. There was a second race to bet.

"You hold this," he said, as the coins dripped into Glenn's hand. "My luck ain't been good."

Glenn, who always needed two dollars, could have bet Lewis's money on his own horse, just as he could have lied and kept the winnings if Lewis's Double had come in. But the blind man trusted Glenn. And Glenn looked out for the blind man, fetching him coffee from the snack bar, reading to him from the newspaper, watching over his cup to make sure nobody filched a coin. Partly, he was loyal because Lewis was blessed with blindness to bring in the money and always tipped Glenn after a good day. But Glenn had been hustling at Hawthorne for over a dozen years, so he knew the track was full of desperate guys who would do anything for a two-dollar bet, including steal from a blind man.

After consulting the *Chicago Sun-Times*—his *I Ching*, his Magic 8 Ball—Lewis determined that the 3 horse, Golden Ellen, would win the second. Glenn dutifully bought him a ticket, even though it contradicted Lewis's earlier declaration that Light As a Cat would win, but Lewis left for the bus before the race even started. If the 3 won, his "housekeeper," the woman who cleaned his apartment and chauffeured him to the track, would cash the ticket tomorrow. And unlike Glenn, she wouldn't ask for a tip.

"If my number comes in, them dudes'll be beggin' me," Lewis whispered, when Glenn was out of earshot. "I got to get on the bus and get out of here."

He stood up and walked toward a wall. I grabbed the sleeve of his parka and then led him to the Hawthorne Shuttle, a minibus that plies the quarter mile between the grandstand and Cicero Avenue. Lewis lifted himself onto the bus a little bit at a time, resting both feet on each step before attempting the next. As soon as the smoked doors unfolded behind him, I jogged up the ramp and banged on a locked door, motioning for the security guard to let me in. I flashed the stamp on my hand to prove I'd already paid admission. I didn't want to miss the second race.

Glenn was standing by the rail, at the bottom of the sloping asphalt apron. He was alone out there. All the other gamblers were inside, watching the races on closed-circuit television, leaving the apron as deserted as Daley Plaza on a winter holiday. Glenn's army jacket was zipped against the chill, and a watch cap flattened his graying curls. The sun was pale and bright, but there was no warmth in its light. You could see the cold. You could hear it. The refinery smokestacks unfurled pale pennants of smoke, outlined sharply against the crisp sky. Above our heads, a portly Southwest Airlines jet, brightly colored as a Japanese carp, swayed to the bottom of the sky, drifting toward Midway Airport, three miles to the south. Its engines sounded as muffled, as far away, as static from a transistor radio.

"It's gonna be hard to hustle this year," Glenn said, as the second-race horses jogged past in their warm-up and the clock on the brick tote board clicked down the seconds to post time.

Before 2003 Hawthorne had let the masses in free and charged $1.75 for a program, or a "book" as Glenn called it. Glenn picked programs up off the floor and peddled them to late-arriving gamblers for a buck. Management should have loved him. He kept the track clean, and he bet all his earnings on the horses. But now Hawthorne was under new ownership. The track had merged with Sportsman's Park, which was right next door on Cicero Avenue. The two had operated side-by-side since the 1920s, when Al Capone founded Sportsman's as a dog track. Sportsman's eventually came into the possession of the Bidwill family, which also owned the Chicago Cardinals football team. In 1998 Charles Bidwill III, the family scion, converted Sportsman's into a dual racetrack/motor speedway by building a 60,000-seat erector set grandstand and pouring an asphalt racing oval. With its high walls and concrete infield, the new project looked like a prison yard. Horses and cars had never mixed well on the streets, and they didn't mix at Sportsman's, either. Horses broke their legs on the thin cushion of dirt spread over the asphalt. NASCAR decided to hold its local race in Joliet, Illinois, which was closer to its rural audience. Sportsman's was tagged for demolition, and the Bidwills began running their spring meet at Hawthorne.

The motor speedway fiasco cost the Bidwills over $30 million. It was costing Glenn money, too, because Hawthorne was now charging a two-dollar admission and throwing in a program, which meant he no longer had a market for his secondhand "books."

"They ruined the hustle," he complained. "They're giving everybody a book when they come in. I used to be able to sell books outside the door. I made twenty or thirty dollars a day sometimes."

Glenn stopped talking, so we could watch Lewis's horse finish eighth. As a seer, Lewis was not exactly Tiresias. Glenn had done better. His horse had finished second. But he'd bet it to win. The ticket spun from his hand like a white leaf.

"Should have bet to place," he groaned.

Then Glenn ran off to aid another infirm gambler: a man in a wheelchair who needed his betting money carried to the window. He might have been the Hawthorne chapter of Little Brothers to the Elderly, except he had a financial interest.

"I'm gonna run a trifecta bet for this dude," he said, "and I'm gonna put in forty cents. That's all I got left. My forty cents may turn into ten dollars. Then I'll be able to bet again."

Glenn had not expected to spend his forties grifting at the track. He'd begun his working life as a crane operator at the U.S. Steel Works on the South Side. In the late 1970s, he was earning $40,000 a year—"more than a schoolteacher. I thought that was it."

Chicago doesn't make steel anymore. Glenn was laid off in 1986. When he worked at the mill, he'd spent every payday at the track, so once he was tossed out, he decided to turn it into a full-time occupation. In seventeen years he'd worked every hustle known to a man with an empty wallet and an urge to bet the Daily Double. For a while, he stood outside an offtrack betting parlor in the Loop, selling photocopied programs at far below the cost of real programs. The police broke up that scam. Glenn lived with his sister, who would always provide him a bed, since he'd put her through nursing school when he was a steelworker.

"I got brothers who are cops, I got a sister who makes $70,000 a year at the Board of Trade," he said. "They're wondering why I do this. It's my livelihood. I'm the black sheep of the family, but they ain't never gonna kick me out. When I was making $40,000 a year, I'd do anything for anyone."

U

There are worse addictions than horse racing. Glenn knew it, because he'd suffered most of them. As a young man, he'd played cards and shot dice with high-rolling South Side gangstas who laid out drug buffets at their gambling parties.

Back then, Glenn had blown his money at the racetrack every afternoon; in the evenings, he'd take whatever was left to the drug houses.

"I used to do cocaine, heroin," he told me once. "I went to four programs before I finally got clean. I been clean for five-and-a-half years. Betting is a different high from drugs. With drugs, you don't get nothin' back. When I got twenty dollars, I'd go straight out to the West Side, get me a bag. It was take a smoke, you'd be in the twilight zone. But that was it. You wouldn't have nothin' left. Here, you bet five dollars, you might be able to get some more money to keep gambling."

◡

That Monday, the blind man was all alone at the bottom of the ramp, squatting on an overturned bucket.

"Where's Glenn?" I asked.

"He probably won't be here today," Lewis said. "Today's the third. He got his check."

"I didn't know he got a check."

"Probably a lot of people get Soc' Security checks you don't know about."

"Probably," I said. "So how are you going to pick your Daily Double?"

"I got a paper."

Lewis gripped the head of his cane as though it were a wizard's staff and lifted himself off the bucket with a hydraulic slowness. A blanket drooped over the rim. I peeled it away and found a ragged-edged *Chicago Sun-Times* racing page. It was something anyone could buy for thirty-five cents, but Lewis was hiding it as is if were a CIA codebook.

"What do you want me to do?" I asked, unfolding the sheet so Lewis could sit down again.

"I want you to add up the top and bottom numbers in the first three races."

"Thirty-one," I said, after summing in my head.

"Now, I want you to add up the top and bottom numbers in the last three races."

"Forty."

"That's seventy-one. Now, count down seventy-one horses."

My finger ticked down the page until Lewis asked, "What race you up to?"

"The eighth."

"Go to the second horse in the eighth race."

"We need to do six more to get to seventy-one," I pointed out.

"Well, OK," he said. "Go to the sixth horse down."

"The sixth horse is number 2, Mr. Sandstorm."

"Now, what's the horse above that?"

"Eight."

"The 8 horse in the first race," Lewis pronounced. "That's the winner!"

"There is no 8 horse in the first race," I said.

I had to break that to him. The track won't let you bet a number that doesn't go along with a horse.

"No 8?" he keened. He sounded disappointed. After a meditative moment, he revised his system.

"Well, count down three more horses in the eighth race. What's that?"

"The 10. There's no 10 in the first race, either."

"No 10?"

"Nope. There are only six horses in the first race."

Lewis was stumped.

"What's the first horse in the second race?" he blurted.

"Two," I said.

"I think it could be a 3-2 Double. Yup, that could be it."

"How'd you get that?" I asked.

"I added three and two to get five."

This was like the scene from *A Day at the Races*, in which Chico sells Groucho a set of handicapping books from an ice cream cart, then sells him a codebook so he can understand the books, then sells him a key to understanding the code.

I didn't ask how the number five had been dragged into this. It was illogical to demand logic from Lewis's handicapping. He made it all up as he went along.

"I think the 3 in the first race," Lewis affirmed to himself. "I think I'll just play that 3 to win."

He delved into his pants pocket and hauled up two crinkled bills. Coins he distinguished by feel. Bills he didn't need to. He only got singles. I took the money into the murmuring bazaar that was the Hawthorne grandstand and stood in a betting line behind a Mexican in a cowboy hat and a white-haired retiree whose windbreaker sagged around his bones.

In the grandstand, the grill sold fried chicken, collard greens, and peach cobbler. The cigarette smoke was not as heavy as it had been years ago, when it clouded as thickly as mustard gas on the Western Front and soaked into clothing, skin, and the newsprint of my *Racing Form*, but there were still afternoons when sheer gray scarves floated beneath the ceiling. Over by the barbershop, old men threw spades and bid whist across a scarred tabletop. In the carrels facing the television monitors, which showed races from all across the country, you'd find paper baskets full of chicken bones and discarded tickets from Aqueduct, Calder, Laurel, Turfway, and the Fair Grounds. The pleas of the gamblers, some sacred, some profane, were as loud as the barking of brokers at the Mercantile Exchange. You could have heard a $100 bettor named Pops pounding a tabletop with his padded palm, booming, "And won! And won! And won!" when his horse came in. Or an old woman praying publicly for her two-dollar bet to hang on in the stretch, crying, "Come on, Lord! Come on, Lord!" as she rocked in her chair.

I bet Lewis's money on his 3 horse and then hustled outside to wait by the starting gate for the horses to run free.

Lewis's 3 horse, Shelby's Dancer, was the 2–1 favorite. When the doors of his stall boomed open, he bounded to the lead. Around the first turn, he shaped his path to the rail, clocking the quarter mile in twenty-five and one-fifth seconds, a cantering pace that should have left him plenty of kick for the final yards. The horses ran single file up the backstretch, as distant as approaching cavalry in a western. Nobody tried to pass Shelby's Dancer. Like long-distance runners on the first lap of a mile race, the jockeys were putting in the distance, waiting for the turn to make their moves. I watched the tote board. The half-mile time was fifty seconds. I beamed as I thought about presenting Lewis with six dollars.

Shelby's Dancer still had the lead at the head of the stretch, but the other colts were closing on him. Overwhelmed by the pressure, he lost his will to run, and two rivals thundered by. It happens a lot with cheap (meaning slow) horses. This was a $5,000 claiming race, meaning the horses were for sale to any owner who could put up that paltry fee. Shelby's Dancer didn't find any takers.

I slipped out front to report the results.

"Lewis, your horse finished third."

His head swiveled toward my voice.

"Who won?" he asked.

"The 4." The winner's name was Moe Dickstein, but only the track announcer referred to horses by their names.

"The 4? You liked that 4 the other day."

"Yeah, but that was a different 4."

The first race over, Lewis's housekeeper appeared to drive him home. He picked up his bucket, took the arm of her camel-hair coat, and trundled out to the parking lot.

# 2

# If Wishes Were Horses

Since the Hawthorne management had ruined Glenn's bookselling scheme, he needed a new way to make money at the track. So he started stooping—searching the floors, the counters, and the trash cans for tossed-out tickets. Stooping, or, as Glenn called it, "ticket-picking," is one of the oldest hustles. The grandstand of any racetrack is littered with betting slips, like the aftermath of a ticker-tape parade for eighth-place horses. Most of them are losers, but there are always a few live ones down there, discarded by mistake. A man named Herb Forneck used to make his living at the Chicago tracks by turning over tickets with his shoe. When Sportsman's Park was open, a character known as the Garbageman appeared each afternoon around the eighth race, toting a plastic bag. He'd scoop tickets off the floor, sort through them at home, and return the next day to cash the winners. Sportsman's was the site of the greatest day in Chicago stooping history. It happened one afternoon in 1990. After the ninth race, the stewards awarded place and show to the wrong horses, and the track started paying out money. By the time the mistake was fixed, hundreds of disgusted gamblers had thrown out tickets with the real winning combination.

"There were some sharpies who realized they'd put up the wrong numbers," recalled a handicapper who witnessed the scramble. "One guy runs through the third-floor grandstand, grabs the bag out of the trash can, ties a knot in it, runs to the next trash can, grabs that bag, and he was flying downstairs with the trash bags, presumably to take home and look through. People turned into stoopers who never were."

Glenn had been stooping casually for years, but he'd only made one big score. On Breeders' Cup Day in 2002 he idly swept a ticket off a counter, slipped it into a betting machine, and saw the figure "$420" pop up on the screen. Ecstatic, he cashed the ticket, bought beers for himself and a few friends, and then spent the rest of the afternoon betting like a big shooter. That night, he went home with nothing but the bus pass he carries so he won't gamble away his busfare.

There was a difference between Glenn and Herb Forneck, or between Glenn and the Garbageman. Herb Forneck and the Garbageman were pros, the racetrack's version of scrap-metal collectors who troll the alleys in pickup trucks, searching for junk. Glenn was a gambling addict looking for his next bet. He always needed money. No matter how much he won, no matter how much he hustled, he gambled it away, every cent of it.

One day, in late winter, Glenn showed up at the track with $100 in his pocket, a grant from his brothers and sisters. He clicked through the gate at ten o'clock, half an hour before the track started charging admission. Glenn always tried to get to Hawthorne before ten thirty in the morning, so he could skirt the two-buck admission.

The first race wasn't until one o'clock, but Glenn didn't have to wait that long to get a bet down. Like most racetracks, Hawthorne offers full-card simulcasting. It broadcasts, and takes wagers on, every race at every major track in North America. The action started at eleven thirty, with the first race at Tampa Bay Downs, and lasted until midnight, when the last horse crossed the finish line at a floodlit harness track in California. Illinois legalized simulcasting in 1995. (Before that, tracks had only taken bets on big out-of-town events, such as the Kentucky Derby.) So now, instead of nine races a day, there were over 300. Glenn bet on as many as he could afford.

When I walked into the track around twelve thirty, he was gazing at a bank of televisions above the betting windows on the first floor of the grandstand. It looked like the television department at Circuit City. Out-of-sync screens flashed carnival-colored logos: Gulfstream Park, outside Miami, was a hot mauve; Tampa Bay Downs, a golf-course green; Aqueduct, in frozen Queens, a chilly blue. Striped down the side of each screen were the odds tables, with each horse's number embedded in a tab the color of its saddle towel: red for 1, white for 2, blue for 3, yellow for 4, green for 5, and so on, to lime green for 12—the same colors at every track.

"I'm gettin' kinda short," Glenn said. "I only got about ten bucks left. There's a race at Turfway coming up in a minute."

Glenn didn't have a program, so he let the other bettors do his handicapping. If the crowd liked a horse, he usually liked it, too.

"I think I'm gonna play the chalk here," he said.

The chalk is the favorite, so called because, in the days before tote boards, track bookmakers scribbled their shifting odds on chalkboards. Favorites don't pay much—this one was 9–5, which meant it would return $5.80 on a two-dollar bet—but they win a third of all races, and Glenn's money was so tight he needed a winner to keep going. Chasing long shots is for guys with big bankrolls, guys who can afford to suck up a lot of losers before they hit the jackpot.

Glenn raced to a betting terminal, but the horses at Kentucky's Turfway Park  were out of the gate before he could punch in his bet. He backed away from the machine and scanned the televisions for the next race. The second at Laurel, in a suburb of Washington, D.C., was a minute away. Glenn bet five dollars to place on the favorite there and then stepped back to watch the race with his arms folded across his black sweatshirt. He'd lost plenty of bets, so when his chalk straggled home fifth, he just scrunched his moustache and wobbled his head in resignation.

"That's it, man. I'm broke."

It was time to stoop. Glenn donned the wire-rimmed glasses that helped him read racing programs and other fine print and headed for the east end of the grandstand. On the way, he spotted Billy. Billy, who is also known as Bucky because of the two parchment-colored incisors that nibble at his lower lip, was slouching in front of a glass case holding an exhibit on sixteen-inch softball, a pastime unique to Chicago. His untrimmed blond pageboy was stringy and greasy, his Miami Dolphins jacket as disheveled as the body it warmed. A multi-sport hustler, Billy spent his summers selling "Cubs Suck" T-shirts outside Sox Park. But in the winter, he was at the track, and when he was at the track, he stooped. No one at Hawthorne was more thorough: Billy wrote down the winners from every track, so he could compare them to the numbers on picked-up tickets. He was a walking results ticker—even serious gamblers would ask him, "Who won the sixth at Laurel?" or "Who won the third at Beulah?"

"The 4 got scratched in the third race at Aqueduct," Billy told Glenn.

"A late scratch?" Glenn asked.

"Uh huh."

Since Billy gleaned the track for winners, Glenn needed another specialty, in order to avoid competing with a friend. So he looked for late scratches, horses pulled off the track just before post time, usually because they'd broken loose during the post parade or because the jockey or the track veterinarian had decided they were too gimpy to run. Gamblers were entitled to a refund on a scratched horse. If the horse was on a Pick Three, Pick Four, or Pick Six ticket, the bet was switched to the favorite. Not everyone remembered that, which made Glenn's next move worthwhile. Lifting the lid off a garbage can, he stirred the rubbish, hoping to find a ticket with the 4 horse at Aqueduct.

"A lot of money in these garbage cans," he said. "It's nasty. I gotta keep washing my hands. But it's worth it."

As he sifted garbage, Glenn looked anxiously at a janitor pushing a broom. The guy might sweep away a live ticket. Glenn also watched for security. Racetracks hate stoopers. Stoopers cash bets that would otherwise remain in the track's coffers. (In one recent year, Hawthorne kept $578,206 in uncashed tickets.) And by the time they feed a ticket into a betting terminal, it's usually been stepped on by nine shoes or soaked for two hours in a rotting salad of taco wrappers, hot dog buns, and soda cups.

("They gunk up my machines," fumed Packy Hart, Hawthorne's director of mutuels, "and then I have to shut them down for repairs.")

As a result, stoopers are ejected on sight.

"I know a lot of guys been gettin' barred out for this," Glenn said warily.

Glenn couldn't find an Aqueduct ticket in the can, but he discovered a pair of betting vouchers, one worth sixty cents, the other ninety. The players who'd pitched them thought they were small change. They weren't to Glenn.

"Fifty more cents, I got a bet," he said optimistically.

Glenn rode the escalator upstairs, where there were fewer janitors and security guards. At last, on the third floor, he found the ticket he was looking for. It was resting on a table, next to a crimped aluminum ashtray. Some pissed-off loser had torn it into quarters. Glenn reassembled the ticket. He knew a clerk who would cash torn-up tickets, but only if they were taped back together. He'd been in this situation before; he knew where to find the tape.

Down on the first floor, there was a poster promoting a book signing by a writer for the *Daily Racing Form*. Glenn eased it from its pillar, rolled the tape off the bottom corners, and smoothed it back into place, moored only at the top. He sat down to repair the ticket and then hurried off to see the clerk.

Glenn worked hard for that two bucks. I never found out whom he bet it on, but an hour later, I saw him sitting alone on a bench next to the customer service window. I asked him how things were going.

"It's rough, man." He shook his head dejectedly. "I'm just trying to get together enough money for a bet."

Glenn wasn't around much in the next two weeks. Some mornings, he'd be in the door at his usual ten fifteen, but then he'd leave after the second race. Other days, he wouldn't appear at all. His brother-in-law was in the hospital for a heart operation and his sister had the flu, so Glenn was driving their children to school on the North Side every day. It was his role, as the errant brother, but it only left him free between nine and two o'clock.

Glenn and I had an arrangement, which fell somewhere between friendship, philanthropy, and paying for interviews. I bought him burritos, so he wouldn't have to spend his gambling money on food, and I gave him two dollars whenever he was tapped out. In exchange, he let me follow him on his stooping excursions. As a result, word got around the track that I was a soft touch. While Glenn was off caring for his nieces and nephews, a hustler named Eli offered to take my alms.

Like all good hustlers, Eli had a nose for money. I'd met him a year and a half before, on the afternoon of my $660 win. He was a member of the blind man's court that day, running bets, fetching coffee. I bought him a bowl of apple cobbler, gave him two dollars, and didn't see him again until twenty-five seconds after I left the window with a wallet full of cash. Eli congratulated me ("My man!"), gave me dap, bumping his fist against mine, and then asked for a gapper, a gift from a winner to a loser. High on victory, I gave him ten bucks.

Eli never paid me back, but every time he saw me, he tried to extend his tab. The first time he spotted me that winter at Hawthorne, he was toting a Styrofoam vat of coffee across the grandstand. Theatrically, he stopped short and stared at me, as though I were a classmate fifty years missing.

"Look at me," he said, slumping his shoulders, buckling his knees in a pantomime of pleading. "I am busted out. This isn't even my coffee. I'm carrying this for someone else. Can you help me out with two dollars?"

"How about a dollar?" I offered.

"Now, how am I gonna bet with a dollar?"

"Eli, you already owe me twelve dollars."

He pretended to look wounded.

"I'll pay you back as soon as I hit something," he vowed.

"When's that gonna be?"

"If I knew that, I wouldn't be asking you for money."

Eli had been lucky once. In 1969 a friend from "Jewtown," the old Maxwell Street Market, tipped him off to some horses. Eli won $80,000 in two days, or so he said. He put a down payment on a house for his soon-to-be-ex-wife, bought a new Buick Electra, and banked the rest.

"Then I got cut off," was how he told the story. "Guy saw my new car, he gave me three losers in a row."

For some guys, there's no greater calamity than winning a lot of money at the track. That was the end of Eli's good fortune, but not the end of his horseplaying. For the next thirty years, he scraped by on odd jobs—construction, exterminating—that gave him the freedom to spend his days at the track, chasing the next big winner. The eighty grand dwindled, like an iceberg towed down to the Sargasso Sea, until the day he called his daughter and asked her to bring him $300 from the bank. "Dad," she told him, "you've only got eighty dollars in your account."

(Winning a lot of money on the horses is no different than inhaling that thunderous hit of crack that takes you up to Asgard with Thor and Odin. After the buzz wears off, you don't feel less anxious or more confident. You feel like smoking more crack. Unless you're supernaturally disciplined, a big ticket won't solve your financial problems. Track money almost always finds its way back to the track.)

Eli's woman had passed away two years ago that summer. His house was boarded up, uninhabitable, so he floated between lady friends, crashed with his daughter, or, when there was no welcoming bed, played cards all night.

I gave Eli a dollar. I didn't like giving him money. I always felt ripped off. He wouldn't hang out and answer my questions, like Glenn. He disappeared, and I wouldn't see him again until he needed more money. Once, he walked up to me just before the ninth race and announced, "I just got here. You got $100?"

"No."

"Can you get it soon?"

"No."

Eli lost interest in the conversation right there. But I saw him again after the race. He asked me for a fiver.

"It's just a loan," he said.

"You always say that."

"Things have changed," he insisted.

Eli had burned through countless benefactors. He once talked me into giving him a lift to the West Side, so he could visit "my last source of support, other than my daughter." Glenn didn't even consider him a real hustler. Eli was a panhandler—and worse.

"He's probably begging," Glenn told me, when I related a meeting with Eli. "I knew this guy who went to the parlor at Jackson and State. He worked downtown. He asked me if I knew Eli. I said, 'Everybody knows that motherfucker.' He said Eli stole his briefcase. Now, he don't even go down to that OTB no more."

Eli hustled when he needed to, though. There were only so many "loans" he could take out. When he had to work for gambling money, Eli could be as shrewd as the street peddlers who sell dollar-ninety-nine stocking caps for four bucks. The week after I gave him that stingy dollar, he sat down next to me while I was deciphering the *Form*. A windbreaker, accented with the Hawthorne logo, was draped over his arm. Eli had gotten it in the gift shop—for free. The racetrack ran an incentive program—Club Hawthorne—aimed at big bettors. Every dollar that went through the tote was worth points that could be redeemed for cameras, stuffed animals, radios, big-screen televisions— and windbreakers. Eli had signed up. Whenever he ran a bet for a heavy player, he recorded it on his card. He'd accumulated enough points for this jacket, which he now wanted me to buy.

"I'll sell it to you for twenty dollars," he offered.

"I've already got a jacket," I said, tugging on the collar of my Old Navy slicker. "I don't need another one."

"I'll sell it to you for twelve dollars."

"I still won't need it."

"Look," he said, as he drew his chair closer. His voice deepened, softened. "Can you do something for an old man? Bet a dollar exacta for me in this next race: 2-3 with 2-3-6-8-9. It'll cost you eight dollars. If it comes in, I'll split the money with you."

Maybe I was impressed because Eli was offering me an investment. Maybe I wanted to get him off my back (although I knew that giving money to Eli would simply buy me more Eli, redeemable the next time he was broke). Whatever the reason, I made the bet. If 2 or 3 won, with 2, 3, 6, 8, or 9 in second, the ticket would hit. I doubted that would happen. I had no faith in Eli's handicapping, because Eli had no faith in Eli's handicapping.

"You can never make money handicapping," he liked to say. "When you handicap, you just come up with the same horses as everyone else. The only time you'll make money at this game is by playing numbers."

And yet, the bet won. I watched the race from the apron. The 2 came in first. The 8 was second. The exacta paid $15.80 for every two dollars wagered, which meant my ticket, which was a series of eight one-dollar bets, was worth . . . $7.90. I ran inside, to hunt down Eli.

"You owe me a nickel," I shouted, as I found him lingering by the video driving game. "I spent eight bucks and I got back $7.90. We were going to split the winnings, so we should split the losses."

"You see?" He spread his arms, flashing his palms in a gesture of poverty. "Those are the kind of bets I get. I lose even when I win."

"So where's my nickel?"

"You'll get it," he said.

I never did. Eli still owes me a nickel, on top of all his other debts.

◡

At this point, my $4,000 stake was undiminished. In fact, it was still piled in a vault at my neighborhood bank. I was walking around the track with a couple hundred dollars in an envelope, letting it go five or ten bucks at a time, because I didn't want to start betting big money until I'd seen most of the horses on the grounds run once, getting an idea of who was good and who was glue. Thoroughbreds usually race every two weeks, but after two weeks, I was still making tiny wagers.

"You know, you're going to get in trouble with that envelope," a friend of mine pointed out, when he saw me slipping it into a pocket of my parka. He was right. And the time had come to step up. The next morning, I went to the bank and withdrew $4,000 in hundred-dollar bills. That was way too much cash to carry around Hawthorne, so I decided to convert it into vouchers, credit slips that feed into the touch screen betting machines that are set up all over the track, like slot machines in a casino. The machines subtract the amount of your wager and then spit back a new voucher with your remaining bankroll. At the end of the day, or the end of the meet, you trade in whatever is left for cash. I wanted to make the transaction as secretly as possible. Hustlers can smell money. After I'd hit my $660 exacta, a hustler saw me celebrating and growled, "Hey, you want me to cash that for you?" He knew I was holding a signer—a ticket so stupendous it had to be reported to the IRS—and he was offering himself as a tax shelter. For a tip, he'd sign his name to Form W-2G ("Certain Gambling Winnings"), and since hustlers don't file tax returns, we'd cheat the revenuers out of their 27 percent. I cashed the ticket myself.

To further avoid the hustlers, I paid two dollars to "cross over" to the clubhouse. Hustlers were not appreciated there. Even if they had been, they wouldn't have sprung for the admission fee.

Crossing over to the clubhouse was like stepping from a Greyhound bus depot into the lobby of the W hotel. I saw two black people: the shoeshine man, lounging high on his stand next to the bar, and a cowed-looking hustler, who was running bets for a prominent suburban auto dealer who owned a string of horses. The dealer supported Hawthorne by raffling off cars and broadcasting an ad—between every damn race—that opened with a hyped-up announcer shouting, "Sale! SALE! SALE!!!" He was a short gray-haired man in gleaming shoes, a tailor-cut suit, and a fur-collared overcoat. His cigar was as thick as a dolma. He popped its sodden butt out of his mouth, aiming it at his hapless sidekick.

"See how you fucked me up?" he grumbled, expectorating the f-word as vigorously as one would stomp a bug. "You fucked me up, you motherfuck . . ."

I didn't linger for the rest of that performance review. In search of Hawthorne's remotest ticket window, I ascended to the second floor, with its patterned carpet and stuffed green armchairs. I passed the Gold Cup Room, a restaurant—with real silverware and tablecloths—overlooking the finish line. The hush of the clubhouse was stultifying: it was a shopping mall at eleven o'clock on a Tuesday morning, peopled by coffee-club senior citizens. It was the periodicals section of your public library, with men studying *Racing Forms* spread out across long tables, looking up to stare at screens that carried the news of their "investments." I found an idle ticket window next to a booth that sold hot dogs and coffee. Ripping open my envelope, I pulled out a stack of hundreds and handed it to the green-vested clerk.

"Eight $500 vouchers," I ordered, my voice booming with pride—as much as a nasal midwesterner's voice could boom. Five hundred dollars was the biggest denomination available.

The clerk's nimble thumb flicked through the bills. I thought I was a heavy hitter, but he obviously handled this kind of money every day.

"Perfect," he barked. Then the betting slips began curling from his machine. I was ready to gamble.

U

An old rule of thumb says that your biggest bet should be 5 percent of your bankroll. Five percent of four grand is $200, which is a lot of money. I decided to bet $150, which is still a lot of money. But, to test my cool, I wanted to make a man-sized wager. Before I plunged, though, I wanted to find a horse with a 50–50 chance of winning, going off at odds of 7–5 or better. It was the same system I'd used at

Sportsman's Park. My first serious bet was Tejano Run, a filly running in a six-furlong sprint. On paper, Tejano Run looked invincible: she'd won six of eight races at Hawthorne and ten of her thirteen sprints. When I saw that her odds were 5–2, I was giddy. You know what they say about gift horses. I hurried to a betting window. Glenn saw me leaving the window with my $150 W-5 ticket.

"You must be loaded," he said.

That might have been a share-the-wealth solicitation, but I was too nervous to talk to Glenn. I was too nervous even to step outside to the apron. This race was something to peek at out of one eye. I was so nervous, I ran to the bathroom to take a piss. Then I scrubbed my hands with Hawthorne's goopy soap. They say cleanliness is next to godliness, and if I were virtuous, maybe I'd be lucky, too.

At post time, Tejano Run dropped to 9–5—partly my fault, I thought proudly. Watching through the windows, I followed her progress as far as the turn, where I caught a glimpse of her green saddle towel as she tried to charge the leaders. At the crest of the turn, Tejano Run reached third place, but that was as far as the wave carried her. The green towel with the white "5" receded through a chestnut tide of Thoroughbreds, sweeping away my $150.

After the race, I looked back at my *Form*. This had been Tejano Run's first outing of the year. The last time she'd returned to the track after a long vacation, she'd finished sixth. Obviously, this was a horse who needed to race herself into shape.

"So *that's* why she lost," I said to myself.

Tejano Run was also a sucker horse: she'd opened at generous odds because the insiders who bet early knew she was suspect and shunned her. The rest of us, who had only the *Form* to guide us, thought we were getting a bargain, so we showered her with money in the final minutes.

I tried to get my money back on the ninth race by betting on Burgandy Tower, a one-eyed horse who always won when he drew the inside post. He was the 1 horse, and he was 7–1, so I wagered twenty dollars. If he won, I would be almost even for the day. If he lost, it was just another twenty on the fire. Burgandy Tower reared as the gate opened, flailing the air with his hooves, but he found his footing and slipped inside the leaders on the backstretch. Burgandy Tower had the shortest trip around the track, and he needed every spare inch. Coming into the stretch, he had the lead, but Good Better Best and Zennamatic were straining after him.

"Jerry La Sala gives the whip to Burgandy Tower, trying to get him home," track announcer Peter Galassi shouted. "On the outside, Good Better Best. In between horses, Zennamatic. It's Burgandy Tower. Good Better Best on the outside."

Galassi stretched his words to urge the leader across the line: "Burgan-dy Tow-er *will prevail.*"

Having a winner was good, having twenty dollars on him was better, but best of all, his odds had jumped to 8–1 after the gate opened. I was even for the day. I ran through the grandstand, whooping at my transformation from sucker to seer.

Usually I throw away my losing tickets, because they're bad luck. But I saved my ticket on Tejano Run as a memento of my moment as a whale, a big bettor. It was the last time I bet $150 to win.

Wednesdays and Thursdays were the "dark days" at Hawthorne, the weekend for horses and jockeys (although not for gamblers—the grandstand was open for simulcasting every day save Christmas, which could be a forlorn and anxious holiday for the habitués, the bachelors especially). The racing week began on Friday. If you arrived early enough, when the monitors were counting "168 minutes to post time," you could watch a groundskeeper swaddled in a Carhartt coat polishing the finish line mirror. Tractors harrowed comb trails through the loamy dirt, churning clods to grains. Patches of brittle snow were glued to the turf course—the oval of grass within the dirt track was useless until the April thaw—and a few gulls, miles astray from Lake Michigan, searched for gaps in the piano-taut strings stretched across the melting infield pond, which, as a romantic gesture from the track's owner to his wife, had been dug in the shape of a heart. A dewy scene, even at ten thirty in the morning, it was a pastoral act played out on an agricultural preserve set among the smokestacks. The only urban experience that came close was standing on a sidewalk outside Wrigley Field and watching the groundskeepers through an open bay door, seeing the outfield green exposing itself to the city gray. There was, in both places, the same spotless feeling—your *Racing Form* was unsullied by losing picks, the Cubs had not yet given up a walk, a hit, or a run— and the same naïve hope, protesting history and mathematics, that both states of perfection could remain the same. I will become a winning horseplayer today! The Cubs will win the pennant this year! Never mind that both seem as extraordinary as the events in *Bulfinch's Mythology* and would require the same supernatural assistance.

Hawthorne can contain 30,000, nearly as many as Wrigley, but even on the sulkiest weekday afternoon, at the gray end of a losing season, Wrigley will fill a third of the way to its eaves, while Hawthorne is lucky to have 1,500 in its seats, scattered as sparsely as pins on an airline traveler's map. (They're usually the same 1,500: when I walked into Hawthorne on opening day, I hadn't been to the track in six months, but then I saw the regulars—the blind man, Glenn, Bucky, and the tall sleepwalking man in tattered overalls—and felt as though I'd just walked back into a party after a five-minute cigarette break.)

In urban America's heyday, between Prohibition and the Second World War, horse racing jostled baseball and boxing for column inches in the sports page and footage on the newsreel. Workhorses still trod the streets, and people wanted to see how fast the breed could run, unencumbered by ice wagons. Racetracks were as swarmed as today's NASCAR ovals. Hawthorne's display cases contain blown-up, documentary-gray photographs of a Saturday crowd from the 1920s. Captured from above, it looks like a street cobbled with straw boaters.

"I remember when you had 30,000 at the track," remembered Joey Johnston, a trainer-turned-mutuel clerk who was raised in a house twenty feet from the Hawthorne starting gate. "Everybody came to Chicago back then. Sixty thousand came to Arlington Park."

In the 1960s the horsy types who ran the racetracks refused to put their races on television. If horseplayers could watch the races on television, they might stay home and bet with their bookies. Pro football took the airtime, and sports fans soon found a new place to spend their Sundays. When racing finally discovered a way to mix television and gambling, the offtrack betting parlors drew even more bettors away from the track. Why spend an hour on the bus when there's a legal bucket shop in the neighborhood? Bets on Thoroughbred races increased from $9 billion in 1991 to over $15 billion in 2002, but only 13.5 percent of that was laid down at a racetrack. The rest was wagered at OTBs, through telephone accounts, or over the Internet.

"It's helped the overall handle, but it's hurt the atmosphere at the track," said Hawthorne announcer Galassi.

Not even the *Swingers* vogue, which made youth culture props out of martinis, cigars, and Sinatra CDs, could turn "the Track" into a hip place to spend a weekend. Galassi now sighs for the cheers that once mingled, like static, with his stretch calls.

I was at the track every Friday. So was Glenn. On the first day of spring, the week after I was suckered by Tejano Run, we appropriated a table behind a bank of flip-down ballpark seats on the first floor. There wasn't much competition. The lacquered top was gouged with pen strokes, and the flared feet were wobblingly uneven.

"I can't imagine those seats being full," I said to Glenn. "Coming here on a weekday is like going to the movies at noon. It's kind of eccentric."

"Yeah," Glenn agreed.

In the first, I figured Zee Anna would get the lead. Since she was breaking from post number two, she'd be able to run straight to the rail and take the shortest possible trip around the track. She did. Even better, she did it at 5–1, so my twenty-dollar win ticket was worth $122. And I was alive in the Daily Double.

(Classic racetrack joke: A gambler is waiting in line to bet the second race when he suddenly keels over. A doctor kneels down to take his pulse and then reaches into his shirt pocket, where he finds a ticket.

"Is he dead?" the panicked patrons ask.

"Yes," the doctor says solemnly. "But he's alive in the Double.")

The second was for maidens, horses who had never won a race. The favorite, Rainy Day Rules, was making her debut as a racehorse, but Michael Reavis trained her, so the gamblers had faith in her. Reavis was not only the best trainer at Hawthorne, he was also the most flamboyant. His outfit—a hat banded by silver buckles, a buckskin jacket— looked like an exhibit stolen from the Buffalo Bill Museum. His hair was a relic of Custer's scalping. The cigars that poked away strangers came from the humidor of the Auto Dealer, who owned the best horses in Reavis's barn. You often saw them standing together, by the clubhouse bar, the Electric Horseman and the Godfather, making a guest appearance in each other's movies. The Auto Dealer liked to bet, and when one of his horses dropped from 2–1 to 6–5 on the tote board, it was a signal the horse was likely to win.

I hated Reavis. You couldn't bet against his horses because they won almost half the time, but you couldn't bet on them, either, because their odds were so low they would have had to win *more* than half the time to turn a profit, and Reavis's winning percentage was only 40 percent. As the saying goes, "Barely a man is now alive who paid the mortgage at 4–5." It wasn't worth putting up two bucks to get back $3.80. (Most people thought it was, obviously, or those horses wouldn't have been the favorites. But most people lost money at the track.) So you just had to wait for another race.

Rainy Day Rules wasn't owned by the Auto Dealer, but she was 8–5, so somebody knew something. Glenn had come to the track with forty dollars. He bet thirty to place on Rainy Day Rules.

"I wasn't even gonna come here today, but I got to sittin' and there wasn't nothin' on TV but that was shit," he said. "So I got here and me and this other guy was walking in together, this guy told us both to play Reavis. I saw this Reavis horse in this race, so I bet it. If I see a good race, I ain't gonna wait around. That's how I bet when I first come in. I try to hit early. If I don't, I start hustlin' and hustlin'."

Glenn hit early. Rainy Day Rules won by twelve and one-half lengths, paying $3.60 to place. It was a fair reward, he thought.

"If you get that money down right, it don't matter if it pays three dollars," he said. "As long as you get that money down."

I hit the Daily Double, for $45.20, and, since I'd used Rainy Day Rules in an exacta with the runner-up, Z Me Zipp, I won another $21.40 for predicting equine behavior. Right then, I could have used a cigar to advertise my smugness, but I never smoked or drank at the track. I limited myself to one vice at a time.

Complacent, self-satisfied, I skipped the next two races. I didn't need the money. Glenn was feeling so flush that he blew two dollars on food, running to the grill for a pair of the discount hot dogs Hawthorne peddled on Fridays.

In the fifth race, we both bet on Barrett Kathryn at 6–1. Barrett Kathryn's jockey, Zoe Cadman, was Hawthorne's only female rider, and she loved to prove her machismo by forcing horses through tight gaps along the rail. Zoe kept her mount close to the rail the entire race. When she and Barrett Kathryn turned into the stretch, they were facing the rumps of three faster horses. Zoe had a decision to make: she could go around them, which would mean running extra yards, or she could wait for a gap to open in the moving wall. She waited. It would have been easier for a rich man to get into heaven than for Barrett Kathryn to slip between the horses blocking her in the stretch. But she did.

"Zoe, man!" Glenn exulted, as Barrett Kathryn zoomed along the fence and under the wire. "Mmmm!"

He dropped a five-dollar bill on my *Racing Form*.

"Here, man, have a bet," he said. "You're always helpin' me out. Here's something now that I'm up."

That was the code of the grandstand. A big payoff wasn't a purely personal windfall, like an inheritance or a bonus at work. It was a product of impersonal fortune, like a lottery win. You were obliged to share it with your friends. If you were generous, the guy next to you would share his luck when the wheel spun his way. I stuffed the fin in my pocket.

I was touched, but the next race was for horses who had not won in the last year. None of them looked likely to do it this year, either.

"This is a pretty sorry field," Glenn said, shaking his head. Usually he saved his regret until he'd lost a race. But Hawthorne was offering such awful choices, he was mourning the loss of his money in advance.

"Have you ever heard the saying, 'This race is so bad I wouldn't bet it with your money'?" I asked Glenn.

"Uh-huh."

"Well," I said, "this is that race."

"I hear that," Glenn agreed, but he went ahead and bet five dollars on Uptown Brown, who finished eighth.

On my way out of the track, I ran into Eli. Before he could ask, I gave him the fin. For once, it wasn't my money.

Glenn punched out after the tenth race. He didn't want to blow his winnings on Santa Anita, a Southern California track that started its program midway through the Hawthorne card and ran until seven in the evening. That night, he gave his sister fifty bucks. The next morning, he went to a barbershop, putting a little track money into the neighborhood economy.

"They done kicked the blind man out!"

Glenn was drunk and distraught. His day had begun brilliantly. On the way to the track, he and a friend had pooled their money for a fifth of Canadian Club. They sneaked the bottle through the gate and drank it in the empty seats outside. Then, at noon, as his buzz peaked, everything went bad. He was at his post behind the blind man when a squad of blue-shirted security guards approached, led by a rubicund, walkie-talkie-toting heavy with the sour mien of an assistant principal. The blind man was told to leave the track. Sure, he'd been sitting out front for three decades, but Hawthorne was under new management. Beggars were no longer welcome. Lewis was hoisted from his bucket and led to the Hawthorne Shuttle. The little wagon dropped him at the bus shelter on Cicero Avenue, where he awaited his last ride home.

"That's some rotten shit!" Glenn raved. He was posing angrily in the center of the grandstand. A strand of spittle leaked from a corner of his lips, whether from drunkenness or outrage, I wasn't sure. "He's been comin' out here thirty years. He just makes five, six dollars a day. He doesn't bother no one. They told him they don't want him hustlin' no more."

Henry, a friend of the blind man, was going to help him onto the bus—after the second race. Glenn had lost $120 on the early East Coast races—his bankroll for the day—so he searched the room for someone who could stake him. He spotted Wes, "my main man," and threaded through the carrels.

"I'll show you something," Glenn said. "I don't got to sell programs. I can get money from people out here. They know me."

Whatever he whispered into Wes's ear produced a crinkling fiver—Glenn's generosity returned. Glenn put out his fist for dap.

"Who you like here?" Glenn asked Wes.

"I ain't bettin' Hawthorne," Wes said, holding up a creased simulcast program that was open to the fifth race at Laurel.

"I'll give you a winner here, the 4," Wes said.

"I'll bet the 4."

Glenn ran the fin to the window.

"I bet five to place on the 4," he reported, after he came back.

I pointed at the Laurel monitor.

"The 4 is only 7–5," I said.

"Where's that at?" Glenn asked.

"Laurel."

"Oh. I bet the 4 at Hawthorne."

The 4 at Hawthorne was Great Grandson. Great Grandson had finished tenth or worse in five of his last six races. In the other race, he'd finished sixth—out of seven. I read this information out of the program as we walked to the apron. Glenn refused to change his ticket. If the number 4 was good at Laurel, it might be good at Hawthorne, too, he said.

Even without binoculars, we could see Great Grandson faltering on the turn, ratcheting backward through the field.

"He's dying," I said.

"Never say never," Glenn shouted. "Never say never."

To bet is to hope. Glenn wasn't going to lose his faith until Great Grandson crossed the finish wire. When it finally happened, the horse was jogging toward an indifferent tie for last place. After the race, Henry joined us outside.

"Come on," he said. "The blind man's waiting for me. I'm gonna take him on the bus."

The three of us rode the Hawthorne Shuttle out to the bus shelter. It was a one-room cabin. Henry opened the door, and we walked into the stuffy aroma of unfinished planks heating in the sun. Beneath the windowsill, someone had written "Horses are harder to catch than buses. Play ALL–ALL." Lewis sat on his bucket, hands composed over the head of his cane. The blind must learn patience, living alone in a dark world that is far more personal to them than the world of shape and color is to the sighted, who share it with billions of others. A blind beggar must be doubly patient, waiting for charity to approach from places he can't see.

"Who 'zat?" Lewis asked, hearing feet squeezing the floorboards.

"It's Henry."

"It's Ted."

"It's Glenn."

"Glenn. Who'd you have in the last race?"

"The 4."

"The 4? I had the 4, too!"

"What happened, man?" Henry asked, changing the subject to the blind man's banishment.

"They done told me to leave," Lewis said, his voice rising through sadness to confusion to indignation. He'd been at Hawthorne longer than the grandstand itself, and now he'd been told he was a nuisance.

"That's some rotten shit," Glenn said. He promised to have a talk with "Mr. Carey"—Thomas F. Carey, the owner of Hawthorne Race Course.

"I'll be back," Lewis promised, as Henry led him toward the street to meet the bus. "I'll see you boys again."

On Saturday mornings, at ten thirty, the racetrack holds a "Fan Forum." Usually the guest is a jockey or a handicapper, who takes an inning of softball questions from track announcer Galassi and then takes another inning of softball questions from the scanty audience. On "Ask the Management Day," the guest was Thomas F. Carey III, the general manager of the racetrack and son of Mr. Carey. Glenn was there early. A few people sat in the folding chairs. Even more people queued up for a Styrofoam cup of coffee and a free doughnut. Most of them were wearing old coats, so it looked like a relief line.

After questions about how much a jockey earns (10 percent of the owner's share of the purse, if the horse wins, a fifty-dollar fee if it doesn't) and what Hawthorne was doing to get the young hooked (taking 4-H clubs on tours of the stables), Glenn raised his hand.

"Uh, yeah," he said, in his slow voice. "I was wondering why this old guy be sitting out front, they barred him off the track. I was wondering why."

The young Carey was wearing the only coat and tie in the entire room, and he had the air of a man who was, except for this one hour a year, insulated from the combat-level crises of his family's business. Shoved out into the street, the prince seemed startled to encounter a subject.

"If security has barred him off, there has to be a reason," he said. "Who are you talking about?"

"The blind guy who sat at the bottom of the ramp," Glenn said. Everyone knew the *blind guy*—at least everyone who came in through the front gate.

"I . . . I don't have an answer for that," Carey said, his face shutting down, his eyes searching for a friendlier question.

Glenn and I talked a lot about visiting the blind man. Glenn knew where he lived, in an apartment building on the Near North Side. We worried about him. We thought he might be lonely. But I always left the track after the ninth race, around five o'clock, so I could go home to handicap the next day's races. Glenn liked to stay late. The hour between six and seven was his favorite time of day. He knew a little trick with the betting machines. Before six thirty, bets taken on out-of-town races go into the coffers of the Thoroughbred industry, which runs its horses during the day. After six thirty, the money goes to the local harness tracks. Since the eighth and ninth at Santa Anita are run after six thirty, central time, the machines had buttons for "afternoon" and "evening" races, to keep the funds separate. Sometimes, gamblers pushed the wrong button and bet on the eighth race, when they had meant to bet on the sixth. Sometimes, they discarded their tickets after realizing the mistake. Sometimes, Glenn picked them up.

"I know a guy who found a fifty-dollar exacta box from Santa Anita," Glenn said. "He cashed it in for a refund before the race started. It came in and paid $2,700. If he'd a held onto it, he woulda had a lot more money. But you don't think that way when you've got fifty dollars in your hand. I'm just hopin' I can find a ticket like that."

We never did go see the blind man.

# 3

# Professor Speed

In my first month at Hawthorne, my only big day was that afternoon with Glenn. Most weeks, my betting ledger looked something like this: -$56, +$13, -$112, -$47, -$93. I was losing money, but I couldn't understand why. In my first month as a serious gambler, I lost $1,200. As the odometer on my bankroll spun backward to $2,800, I felt ... miffed.

I thought I deserved to win. I'd read three books on handicapping—*Picking Winners* by Andrew Beyer, *Commonsense Handicapping* by Dick Mitchell, and *Betting Thoroughbreds* by Steven Davidowitz—so I figured I was better educated than 99 percent of the guys at the track. These books were the canon, and I'd memorized all their rules: never bet a horse with odds lower than 8–5; never bet a horse who has lost six straight races in the same class; never bet a maiden claiming race; never bet a horse wearing bandages on its front legs; don't bet every race. I followed all of them, fighting the impulse to break one—to bet just two little dollars—as though I were denying myself sweets for Lent. It was agony to watch the odds on a horse I loved drop to 4–5. It was further agony to keep my hands away from my wallet. And it was agony compounded to watch the horse win and pay $3.60. But I never bet them. I was an iron man. I wasn't going to break the Rules, the System. And still, I lost.

Losing was even more galling because I was working so hard at my handicapping. Five nights a week, I sat at my desk until midnight, analyzing the *Racing Form*, writing out lists of all the day's winners, watching old races on Hawthorne's Web site. (I had subscribed to a DSL service just so I could see the replays in high resolution.) The next day, I'd blow a hundred bucks and listen to a woman, leaving the track after her once-a-year gal's outing, squeal into her cell phone, "I just won $8,000 on a two-dollar bet. Aaaahh!"

Dumb, lucky bitch.

Handicapping is a nerd's game. Nerds have always been with us. In centuries past, the monasteries took them in and forced them to copy the Bible. Now, they work in computers, and a few of the most fanatical end up at the racetrack. In *Picking Winners*, Beyer seriously advised handicappers to avoid the company of women. Sounding like a fourteenth-century abbot advising a novice, he wrote:

> The most deleterious effects on a horseplayer's concentration are caused by women. When a gambler has had an exceptional day at the track, or is in the midst of a great winning streak, he may exude a sense of self-esteem and confidence to which women respond. If this occurs the horseplayer is dangerously apt to fall in love, and the distraction is sure to ruin him at the track.

Beyer finally married at the age of forty-two, after sublimating his sex drive long enough to develop speed figures (numeric ratings of horses' running times), which turned out to be the most influential handicapping advance of the twentieth century. He waited long enough to avoid children, at least. Saving for a college education will really cramp your bankroll.

"It's a bachelor's game," said Noel Michaels, a (married) columnist for the *Daily Racing Form*. "I don't know what came first, the chicken or the egg. I don't know if the bachelors are the kind of guys who play the horses, or if playing the horses makes you unattractive to the opposite sex."

I was well suited for the discipline of handicapping. In my pre-adolescence, after I was cut from Little League, I'd become obsessed with Strat-O-Matic baseball, a pre-Rotisserie, pre-Triple Play board game played with cards and dice. One summer, I replayed an entire National League schedule in my bedroom, updating my team statistics and league leaders every Sunday morning. I also subscribed to the *Sporting News* and read its box scores as assiduously as my father, an economist, studied our state's revenue projections. Eventually I got interested in girls, but not too interested. At thirty-six, I had a girl-friend, but I was still a bachelor, *de jure* and *de facto*—never married, never shacked.

The world of baseball statistics is not so far from the world of the *Daily Racing Form*. Neither is the knack for solitude required to study them—the nerd's preference for words and numbers over companionship. In fact, Steven Crist, publisher of the *Racing Form*, was also a Strat-O-Matic freak as a kid. During a three-year, between-jobs period when he played the races full time, Crist wrote that he felt like "the Strat-O-Matic scorekeeper again."

It takes a combination of arrogance and denial to believe that you can beat the races. This fits perfectly with the egocentric fantasyland most of us over-thirty single guys inhabit. We could have been playing with military miniatures. We could have been compiling discographies of sixties garage bands for *Record Collector*. We could have been doing drugs. Instead, we were devoting ourselves to the most mathematically unforgiving form of gambling in the world.

It would be easy for someone with a moderate edge in skill to beat the races, except for one thing: the track keeps 20 percent of the pot. The "takeout" is its fee for booking the bet, maintaining a racetrack, and paying prize money to winning owners. (The actual figures in Illinois are 17 percent on win, place, and show bets; 20.5 percent on exacta and Daily Double bets; and 25 percent on trifectas, superfectas, and Pick Threes. Thanks to breakage, the practice of rounding payoffs down to the nearest twenty-cent increment, the bites are even bigger than advertised. Since a horse that ought to pay $6.79 actually pays

$6.60, the track's real share of win bets is close to 19.5 percent.) It's a far more pitiless tax than slot machines (3 to 5 percent) or roulette wheels (5.26 percent), which are less expensive to maintain than horses. It's also a lot more than a stockbroker's 3 percent commission or a bookie's 10 percent vigorish. What makes horse racing different from mechanical games, though, is that players can choose to bet only when they think they have an edge. If you believe a horse has a 25 percent chance of winning, then 3–1 is a fair price (good odds). If he is 4–1, then you have an overlay, a situation in which the odds are in your favor. If your assessments of equine ability are accurate and you bet only on overlays, then, theoretically, you will turn a profit. With a roulette wheel, by contrast, the house has a 5 percent edge on every spin. Luck can make you a winner on any given day, but not even luck can beat 5 percent in the long run.

"A horseplayer by nature is a different psychographic than other types of gamblers," one racetrack executive told me. "They want to give themselves an edge. They think they're smarter. They think they have information other people don't."

No one knows for sure, and no one will ever know, because gamblers lie more than fishermen or gigolos, but it's estimated that only 2 to 5 percent of horseplayers turn a consistent profit. The uninformed masses enrich the savvy elite (which is the way it works in the world outside the racetrack as well). Is it any wonder that you see so few eager-looking twenty-five-year-olds at the track, and so many disgruntled sixty-year-olds?

After blowing $1,200 in just a month's time, I decided to seek professional help for my gambling problem. Hawthorne had its own house handicapper, who could be found, every afternoon between the first and the ninth, in his Handicapping and Business Center on the third floor. I scuffed up two flights of clifflike stairs to see him.

Scott McMannis was built like a desk sergeant. A broad-shoul-dered, Earth-bellied man in a police-blue dress shirt and a red tie, pat-terned with horses, he was leaning back in his office chair, watching a race replay on a giant-screen television. Every few moments, he stabbed his pen at the program in his hand. He was writing trip notes, comments on the running of the race: "Believe a Countess stumbled gate; Ms. Tish wide turn." His desk was a prospect of notebooks and pillared papers.

Throughout the room, a few men hunched quietly at long tables, swotting over programs. When I introduced myself after the replay, I found out why every table faced Scott.

"I teach a class on handicapping every Saturday morning," he said, filing my business card in a leather portfolio. Then he pointed at his list of students, looked up at me, and asked, with a hint of obligation, "Why don't you sign up?"

Scott McMannis was a teacher, an academic who had chosen horse racing as his field of study. He'd started out as a respectable scholar, earning a master's degree in finance at Northern Illinois University, which won him a job as a business professor at a two-year college in the suburbs. After ten years in academia, Scott had advanced to dean of lifelong education. What he really wanted to do, though, was go to the track. In 1979, at age thirty-eight, he was an administrator, and he could have retired as one. But when the school year began, Scott was absent. He'd quit to become a professional gambler. Scott and his wife, Wendy, were childless, and she had a good job as a kindergarten teacher—so, Scott said, "She told me, 'Give it a try.'"

Scott had been warned about wasting his life this way. When he was a boy, his Uncle Ted, a well-to-do fastener manufacturer, took the family on regular outings to his private box at Arlington Park. At the age of eight, Scott learned to read the *Racing Form* and picked a horse named Deaux Moulins out of its columns. His uncle had given every child in the party twenty dollars for betting. Scott invested half his stake in Deaux Moulins. The horse came in at 6–1, he remembers, "So I was the big winner that day. On the way home to Rockford, I was apparently a little pugnacious, braggadocios. My uncle said, 'You know that the big winner buys dinner.' I said, 'I guess that's me.' He called all our relatives and we met at a place called the Rathskeller. He said, 'My nephew here is the big winner. He's buying dinner for everybody.'"

When the owner brought the check, it was more than double Scott's winnings. After a few uncomfortable minutes, Uncle Ted agreed to make up the balance. But he made his cocky nephew listen to a lecture first.

"He said, 'I want you to learn a lesson from this. When it comes to betting on horses, it's easy come, easy go.' He didn't want me to get the idea that it was easy to make money betting on horses."

Scott never imagined it was easy. He pursued handicapping the same way he'd pursued math, statistics, and finance—as an academic discipline. He read the current literature in the field: *Picking Winners* by Beyer and *Winning at the Races: Computer Discoveries in Thoroughbred Handicapping* by Dr. William Quirin, a professor of mathematics at Adelphi University. Both books presented formulas for making speed figures.

Today, speed figures are published, in bold type, in the *Daily Racing Form*. But in 1979 they were possessed only by a brotherhood of math geeks who got a thrill from copying down race results. Scott spent a year doing just that, going to Sportsman's Park with his own speed-figure chart. His in-laws were worried he'd gamble away his house, so he started gingerly, betting ten dollars to win and ten dollars to place. But his figures were leading him to so many good bets that by the end of the season, he'd stepped his action up to $200 a race.

"I do remember some horses that paid thirty dollars or forty dollars to win," he said of that golden age of speed handicapping. "I can't remember the last one."

Speed handicappers believe they've solved the age-old problem of comparing horses who've raced at different distances on different days. In harness racing, a handicapper can compare horses by their final times, because all the races are run at the same distance—one mile—

over a crushed limestone track. But Thoroughbreds race at distances from four furlongs to a mile and a half, and they run on dirt, which can be softened to tiring muck by a rainstorm or pressed down to a hard-packed springboard by a maintenance crew that wants to dazzle the crowd with fast times on the day of a big race. Before Beyer popularized speed figures in the 1970s, most handicappers thought a horse's clockings were worthless. "Time only counts when you're in jail," they scoffed, instead betting horses based on class—the quality of competition they'd been running against—or breeding. Speed handicappers dealt with changing surfaces by calculating a track variant, a number that expressed whether the dirt was fast or slow that day.

(Here's the best example I've seen of how speed figures work: On December 12, 2003, a cold rain fell on Chicago, seeping into the Hawthorne track and freezing it just below the surface. Instead of the usual four inches of loose dirt, horses were running on a thin inch. That day, an $8,000 claimer came within one one-hundredth of a second of breaking the track record for six furlongs. A few races later, Coach Jimi Lee, a talented sprinter, ran the distance in 1:07:27, the fastest time in Hawthorne's 112-year history.

Speed handicappers were unimpressed. Scott calculated that, because of the frozen track, the day's times were seven and one-fifth seconds faster than normal, the biggest variant he'd ever made. He assigned Coach Jimi Lee a speed figure of 53; on Scott's scale, which is smaller than Beyer's, one point equals one length. It turned out that the horse's record-breaking effort was inferior to the race he'd run earlier that fall, when he'd beaten a field of stakes horses to earn a 59.)

U

Speed figures alone didn't make Scott McMannis a winner. He knew how to bet, too. As a business prof and a stock market investor, he'd studied the principle of risk/reward ratios, and he applied it to horse racing. He never bet a horse unless the odds were 2–1 or higher; anything less, and the squeeze wasn't worth the juice. From the beginning, he possessed a bubble-gum ass—the ability to sit through an entire card without getting up to go to the window. Once, at Sportsman's Park, Scott went sixteen days without making a bet. On the seventeenth day, he bet an exacta box (betting on three horses to finish first or second in any order). It won.

"He can win without my money," he would declare, when a horse with the best speed figures was going off at 4–5 or 3–2. If the horse won, Scott was unruffled.

"A lot of people say, 'I'll kick myself if this horse wins and I don't bet him,'" he said. "That's a psychological phenomenon called Fear of Regret. I've never had a problem passing a race. That's how I like to live my life. With no regrets. This woulda, coulda, shoulda business is something I don't subscribe to."

Scott spent his first months as a gambler cloistered in the Membership Room at Sportsman's Park. He was still a teacher, though. I know horseplayers who won't talk to, listen to, or make eye contact with anything human, for fear of giving away a secret that might diminish their odds. But a teacher can't hoard knowledge any more than a preacher can keep his mouth shut about the Bible. And Scott missed lecturing, missed the feeling of being Socrates in the agora, surrounded by students. Gambling was a lonely, isolated life. In the summer of 1981, he began hosting ten-dollar-a-head handicapping seminars in the Howard Johnson's across the street from Arlington Park. Thirty people showed up. They were intrigued by his speed figures and his trip notes, so he started selling them in a weekly newsletter he called the *M. Scott McMannis Speed and Trip Service*. A year later, he was working inside the track. Arlington built him a classroom with 190 seats and three projection screens. On Saturdays, Scott lectured to standing-room-only crowds, more students than he'd seen in a week of Finance 202 at his community college. Every racetrack regular needs a nickname. Scott became "the Professor."

Scott was now a professional handicapper. He didn't have to gamble to pay his bills. But every April, he claimed gambling winnings on the "Other Income" box of his IRS form. Ten years into his new career, he made the bet that persuaded everyone he'd been right to quit his job and hang out at the track all day.

In 1989 Arlington introduced a wager called the twin trifecta, which required bettors to pick the top three finishers of two races. The twin tri, or double triple, as it was sometimes called, usually covered the most unpredictable races of the day—maidens or claiming horses so lame and erratic they were on sale for $5,000. On days when no one hit it, the money was banked to fortify the next day's payoff. The meet began in June. That month, no one hit the twin trifecta. No one hit it in the first two weeks of July, either. The pot grew parabolically— the bigger it got, the more was bet into it—until, by midsummer, it was swollen to almost $80,000. That reward was worth a big risk, Scott decided.

"I looked at it one day, and I thought, 'It's worth going for, and I'm going to use horses no one else is using.'"

He bought a ticket using six combinations in the seventh race and sixty combinations in the ninth race—a $720 wager. Scott's horses won the first leg, but he did not allow this to excite him. He was a pro, and the ninth race was just a big business deal, about to be consummated. Besides, he had work to do.

"During the ninth race, I was busy writing down my trip notes for the race," he recalled. "Well, the horses were coming past the wire, and I was trying to make the notes, and I thought, 'I think I hit the double triple.'"

Scott continued scribbling his notes. Standing next to him was a man named Fireman Bob, who was ecstatic.

"Let me see the ticket!" Fireman Bob shrilled, feeling the thrill his friend was suppressing. Scott brushed him off.

"I have to get these notes written," he said.

"Hand me the ticket!" Bob demanded.

Scott flipped it over.

"Jeez," Bob said, as Scott wrote even more notes. "You do have it."

After the Official light flashed on the tote board in lurid motel neon, the track announcer came on the PA. Someone had finally hit the twin trifecta. There was one ticket, worth $81,257.20.

When Scott got home, he surprised his wife in the laundry room. Wendy was not exactly embarrassed to be married to a professional gambler, but whenever anyone asked what her husband did for a living, she said, "He works in the horse racing industry." For a moment, Scott stood in the door frame, grinning. Then he handed her a brown paper bag, heavy with cash.

"Pay off the mortgage," he said.

He hadn't gambled away the house after all.

U

Class started at eleven thirty in the morning. I was ten minutes late the first Saturday, because I refused to skip my morning run. The doors to the Handicapping Center were locked.

The second Saturday, I got up early and made it to the track for a lecture that could have been titled "Speed Figures, and Why the Ones You Can Buy from Me Are Better than the Ones in the *Racing Form*." The lights went down, Scott clicked his overhead projector, and an off-kilter rhombus of light glowed on the pull-down screen. Scott was wearing his red horse tie. He always wore a tie to the track, even on weekdays. It was the academic man's symbol of authority, and it made clear that he was a 2-percenter, while the rest of us—dressed in ball caps, T-shirts, and snap-button windbreakers, many of them free racetrack giveaways—were 98-percenters.

"When is a six-furlong performance in 1:15 the same as one in 1:12?" Scott asked, speaking into a breathy hand-held microphone. His jowls sank into his collar as he stared at us over the tops of his reading glasses.

A man in a Hawthorne cap spoke up.

"The track might have been slow."

"Exactly," Scott said. "What central point does this make?"

"You can't use the same times," another pupil volunteered.

"And that's what launches us into the discussion of speed handicapping. Because, as proven by the computer studies of Bill Quirin, the number-one most important fact in the past performances is how fast a horse has run, minus the outside influences. What we need are adjusted speed figures, constructed with an accurate daily track variant."

The *Daily Racing Form* printed such figures under the name of their inventor, Andrew Beyer. But those were calculated by a team of statisticians that worked off charts and never visited our track. One could do better.

"When you're sitting in San Francisco making figures for all the races, are you seeing all the races?" Scott asked. "What if there's a timer malfunction, and the time is faster than it should be? If someone isn't seeing the races or factoring that in, they won't know that. It's a big job."

Scott smoothed a transparency onto his projector. It was a page from the Hawthorne program, with McMannis speed figures inked beneath each horse's name.

"I handicap using the projection method," he said. "It's easy once you learn how, which isn't easy, but it can be mastered."

The shadow of his pen pointed at the top horse on the page, Shed Some Light.

"This is Shed Some Light's second race off a layoff. You can see we've drawn our layoff lines whenever a horse is away from the track thirty days. Horses usually improve in their second race after a layoff. So we want to find out what he did last time he was running his second race off a layoff. Can anybody see?"

"A 41," someone mumbled.

"Forty-one. OK. So we can predict this horse will run about a 41."

Scott inked in the figure. The next horse was also projected to run a 41; the horse below him, a 39. When he'd filled out the page, we all saw how swiftly each horse could be expected to run that day. His attempt to predict the future was no different from a fast-food executive studying traffic patterns before deciding to build a Burger King on a street corner, or a loan officer studying a credit history to make sure the applicant wasn't a deadbeat. A bank maintains its 5 percent edge by refusing to take a risk on bums; so does a horseplayer.

(As it turned out, Shed Some Light underachieved. He finished second by nine-and-a-half lengths, earning a lowly figure of 35. Horses are dumb animals. They don't always run the way they're supposed to on paper.)

After that class, I started hanging around Scott's room, the Handicapping and Business Center. It had a computer and a fax machine, so horseplayers wouldn't have to stew in their offices when they should've been at the track. There was a video library with a tape of every race run that spring. And among the monitors' flashing parades of horses and Pop Art-colored odds tables, there was a television tuned to CNBC. Wendy was usually at the track, and when she wasn't carrying Scott's voucher to the lone mutuel clerk on the third floor (early in the meet, Scott tripped in the press box, putting himself on crutches), she was charting the couple's stock prices as diligently as Scott recorded trip notes. On slow afternoons, their only company might be Joe, a retired teamster, and Sig, a commercial artist who had lived in the same Polish neighborhood for all his sixty-plus years. Sig loved to quote the horse racing movie *Let It Ride*, which had been directed by one of his old coworkers from the Leo Burnett ad agency.

"Even when you know, you don't know," he'd shrug, after losing a bet.

Every afternoon, just before the national anthem, Scott led a review of the day's card. From behind his desk, he told anyone who attended which horses he was going to bet. The saying goes that there's more bad information per square foot at the racetrack than anywhere else in the world, but I got one of the only good tips of my life at his race preview, when he touted a horse named Tour's Bluff in the ninth. Tour's Bluff had won the last time he'd worn eye screens—mesh goggles that look like a fly's eyes. The notation wasn't in the *Form*, but Scott had written it on his program and filed it away.

"That was the only way they could keep the horse from running too fast and burning himself out," he said. "If anyone's going to be down in the paddock before this race, see if the horse is wearing eye screens."

I didn't go down to the paddock (the area where the horses are saddled before a race). But during the post parade, I leaned over the rail and stared at Tour's Bluff's head. He was wearing eye screens. He was also 6–1. I ran inside, told a friend, then bet ten dollars to win. Tour's Bluff sprinted seven lengths ahead of the field, running the quarter mile in twenty-two seconds flat. It must not have been too fast, because he hung on to win. On my way upstairs to thank the Professor, I ran into another winner.

"I heard what you said about the 10," he told me. He whipped out his ticket—five dollars to win and place—and we bumped fists.

At the racetrack, information loses value with every ear it touches, but Scott didn't mind giving away his secrets. Picking winners in public sold the *Speed and Trip Service*, and he made more money as a "professional handicapper" than as a bettor. Also, his most faithful adherents were two-dollar and five-dollar players looking for free advice. Guys who could have messed up his odds, bookies and sharpies, hiding in the Gold Cup Room, or the OTB outside Arlington Park, or the Las Vegas sports books—they didn't want to hear from an expert. They considered themselves experts.

Scott encouraged his pupils to bet with him. The week after Tour's Bluff won, he wrote this in his newsletter: "We were all excited about betting this horse at 6–1 when he came out with the protective eye screens last Sunday. That's the second time we've cashed on him by catching the 'screens on' angle." But he also knew that horseplayers are contrarians and wise guys who'd rather lose money on their own nonsense than win with someone else's common sense. After all, betting against the grain is the only way to make a big score.

"In terms of the review, you notice how many people go off and bet their own horses," he said. "Or they might take my horse and bet it in combination with another horse, instead of betting it in the win pool, like I would. When you consider that there are people all over North America betting into the pools, it's easy to be under the radar."

The Handicapping Center was also the best place to hear lewd jokes. Scott loved locker room humor, so when Wendy wasn't around and the room was men only, he'd lean across his table, drawing everyone's ear closer to his voice, and ask, "Did you hear the one about the woman who bought a parrot from a whorehouse?" We hadn't, of course. Scott knew more about handicapping than we did, and he knew more Playboy party jokes, so we listened.

"A woman goes to a pet store and she asks to buy a parrot. The owner says, 'Well, I can let this one go cheap, but there's only one thing. He used to live in a whorehouse.' The woman figures, well, it's a good price, and the parrot can't be that bad, so she takes it home. The next day, when she comes home from shopping, the parrot says, 'Awwk, new madam.' Then her daughter comes home from school, and the parrot says, 'Awwk, new prostitute!'"

We waited for the punch line with frozen, expectant smiles.

"Finally, the woman's husband comes home from work, and the parrot says, 'Oh, hi, Keith!'"

That's the cleanest one I can remember, anyway.

# 4

# First Your Money, Then Your Clothes

No horseplayer was as contrary as the man who sat alone in the Handicapping Center, his hands folded atop a Churchill Downs leather portfolio. His jaw was collapsed over a mouth of missing teeth, so his bearded chin jutted forward, giving him an air of surly defiance, like an Appalachian mountaineer. The face was a true picture of the inner man. I once asked a racetrack executive to name the most cantankerous gambler in Chicago. He didn't hesitate a moment before blurting "Creighton R. Schoenfeldt," the signature he'd seen on dozens of querulous letters and e-mails.

When Creighton heard I was writing a book, he waved me over to his table. He wanted me to see how an experienced handicapper worked.

"C'mon, siddown," he said, in a voice eager—impatient, almost—to show hospitality.

I sat down, and he spread a sheaf of printouts across the table. The product of a handicapping program called All-Ways, they ranked every horse according to its speed from the gate, its class, its workouts, its finishing kick, and a few other factors so obscure they must have been concocted by the programmers to make handicapping look like a Cal-tech science project. The end result of this effort to reduce every horse to binary code was a betting line, an estimation of each horse's fair odds. If the tote board offered higher odds, you laid your money down; if it offered lower odds, you stayed in your seat.

Creighton believed, as faithfully as he believed in St. Jude, that All-Ways was the best handicapping tool ever invented. He tried to per-suade me likewise. He pinned his finger to the page and stared at me through his tea-colored sunglasses to ensure he had my attention.

"I paid $777 for the software and seven dollars a day for this print-out," he said. His voice was thin and rough, weakened by emphysema. He'd been exposed to a lot of chemicals during his tour with the navy in Vietnam. "But it's worth it. Oh, yeah. I had fifty signers one year. To give you an idea of how much I made, the next year, we had to pay $9,500 in taxes every three months. Now, what I do is this. All-Ways divides the races into three categories: chaos, contentious, and orderly. If it's a chaos race, I'll bet two units; if it's a contentious race, I'll bet three units; and if it's orderly, I'll bet four units. I always get my bets in at the start of the day, because I'm fifty-nine. I don't want to have to worry about remembering all that during the races. Right now, a unit for me is two dollars, because they're only racing on the dirt. Once they start racing on the turf, then I'll really fire. Turf is my specialty. If I could just stick to the turf, I'd be one of the best in the country. Isn't that right, Scott?"

Creighton looked to the head of the classroom. Scott did not respond. He was handicapping the next day's races. Like many studious men, he was able to think deeply in a crowded room. Conversation was static, especially Creighton's.

"Well, I guess Scott can't be bothered," Creighton said. "But why don't you come over some night next week, and I'll show you the pro-gram. My wife'll cook spaghetti. Let me tell you, Ted, she cooks the best spaghetti you've ever tasted."

Creighton opened a black billfold, tumescent with keepsakes, and slid out a wedding snapshot. He was standing on the steps of a church in an acrylic blue suit, looming over a petite, gray-haired woman who looked like a Queen Elizabeth doll.

"That's my Mary," Creighton said. "We've been married for seventeen years, never had a cross word. I'll tell you, I married an angel. If I lost her, it'd be like losing my right arm. She used to be a nun, and she still prays at the church every day."

U

Creighton didn't own a car. Twenty years before, a judge had found him at fault for striking a pedestrian. Creighton testified that the man had jumped out into traffic, but the judge had ears of stone. So Creighton decided that if the district court wouldn't see things his way, he just wouldn't drive anymore. He still carried his last license, laminated once it began to tatter like a treasure map, as a memento of the injustice.

This meant I had to give Creighton a lift home. I won't reproduce the entire monologue from that hour-long crawl up Lake Shore Drive, but it was about his feeling that he'd never gotten his due during his years in the Cook County Clerk's office, and his belief that a Republican would be the next mayor of Chicago.

The Schoenfeldts shared a one-bedroom apartment in an old brick building on the North Side, just west of some El tracks. The glass case in the dining nook commemorated the fact that two very different people lived here. The shelves held a Kentucky Derby plate and a bobblehead doll modeled after Bob Baffert, trainer of three Derby winners. Atop the cabinet was a plaster statuette of Jesus, and the room was watched over by a clock painted with the scene on Calvary. The only possession they shared was a menagerie of stuffed animals. This was their "family." (Creighton did have a son, by one of his two previous marriages. The boy had played ball in the minors before becoming a suburban cop. His portrait was propped on the television set.) Mary was in her fifties when she left her order. She moved into Creighton's apartment building, and even though she was seventeen years his senior, Creighton started courting her. He took her out to dinner. Then he left a teddy bear outside her door. They married in 1986.

Creighton went to the track 364 days a year, and "I'd go on Christmas if it was open then," he liked to say. Mary went to church 365 days a year (it was open on Christmas). His life savings went to the horses; hers went to convents, soup kitchens, UNICEF, and the World Wildlife Fund.

"If I just give ten dollars a month to each of my charities, it just comes to $3,000," she said. "That's nothing compared to what people spend on the horses. It's true."

Creighton's gambling was not a source of friction in the marriage. "I'm not his mother," Mary said. "He never tells me not to go to church, and I never tell him not to go to the track."

He could be crusty; she was never anything but sweet. He was devoted to a vice; she was devoted to piety. Mary seemed to consider their differences charming. She'd written a poem about the romance. After I commented on the mismatched curios, Mary seated me at the kitchen table and recited it, reading through wide-eyed bifocals:

Creighton was a-waitin'
And opposites attract
So when he met his Mary
He knew he had to act
Creighton told her how he felt
Which made Mary's heart to melt
At the altar they both knelt
Seifert changed to Schoenfeldt.

Mary folded the paper and yielded the floor to her husband.

"Now, let *me* show you something," Creighton said, as if I needed to be reminded that I'd come to talk to him. He lifted a cardboard box labeled "1995" from a stack in the corner of the dining room. It was full of receipts for his signers. These pink slips, delicate as tissues, their ink fading toward invisibility, were proof of his prowess as a gambler. I leafed through them: a $4,495 trifecta, an $8,490 trifecta, a $7,370 trifecta.

"Mary considers this a hobby," he said, obviously miffed by this dismissal of his second career. "I consider it professional, because of the fact that I do it all the time. I wanted to move to Las Vegas to play in the tournaments out there. I thought it was gonna work out great, because the cathedral is right across the street from the Stardust. But Mary couldn't stand the heat. Sunrise Hospital said she'd die, and you marry 'em for better or for worse, so we came back to Chicago. The apartments out there were too expensive, anyway."

I asked Creighton whether he was ahead or behind in his life, a winner or a loser. Probably behind, he said. Probably by a couple hundred thousand dollars.

"You could have bought a house with all that money," I said.

"What would a house do Mary and me?" he asked. "We don't have any kids. It's just us."

I realized, then, why a gambler and a nun were perfect companions. Both are indifferent to money and possessions. A nun takes a vow of poverty, a vow to forego material pleasures for a chance at a higher spot in heaven. A gambler uses money as a tool to craft an experience for himself; his goal is not wealth, but the ego-thrill of winning, of being right when everyone else is wrong. He is courageous enough to risk something that the ordinary man believes is precious, but which the gambler knows is transient, just as life is transient to the holy woman. Devoted gamblers aren't trying to win money for a boat or a car. They only want enough to eat, sleep, ride the bus to the track, and keep gambling. Mary thought they were opposites—"he's strictly a horse and sports person, and I'm a music and culture and reading and praying person," she said—but they were both cut from the same ascetic cloth.

There was no spaghetti. I'd come on short notice, leaving Mary no time to shop.

"Are you thirsty?" she inquired. "Would you like a soda?"

The look on her face was so pained that I believe her own throat would have felt parched and dry if I'd said I was thirsty. I wasn't, but I accepted a root beer and sat down at the computer with Creighton.

"How long is it going to take to handicap this card?" I asked.

"About five minutes."

"Five minutes?"

"Sure. Look."

A list of handicapping factors, as long as a Chinese restaurant menu, popped up on the screen. Creighton clicked check marks into the squares beside early speed, workouts, late run, and class. Then he hit "Finish." A moment later, the printer chucked to life and began inching out the All-Ways picks. Creighton slid the first sheet out of the tray.

"It says Doughty has a 68 percent chance to win," he read. "Doughty looks like the winner, doesn't he?"

I was spending three hours a night marking up the *Racing Form*. Creighton handicapped with a computer in five minutes.

It seemed too easy.

U

Creighton was sitting in the Handicapping Center, his chin resting on his folded hands, his scowling face as overcast as the gray spring sky. It was raining. The night before, when he'd programmed All-Ways, he hadn't expected rain, so he hadn't asked the computer to tell him which horses ran well in the mud. At noon, when he'd punched in his bets, he still hadn't expected rain, so he'd followed All-Ways's advice. Now he was heavily invested in horses who only won on dry dirt.

"What's wrong, Creighton?" asked Scott, who was rehandicapping the card, circling horses who'd earned big figures in the mud.

Creighton explained.

"So cancel the tickets," Scott said. "The races don't start for another fifteen minutes."

Creighton wouldn't hear of it. He was determined to suffer for not reading the weather report.

"My father taught me certain principles in horse racing," he lectured Scott. Creighton's father was a typesetter for the *Daily Racing Form*, and had brought the paper home every night. "When you make a mistake, you don't learn if you cancel your tickets."

Creighton pushed back his chair and swept his portfolio off the table.

"The whole goddamn day is shot. I'm leaving."

He completed his penance by standing in the rain for an hour, out on Cicero Avenue, until the number forty-eight bus took him home.

"I stayed with all those tickets," he boasted the next day. "I didn't hit anything."

"How much did you lose?" I asked.

"How much? Well, it was considerable."

Creighton's faith in All-Ways was unmoved. It wasn't the computer's fault that he'd lost money. After the fourth race, he walked over to me in a hunched but determined stride that made him appear both humble and demanding. His finger traced a line down the printout he was holding.

"You see this," he said. "If you'd used the top four contenders here, you would have had the trifecta."

I peeked out the windows at the infield tote board. The trifecta had paid over $200.

"Did you bet it?"

"No." He sounded indignant.

"Well, if you don't put money on a race, your opinion doesn't count."

If I was irritable, it's because I'd just lost twenty dollars on the race. I would have been more appreciative if he'd tipped me off beforehand.

All-Ways hit the tri in the eighth race, too. Creighton told me this as soon as the horses were under the wire.

"If that thing is so good," I challenged him, "why don't you tell me the trifecta *before* a race."

"OK."

Creighton walked to a betting machine and returned with a trifecta ticket: 6-1-3.

"There. Now you've seen it. You can go bet it yourself if you want. I'm leaving. I gotta go catch the bus."

In the early spring, before we changed our clocks, the sun set around the eighth race. The smokestacks were isolated in silhouette, and the factory lamps spread away from the track like airport landing lights. Creighton cinched a scarf around his neck, zipped his fatigue-green jacket, and headed for the elevator. Before he left, I wrote down his trifecta combination but didn't bet it.

It lost.

Creighton had gotten on my nerves, which wasn't difficult, because I was losing money almost every day. But he made even Scott McMannis lose his temper. It was an outburst I'd never seen before, and never saw again. Sangfroid was Scott's ruling emotion. Once he lost twelve races in a row. A less confident gambler would have cut down his wagers or come up with a new handicapping strategy. Scott did neither. He was pursuing a long-term growth strategy, and a twelve-loss streak was, as he would put it, within the realm of statistical variability. He'd been winning for twenty years, and he knew that as long as he disciplined himself, he would continue winning.

"Never ask a horseplayer how he did at the end of the day," he liked to say. "Ask him how he did at the end of the year."

When the winners started coming in again, he didn't whoop "Eeeyaaah!" or pump his fist, like the rest of us. He smiled, faintly, and took his notes. What was there to get excited about? The horses had run the way he'd predicted. Order was restored.

Scott was never irked by the weekend gamblers who pestered him for tips—"Who is it in here, Scott?" "Who's gonna win this one?" But Creighton pissed him off.

He did it by eavesdropping while Scott and Wendy were discussing an upcoming handicapping contest and then repeating the details to another track employee. Creighton liked everyone to know he was the guy with the inside dope. When Scott found out, he blew his top.

"Creighton, that was a conversation between myself and Wendy!" he shouted. "You've put me in a really difficult spot here at the track."

Creighton replied, weakly, that he'd been trying to help Scott by letting everyone know he needed help organizing his contest.

"Creighton, you're never happy unless you're miserable!" Scott snapped.

Creighton slinked out of the room, clutching his portfolio. For the next week, he sat alone at a two-seat booth beside a window. He could still see the Handicapping Center from his new spot, but he refused to set foot inside.

"What do I need Scott for?" he groused. "What's he ever done for me except give me 2–1 horses? I can do my own handicapping. Sefapiano's Miss is gonna win this one."

I looked out at the tote board. Sefapiano's Miss was 2–1.

"He's done this before," Scott said. "He'll get mad and stay away for a week. Then he'll sneak in here and sit in the back and gradually work his way forward. He's got a heart of gold. I could leave him alone in this room with a twenty-dollar bill on the table, and I'd know that when I got back, not only would he not pick it up, he'd prevent anyone else from doing it. But he's never happy unless he's miserable."

○

Sure enough, Creighton soon declared a one-day suspension of his boycott. The finals of the handicapping contest were coming up. Every Saturday and Sunday, Hawthorne challenged the customers to pick the winners of races two through seven. Anyone who hit two made the finals. It wasn't hard. Creighton had filled out one entry blank for himself and one for Mary. They had both qualified. When Mary came to the track, she would need someplace comfortable to sit, someplace that didn't reek of cigarette smoke. Only the Handicapping Center was good enough for Mary.

The finals fell on a Sunday during Lent. Creighton arrived first and saved two seats. Mary was still at Mass. She got to the track half an hour before post time and scanned the program, looking for horses with a history of finishing first, second, or third. Mary had taught school for many years, so she appreciated a horse who always gave its best.

Mary filled out her entry, darkening each selection with a pencil she carried in her purse, then sat down with a book of crossword puzzles and a devotional to pass the twenty-five minutes between each race. She bet two dollars to show on each of her horses—"Creighton always says you're supposed to get a winner, but at the last moment, someone else can get up there"—and recorded her wagers on a square of notepaper. Every time she won a bet, she drew a smiley face next to it.

By the fifth race, she was up to three smiley faces—all her horses had won, but she'd only collected small show payoffs. Then she got a gift. Ifyouprefersilver was the 2–5 favorite in the race, a filly of such golden achievements that one bold gambler—a "bridge jumper"—had risked $50,000 on the proposition that she'd finish in the money. The payoff would be five cents on the dollar, but this was a five-horse race. Ifyouprefersilver had only two rivals to beat. It looked like free money—5 percent was better than the going rate on a CD, and you only had to wait two minutes for your interest.

Ifyouprefersilver finished fourth, right behind Mary's choice, Lakenheath. When the bridge jumper's fifty grand was divided among the winning show bettors, Mary's two-dollar ticket was worth $41.40. Mary drew a smiley face next to Lakenheath's name.

At the end of the afternoon, Peter Galassi paged her: "Mary Schoenfeldt, please report to the Handicapping Center. Mary Schoenfeldt, please report to the Handicapping Center."

Mary had nailed five winners in six races. "Durbin's Line," the computer handicapping service in the *Tribune*, had never gone 5-for-6.

"Somebody's living right," an envious gambler mumbled.

Two other horseplayers had matched her feat. Scott gave them a choice: they could split the $2,200 prize money three ways or compete in a one-race playoff. Mary decided not to be greedy. Seven hundred and thirty-three dollars was a lot of money for her charities.

When she told Creighton her decision, he was apoplectic.

"Look what she's doing!" he cried, throwing up his arms. "She's sharing it with the two other people. She could have gone for the whole thing in a playoff. She would have had an advantage, because she'd have me helping her!"

Creighton had picked two winners all day. After a few minutes, he calmed down—$733 was a lot more than he was leaving the track with—and soon he was roaming the third floor with an ether grin on his face, boasting, "I'm so proud of my Mary."

Mary slipped the check into her purse.

"There'll be a hell of a lot of cookies in the house tonight," Creighton beamed.

"It's Lent," Mary corrected him. "I won't even go down the cookie aisle until after Easter."

$$\cup$$

Women handicap just as well as men, but you don't see too many at the track. They're too practical to play the horses. They hate losing money. I know a couple that goes to the track every weekend. Sheila handicaps for hours the night before, marking up her *Form* with multicolored pens. She picks winners, but after a race, she'll moan, "Oh, I really liked this horse, but I couldn't bring myself to go bet him." Jeff flips through the program at the track, then plunges on Pick Threes, using three or four horses a race. He cashes a lot more tickets.

My stockbroker sees the same fear of risk in her female clients. When the market goes through a rough patch, they call in a panic, begging her to pull their money out.

"Women are nesters," she said. "They're interested in security."

Men are egotists. We want to brag about a $3,500 trifecta, and we don't care how much money we have to lose before we hit one.

Henry Lesieur, author of *The Chase: Career of the Compulsive Gambler*, gave me more insight on the X and Y approaches to gambling when I called him at Rhode Island Hospital, where he leads a gambling treatment program.

"The track is like an intellectual endeavor," said Lesieur, a psychiatrist. During our phone conversation he continued:

It's an information game. There's the competitiveness, the kind of macho "I can beat you. I'm better than you." Women, they're not thinking that way. They just don't think about being smarter than the average sucker. They think about having a good time, being with their friends. Think of bingo: You go there and talk with your friends. It's kind of like socializing. There's also the culture and the people there. You go to a track, you don't have comfortable seating. Women are looking for relative safety. They don't want the place strewn with garbage.

That's why Creighton is down $230,000 over his lifetime, and Mary is probably up $200.

U

I was still down more than a grand for the Hawthorne meet. Every time I placed a bet, I wrote it down on the *Form*, and after a month I copied all my wagers onto a single sheet of paper, looking for a pattern in my failure. I discovered that if I had bet the same amount of money on every race, I would have shown a profit. But I hadn't bet the same amount. I'd been too chicken. I'd laid down thirty dollars on horses who'd lost at 9–5 and three dollars on horses who'd come in at 8–1. It seemed like a safe, logical system: favorites win more than long shots, and you have to spend a lot of money to make the payoffs worthwhile. I was scared to plunge on long shots, and, as every race-track bore will tell you, "Scared money never wins."

I sat at Scott's desk and told him what I'd learned.

"I've made fifty win bets so far this meet, and if I'd bet two dollars on every one of them, I'd have won $132."

"Fifty win bets!" he said, feigning astonishment. "That's a lot more than I've made."

"So what should I do about that?" I asked.

He became the patient professor again.

"What I tell people is to bet the same amount of money on every race," he said. "It's got to be enough so it stings if you lose a bet. That way, you stay out of races you shouldn't be in. A lot of bettors use 5 percent of their bankroll as a guideline. How big is your bankroll?"

"Four thousand dollars." Or it had been.

"Are you ready to bet $200 a race?"

Scott knew the answer, which spared me from confessing that, no, I wasn't.

"Why don't you bet twenty dollars a race?"

Twenty dollars seemed like pussy stuff for a man of my means, an autodidact who by this time had read *six* books on handicapping. I decided to bet fifty. I'd work my way up to $200 as my bankroll expanded.

Here are the results from a day of betting fifty dollars a race:

- 4th: Forty-five dollars to win on Melanie's Smile; five-dollar exacta Connor's Glory over Melanie's Smile. Melanie's Smile finished fifth.
- 5th: Fifty dollars to win on No Crime Committed. No Crime Committed finished fourth.
- 6th: Twenty-five dollars to win and twenty-five dollars to place on Call Me Mister C. Call Me Mister C finished last.

- 8th: Fifty dollars to win on Velvets and Silks. Velvets and Silks finished second.
- 9th: Fifty dollars to win on Crafti Sandi. Crafti Sandi finished fifth.

In four days, I'd lost $580. Then I went back to betting twenty dollars, which launched a week-long winning streak.

It always works that way.

Playing the horses was a life-consuming occupation. Medical interns and tax-season accountants may have more exhausting schedules, but I'd never worked so hard. The races only lasted four-and-a-half hours, but the drive each way was an hour, and handicapping took up the whole evening, from dinner to bedtime. As soon as I got home, I logged onto the *Daily Racing Form* Web site and printed out the next day's card while I ate a microwave dinner. I spread the sheets across the desk in my living room, filling each horse's record with split times and trip notes. I had a film of every race run at Hawthorne that year, downloaded from the track's Web site. I also owned a book of "par times," which I'd ordered for $100 from a shyster in California. An almanac of the average winning times at every track in North America, it was supposed to help me figure out whether a horse coming in from out of town—a "shipper"—was fast enough to compete at Hawthorne. And thanks to the deep stack of horse racing books next to my chair, a half-dozen handicapping dogmas butted against each other in my brain, leaving me as confused as a college freshman emerging from Comparative Religion. I handicapped like the sculptor who created his statues by "chipping away everything that doesn't look like my subject." I drew a slash through horses that looked like losers, hoping to deduce the winners that way. But sometimes, I threw out all the horses. Other times, I'd be left with five contenders. When the card was especially long, or challenging, the handicapping bled into the morning, and I'd read the *Form* or watch old races while blindly spooning cereal into my mouth.

I was learning what John Goritz meant when he said, "I don't have a life. . . . All I do is handicap and go to the track." I didn't have a social life, because all the best races were on Saturday. I was half-owner of a fantasy baseball team, but when I found out the draft was the same day as the Illinois Derby, I told my partner I had to work.

"Oh, come on," he said. "It's just a bunch of horses!"

"War Emblem won the Illinois Derby last year," I protested. "Then he won the Kentucky Derby."

Besides, I believed in perfect attendance. So far, I'd missed only one race, when the bus dropped me off six minutes after post time. It cost me the Daily Double. I was never late again, even when I caught a withering, week-long cold that would have kept me home from any other job.

On Illinois Derby weekend, my friend Dave was visiting from England. He'd moved back home to Wolverhampton after a decade in Chicago, and I hadn't spoken to him in nearly a year. At ten o'clock on Saturday morning, my phone rang.

"'Ello, Ted, it's Dayve. What you doin' today?"

"Going to the track."

"All right then, let's go."

I hadn't planned on company, but I picked him up on the way to Hawthorne. Dave is not a gambler, but he works with computers, so he had a lot of money to lose.

"I've got $100 with me," he announced, as we rode the escalator to the third floor, "and I'm going to bet on *every race.*"

"That's usually not a good idea," I said, but his program was already open to the first.

"All right, who do we like here?" he asked.

"Nobody."

I was lukewarm about all these horses, and so was the crowd. The favorite, Westcoastwildcat, was 5–2.

"But if you had to bet on somebody, who would you bet on?"

"Probably the 3—Fever Like."

"All right, then, I'll bet on the 3."

I followed Dave to the window. I felt responsible for his money. If he was going to lose, I was going to lose, too. We lost. Fever Like ran backward through the field.

"No worries," Dave said. "What about the next race?"

All afternoon, I touted horses I would never have bet on myself. It was a weak undercard (the races that precede the feature race), but this was Dave's one day at a U.S. racetrack, and he deserved a chance to lose money on every race. In the fifth race, though, I finally spotted a bet-the-farm, bet-your-ass, can't-lose horse. One Upman was more than a mortal lock. He was the stock and barrel, too.

"The 6 is going to win this race," I declared.

One Upman stood to get the lead, plus he was trained by the Electric Horseman himself, Michael Reavis.

"That's what I like to hear!" Dave exclaimed.

"But he's 6–5, so we'll have to bet an exacta. Let's see, the 7's got the best shot at second. . . ."

"All right, a 6-7 exacta!"

Dave had one essential quality of a handicapper: he never doubted his opinions, even when they were my opinions.

"But the 1 has a shot, too," I dithered.

"Nope. A 6-7 exacta. That's how it's going to be."

And that's how it was. One Upman took the lead, just as I'd expected. The 7, Find My Halter, shadowed him like an escort pony all the way around the oval. We watched the stretch run from the battlement of the third deck. Their sleek heads slid back and forth, but One Upman had too much determination to lose Dave's money.

"We got it!" I shouted, slapping him a high five.

But Dave had won more, because he'd bet a single two-dollar exacta. With the indecision of someone who has too many facts, I'd played several one-dollar exactas involving the 1, the 6, and the 7.

Even though we'd made a score, by the time the Illinois Derby rolled around, we were both down fifty dollars.

"If you want to play it safe," I said, "bet on Ten Most Wanted. He's 2–1. If you want a long shot, bet on Lx Commander."

Two-to-one wasn't going to bail us out. But Lx Commander, a local hero who had won his first race at Hawthorne by ten lengths, was 13–1. We bet on Lx Commander. He led for a half mile, but he was no match for Ten Most Wanted, who was just passing through Chicago on his way to the Kentucky Derby.

I stopped betting after that, but Dave was determined to get even. In the tenth, he laid his last forty dollars on Big Stew, the 4–5 favorite. Big Stew was the sort of horse who ran robustly when he was alone, ahead of the pack. But another horse beat him to the lead, and he sulked through the race, finally giving up in the last 300 yards.

"What a waste of money!" Dave exclaimed, as he rode the down escalator, $100 poorer than he'd been on the trip up. "I'm glad I lost. Now I won't want to come back again."

I'd lost sixty dollars, more than I would have without peer pressure, and I had to come back tomorrow.

"What you doin' tonight?" Dave asked.

"I gotta go out to dinner with my girlfriend and some of her friends."

"Well, I'm going out for a drink later. Why don't you stop 'round?"

"I'll try."

I sped home, where I had just enough time to print out the chart of that day's races before rushing over to Kate's apartment. There was no time to handicap. But there was plenty of time to think about it during dinner. Kate and I had met at an office party, where she asked me whether I'd thought of collecting my horse racing stories into a book. She is an epicurean—a "foodie," in her term—so that night, we went to a French-Vietnamese restaurant. My only use for food was as a sop to the hunger pangs that distracted me from handicapping. I ate the first thing I could get into my mouth—a steak burrito, a bowl of Cap'n Crunch, a pear. My weight had dropped to 148 pounds, because I had already become weary of the Polish dogs and fried chicken dinners at the Hawthorne grill.

On a different night—or better yet, in a different year—I might have been a lively dinner companion. But my mind was in the pages of a *Racing Form* I hadn't even seen yet. I embarrassed Kate by answering her friends' questions in three words or less—"at the track," "lost," "writing a book." Afterward, as we were driving through the packed streets toward the bar where I'd promised to meet Dave, all my stress burst out.

"Why do people go out to dinner?" I asked her. "What's so entertaining about eating? I don't get it."

We made it through a pint of beer, and then I went home, where I handicapped two races before I had to sleep. After that, Kate and I didn't go out much on Saturday nights—it was a work night—and I didn't take another friend to the track until Derby Day.

U

I was sure that if I disciplined myself—if I studied every night, if I kept my wallet in my pants most races—I could be a 2-percenter. If you were enough of a grind, you could master any task, couldn't you? A few years before, I had injured my knee so badly that I could only run three miles without stabbing pain. I decided that if it ever healed, I would run a five-kilometer race in less than twenty minutes. I gritted through months of physical therapy, I ran on eighty-five-degree days when I felt like puking in the final mile, I trained on tracks, trails, treadmills, and roads, and on Thanksgiving Day, I ran a "Turkey Trot" in nineteen minutes and forty-three seconds. Now, though, I was pursuing a more difficult feat: my race had put me in the top 10 percent of recreational runners, but to win at the track, I had to be better than 98 percent of the other gamblers. And handicapping, I'd come to realize, was a professional-level skill, as difficult to learn as medicine, the law, or plumbing. Those all required seven years of training. I had ten months.

U

There was, in the Handicapping Center, another man on the same mission. Rob Fasiang always sat alone at a table buried in computer-printed *Racing Forms*, speed-figure charts, and handicapping manuals. He studied like a college student at the library, copying Scott's speed figures onto every horse's record in a tiny, modest hand. He was at the track every day. Gambling was his job. At least, he wanted it to be.

"This," he told me, "is my rookie year as a horseplayer."

He was thirty-nine, and he'd tried to live a workaday life, like everyone else from his suburban Catholic high school. He'd killed two years at a community college, then spent his twenties and thirties drifting from job to job: he drove a truck for a printer, he delivered pizzas, he worked as a security guard at a surgical supply factory. For two years, he tried to make a living as a professional bowler (bowling is a common gateway sport for horseplayers, because there's so much gambling involved). Despite a 220 average, he never won more than a few $1,000 purses in local tournaments. Bowling was also hard on his wrist and back, and he didn't like being watched by the crowds. He didn't like crowds.

Rob had always bet on harness races—they ran at night, making them convenient for guys with day jobs—but it was a Thoroughbred that convinced him to try a career in gambling.

"There was this horse out at Arlington I thought should have been the second favorite," he remembered. "I got to the track a minute before post time, and he was 15–1. I was just frantically punching the buttons to get my bet in. I bet ten dollars to win and place, and I bet the same for a buddy of mine. We both won $160. That's when I knew I could make money at this."

When the factory he was guarding moved its operations to Brazil, it seemed like the right time to turn pro. Rob was living in a $300-a-month basement apartment in Hammond, Indiana. He didn't have any kids. He didn't have any pets. He didn't have anything to look after but a car. So he maxed out his credit cards to pay his bills and build a stake.

"I just want to get my life down to three things," he said. "Computers, horse racing, and philosophy/psychology. I read a lot of philosophy—Stephen Covey, *The Seven Habits of Highly Effective People*. But I've done everything else in life. I've had a job. I've had a girl-friend—I lived with her for two years. I've been to college. Now, I just want to focus on this."

He raised his palms to his ears and swept them forward, forming an imaginary tunnel.

Handicapping appealed to Rob's desires for anonymity and independence. He didn't cut a dashing figure. ("People who care too much about the way they look are bad gamblers," he said.) He was stocky, shaved his head, wore disc-shaped glasses, and dressed in sweat-pants and untucked oxfords, as though the grandstand were an extension of his living room. He wasn't gregarious—he liked to study the *Form* with his hands pressed to his temples, creating an imaginary cubicle. He didn't have a college degree. In other fields—business, sales, law, politics—these qualities might have doomed him. But the racetrack is a meritocracy. You don't have to go to Yale. You don't have to play golf at the North Shore Country Club or know Mayor Daley. If you pick a winning horse, the track has to pay you. The Racing Board says so.

Rob believed the races could be beaten through self-discipline. He was a natural disciple for Scott, who wrote articles and gave lectures on "personal and money management."

"If you're serious about this game, you're going to have to learn personal management," Scott said during one of his classes, as he wrote, "DISCIPLINE! DISCIPLINE! DISCIPLINE!" on his overhead projector. "If you can't manage yourself, you're doomed. Handicapping is easy. Betting is hard."

To Rob, playing the horses was part of a self-improvement project. He owned a set of Anthony Robbins's *Awaken the Giant Within* tapes and listened to it on his drives to Hawthorne, alternating it with a handicapping seminar conducted by a professional gambler. ("It's a two- to three-hour tape, but I edited it down to half an hour. If I listen to it over and over, some of it will sink in.") To keep fit, he scorned the dollar hot dogs and scuffed up the tall staircases, rather than standing passively on the escalators. He told a parable about a Wall Street firm that hired ten MBAs and ten ex-marines as stockbrokers. The marines made more money, because they were more disciplined. Rob had a five-year plan. By living as part marine, part monk, he would become the best horseplayer in Chicago, better even than Scott.

"I'm 100 percent focused," he said. "Scott works for the track. He's got to deal with customers, he might miss a bet. Also, he's been doing this for over twenty years. He's proven himself. He's satisfied to bet a little, win a little money. I'm hungrier. This is all I'm going to do."

On weekends, he posted his race analyses on a horse racing message board. They always bore time stamps from obscure hours of the night: 3:41, 2:19, and 2:53. He'd start handicapping at eleven o'clock and work through the darkness, his veins tingling with coffee and the anticipation of post time.

"I have trouble sleeping sometimes," he said. "I'll get so excited, thinking, 'I can't wait to bet this horse,'" he said. "So I stay up and write e-mails."

At first, Rob was as undisciplined as everyone else. He couldn't suppress the emotions that sweep us all to the betting window as the horses nose into the gate: fear of missing a winner, desire to get even after a tough beat. I once saw him bet fifty dollars to place and fifty dollars to show on a 70–1 shot who had last run at Great Lakes Downs, a half-mile tank town track in Muskegon, Michigan. I stopped watching the horse after it faded to fifth.

I once read about a stockbroker who owned two cars: when the market was up, he drove his Cadillac; when it was down, he drove his Volkswagen. Rob always drove a flimsy turquoise Ford, but he changed moods as his bankroll billowed and sagged.

When Rob lost, he never blamed the horses or the jockeys. He blamed himself.

"I'm going to stop betting to show," he said after that bet. "I'm gonna stop being so cautious. I've decided to bet to win. Place and show are distracting. They take my focus away from what I'm supposed to do, which is make money."

Losing bets cut Rob more deeply than they cut the rest of us. We could always earn the money back at our other jobs. He had no other job. For Rob, to fail as a handicapper was to fail as a man.

After blowing $260 on a Monday, he agonized over his failure. "I just need to be more disciplined, cool, emotionless. Then when I see that prime bet, go crazy. If I lose two or three prime bets, then I lose confidence. And I miss an opportunity."

At one point, Rob hit a dire losing streak. In a single week, he dropped a dime—$1,000. The defeats cramped his posture and lowered his voice to a mumble. He sat sullenly among his papers, craning his head up half a notch only when someone addressed him. In the last race on the last day of the racing week, he finally joined his fortunes to a winner, betting $160 on Willa Beauty.

"That got me to minus $100 for the day," he said, limp with relief, after Willa Beauty came in at 7–2. It was almost as good as making a profit.

Rob didn't take me seriously as a handicapper until I signed up for Scott's *Speed and Trip Service*. For $300 I got a weekly newsletter, a spiral-bound book full of computer-generated trainer statistics (how many times Michael Reavis had won with a horse laid off thirty days, how many times Wayne Catalano had won with a first-time starter)—and I got Rob's respect. I was no longer a dilettante writer who used his *Racing Form* for taking notes. "I'm glad you joined the team," he said. "I was starting to wonder about some of your handicapping opinions. I was thinking I might have to keep away from you, because you were going to mess me up. You made a wise investment. Scott's the best teacher in the country. He's like having Michael Jordan teach you how to play basketball."

When Rob's big day finally came, he knew it the night before. "This is the best card I've seen all meet," he thought to himself as he handicapped in his garret. "This is an A-plus-plus card. I could win $15,000 tomorrow."

"Every once in a while," handicapper Dick Mitchell wrote, "you'll have one of those days I'll call Christmas. This is when you'll make most of your season's profits."

On the twenty-sixth of April, when the meet had dwindled to its last two weeks—only ten days left to get even—Rob had one of those days. In the second race, a six-and-a-half-furlong sprint for claimers, I'mamiracle beat I'z a Tuffy. Rob had expected that to happen. He'd bet sixty dollars to win and place on I'z a Tuffy, two dollars on the exacta, and two dollars on a Pick Three covering the second, the third, and the fourth. In the third race, run at a mile and seventy yards, Serai led all the way at 6–1, beating a 3–5 favorite. He was on Rob's Pick Three ticket. In the fourth, Whiskey City Jr. filled in the final slot of the Pick Three, which paid $1,049.60. Rob also had sixty dollars to win on the horse and twenty dollars on the exacta. Those bets were worth $388. When I first saw him that day, after the fourth race, he was cupping a nest of tickets in his hands, staring at them with the awe and gratitude of an archaeologist holding an old bone at the end of a two-year dig, or of a miner contemplating the nugget that had finally chosen his bucket. He'd spent so many nights with the *Form*, and he'd endured so many glum losing days that made him wonder whether he was a fool to think he could beat the races. Now, he knew he could. He'd won $3,000 in just over an hour. He was ahead $2,800 for the two-month meet.

"That's $1,400 a month," he said. "That's as much as I made in security working seventy hours a week."

After the races, Rob called his mother to tell her that his work had paid off.

"Congratulations on being lucky," she said.

# 5

# 170 Large

I didn't meet Matt Lovello at the track, because Matt doesn't go to the track anymore. I met him at a twelve-step group meeting in the basement of a Lutheran church in Lisle, Illinois. I'd called the group's hotline and told them I wanted to talk to someone who'd been hooked on the horses; I knew that for every Scott McMannis, there were fifty losers, some of them big losers. Arlington Park didn't pay off Scott's mortgage. Guys like Matt Lovello did.

Matt was a pudgy thirty-eight-year-old with shaggy blond hair and a pair of the rimless, face-shield glasses that were popular in the late 1980s, when the first President Bush wore them. The night we first talked, he had a dollar in his pocket, just enough to pay the tolls back home to Joliet. It was as much as his wife would let him carry. He had given her his credit cards, his checkbook, and his ATM card. He'd signed the house over to her, too. His job as a heavy-equipment salesman took him all over the suburbs, so he was always driving past racetracks and OTBs, and he wanted to make sure he never went inside one again.

Matt's last big betting spree was on May 5, 2001, the day Monarchos won the Kentucky Derby. He was in the sports book of the Rio Hotel and Suites in Las Vegas, gambling with his father. Playing the horses was how he spent time with his dad. And with his clients, his friends, even his children. That Derby Day, the Rio broadcast 482 races, beginning with the morning sprints at Aqueduct and ending with the final trot at a harness track in California. Matt bet on every one of them, speed-reading through the fat programs, then rushing to the windows to blurt numbers at the tellers. For a while, he was hot. He hit the trifecta in the Kentucky Derby, which paid nearly four grand. But by the end of the day, he'd been to the cash station three times. Getting money was never a problem. He had eight credit cards and three ATM cards. The PIN numbers were scribbled on the back of his son's picture. It kept him from forgetting about his son.

"The best feeling in the world was hearing that click, click, click" of bills whooshing from the money slot, he said.

Matt had flown out to Vegas that Friday with $2,500. He flew home on Sunday with forty cents. But he wasn't worried about building a stake for the rest of the Triple Crown races. Matt had discovered a trick that allowed him to charge unlimited amounts of money on his company credit card and then delay the payments indefinitely. He'd been running the scam for three years. One day he was going to pay all the money back, as soon as he hit something big. It might happen at the Preakness, or the Belmont Stakes.

A month later, just before the Belmont, Matt tried to use his credit card to buy a plane ticket. The airline refused the charge. Baffled, Matt called the credit card company.

"Your card has been cut off," he was told. "You've got to see your administrator at work."

The next day, Matt went to see his boss to confess that he'd racked up a $170,000 debt in the company's name.

U

Matt took his turn reading from the group's book of affirmations and then slipped out the door, leading me upstairs to the church library, where he slumped behind the round lacquered table and tried to explain why he HAD to gamble.

"I don't understand why you're here," he said to me.

"Why not?" I asked. I didn't realize it was a rhetorical statement.

"Why are you here when you could be at the track?" he said. "That's how I felt when I was gambling. I couldn't go a day without gambling. I couldn't fathom not gambling whenever I had the chance."

Matt's first trip to the track was just like mine: a day with his father.

"I started gambling my sophomore year in high school," he said. "My dad had me one day a week. He had a friend of his who was going to Arlington. We hit the Daily Double. There was a horse called Teutonic Knight. After that, I fell in love with the racetrack. I was an avid baseball fan, and all that went out the window. I worked at a fast-food restaurant and I started stealing money from the till so I could go to the track."

Going to high school on the South Side meant he could catch a bus to Sportsman's Park in time for the late Daily Double.

"I didn't go to the prom, I went to Sportsman's. I had very few friends, and if they didn't go to the track, I didn't want anything to do with 'em."

Matt went to a public college in Iowa. It wasn't near a racetrack, but Matt was manager of the basketball team, so whenever the school played Creighton, he would sneak off to Ak-Sar-Ben in Omaha. Soon he was taking the Greyhound bus there on weekends, sleeping in the grandstand on Saturday nights to save money for Sunday's card.

"When the basketball team played in the Sun Bowl tournament, we took a side trip to Mexico," he said. "All the other guys went to a brothel to get laid. I went to a race book in Juárez and made $700 playing Santa Anita."

After college, he tried to get a job in public relations at Prairie Meadows, a track outside Des Moines. They turned him down, so he moved back to Chicago and started selling diesel engines. He took his clients to the track, and whenever one of his friends had a bachelor party, Matt made sure it was at Arlington.

In 1992 Matt met Tracy, a divorced mother who, conveniently, lived in Cicero, across the street from Sportsman's Park. During their courtship, he had a big day at the races and gave Tracy the money as a gift. She hid it in the pantry, because she didn't feel right taking gambling winnings. It didn't stay there long. Every time Matt came to see her, he asked, "Remember that money I gave you?" and eventually, it all found its way back to the betting windows.

Tracy knew she was marrying a man who loved horse racing. They honeymooned in Las Vegas (his choice), where Matt sneaked down to the race book while his bride was asleep in the hotel room. But she never realized how much he was gambling. He hid it well. When he had a Monday business meeting in San Francisco, he'd fly out on Friday night, telling Tracy it was an all-weekend affair.

"I'd spend four days in San Francisco. I'd tell my wife, 'I went to the wineries; I went to Alcatraz.' I never saw anything but the hotel and the track."

Matt always paid the mortgage and fed the children, but he and Tracy didn't seem to live as well as the family of a $100,000-a-year salesman should have. When Tracy wanted a new fence, Matt took out a $15,000 home equity loan, spent $900 on boards at Home Depot, and told her she'd have to build it herself, because they just couldn't afford the labor.

"I had her snowed," Matt said. "I had her thinking everything was fine. I always made sure I bumped her $500 whenever she needed anything. She thought I was winning. My dad thought I was the greatest handicapper in the world, because he'd seen me hit some long shots."

They'd been married four years when Matt conceived the credit card hustle. It worked like this: Matt charged all his expenses to his company card, which had an unlimited credit line. Every month, his employer cut him a check to cover his expenses. Instead of paying off the card, Matt would deposit the check in one of his three bank accounts and take money to the track. The first month he did it, he owed $1,000 on the credit card. He needed to pay off half his balance to keep the account open, so he charged $500 worth of merchandise, then canceled his purchases. That placed a $500 credit on his account, giving him another month to pay back the full amount. When the next month's bill came, he owed $2,000, so he bought $1,000 worth of merchandise.

With limitless cash at his disposal, Matt started betting as though he had the biggest bankroll and the biggest balls at the track. He'd open a day by plunging $200 into the Daily Double. He bet $200 to win, place, and show on long shots at Gulfstream Park. One week, he and an engine dealer cooked up a sale that netted them $17,000 apiece.

"I thought I was golden," he said. "It lasted four days, and then I was scrapin' again."

Whenever he walked into the Joliet OTB, the tellers argued about who had to work late, because Matt always closed the place down, lingering until the last quarter horse at Los Alamitos in California crossed the finish line. But even the OTB couldn't give him enough action. He bought a satellite dish so he could subscribe to TVG, a horse racing network. The study at home became a private race book. He had a bookie in Costa Rica and an account with youbet.com, an Internet horse wagering site. He was betting football, too. His son Tyler got to spend father-son time in there, listening to Dad scream "You fuckin' nigger!" at running backs who weren't helping their teams beat the spread.

For a while, Matt fancied he could win enough to pay off his credit card debts. Whenever he played Belmont or Saratoga, two tracks in New York State, he bet the Pick Six, a six-race parlay that has paid as much as $3 million, hoping "to hit the home run." But when he realized he was so deep in debt that no jackpot could save him, he began betting even more madly.

"To me, it wasn't about money," he said. "The last three years at the track, I never left with money in my pocket. I couldn't leave with money, even though I wanted to ease that debt. I didn't feel right about having money. To me, the reasoning I had was there was no way I could reach the $150,000. It became totally unreal. Because of what I could do with that credit card, I thought I controlled everything."

$$\cup$$

The day after he confessed to his boss, Matt woke Tracy at five in the morning.

"I've got something to tell you," he whispered, standing over the bed.

When Matt confessed he'd gambled away $170,000, Tracy couldn't breathe.

"I felt like I had no right to anything I own," she recalled. "My house, my clothes—I have no right to breathe, because of all the money we owe. It was kind of like we were both nonexistent. I thought, 'Where am I going to live? Where are my kids going to live?'"

As soon as Matt went to sleep that night, she pulled all the credit cards out of his wallet. Then she told him, "There's no way I will stay with you if you gamble again."

Matt called his financial adviser, a man who'd saved him from a dozen scrapes.

"I can't do anything else for you," the adviser told him. "You need to get into a twelve-step program."

Matt joined one. He now attends the meetings as avidly as he once attended the races. His boss didn't fire him—"I'd made him a lot of money, and we were good friends," he said—but he was no longer allowed to travel out of town or dine on an expense account. A few months later, when the company reduced its sales staff, Matt was laid off. But he found a new job in sales and worked out a payment plan with the credit card company—$500 a month, from here to eternity—so he could keep his house. He could have declared bankruptcy, but his twelve-step group told him no, he had to take responsibility for his gambling debts.

He won't even read a newspaper article about horse racing now. He can't. At first, it hurt too much to know that somewhere, Thoroughbreds were being led into a starting gate, and he didn't have a ticket on one. Now, any reminder of his frantic gambling days makes him feel "horrible." The secretary of state's office in Joliet just moved into the same shopping center as the OTB. When Matt and Tracy renewed their driver's licenses, he crouched down in his seat, so he wouldn't have to look at the sign. Matt's brother wanted to take him to see *Seabiscuit*. Matt refused.

"Obviously, a movie, there's no friggin' way you can make a bet," he said. "But one, I don't want to take a chance, and two, I have to respect what my wife wants, and she doesn't want me to do it."

A great passion of his life is over, but now he can go to church, because he doesn't care that the service starts at the same time as first post at Tampa Bay Downs. He doesn't shout "Hurry up" at Tyler when they play miniature golf on Saturday mornings. When the family vacationed in San Diego, Matt didn't once consider canceling the trip and cashing in the plane tickets.

Now he has to choose between placating the demon that demands he bet on horses and living with his wife and children. For the last two years, he's chosen his family.

"Life to me is so different now," he said. "It's slower. Plus, I'm a guest in my house now. Tracy's the only one who can sign checks. She handles all the money. She gives me five dollars for lunch every day. There's absolutely nothing I would rather do than be at a racetrack, but the only way I can get cash now is to rob a bank."

# 6

## Derby Day

On the Thursday before the Kentucky Derby, Mary Schoenfeldt sat down at her dining room table to pick a winner. With a ruler and a Sharpie, she drew a grading chart for the sixteen-horse field. Along the top, she listed the qualities she was looking for in a horse: good breeding, a talented jockey, a successful trainer, a winning record.

"When you're a teacher, let's say you give an arithmetic test," she said. "You'd have the kids' names here and the scores here, so you can show the parents. There's certain things I like to look at. They're just things in my mind that could make up a good horse."

Whenever a horse met her qualifications, she penciled in a faint check. The horse with the most checks would be her Derby winner. Mary never saw a copy of the *Daily Racing Form* until she married Creighton, but since then, her charts had given A grades to ten horses who went on to wear the roses: Ferdinand, Alysheba, Winning Colors, Sunday Silence, Unbridled, Lil E. Tee, Thunder Gulch, Grindstone, Real Quiet, and Fusaichi Pegasus.

For the 129th running of the Derby, Mary gave nine checks to Empire Maker: he was trained by Bobby Frankel, whose stable was winning more stakes races than any other in North America; his sire, Unbridled, was a Derby champion; he would be ridden by Jerry Bailey, Cigar's old jockey; he'd won three races in five starts, including the Florida Derby at Gulfstream and the Wood Memorial at Aqueduct, two of the most important Derby preps. All the wiseguys at the *Form* were touting Empire Maker, too: "He's undoubtedly the best horse in the race," columnist Kristin Sadler wrote. At Churchill Downs, the track handicapper made him the 6–5 favorite.

"Here I am with this first- or second-grade way of doing things, and these people have computers, and we come up with the same thing," Mary marveled.

Creighton was skeptical.

"If you go every day, you'd never get it all done," he blustered, hovering over Mary's 146-square chart. "She tries it for other races, but I don't see any success in it."

Creighton didn't have a Derby horse. He wasn't going to bet the race.

"It's just another horse race to me," he scoffed, with a pro's disdain for the amateurs who were emptying their wallets onto a herd of three-year-olds. "They're bettin' with both hands down at the OTB. But I can see a horse race any day."

Creighton planned to spend Derby weekend playing in a handicapping contest on the third floor of the Hawthorne grandstand. He'd asked Mary to help him, but she'd demurred.

"I'd miss out on Mass and Communion and my holy hour for three days," she said.

I didn't have a Derby horse, either. I'd given up trying to pick winners. I was losing too much money. As Mary liked to say, "Anything can happen in a horse race—the horse doesn't feel like running, or he has trouble getting out of the starting gate, or there's a disqualification." I stopped thinking of the outcome as a certainty—"this horse is going to win"—and started thinking in terms of probabilities—"this is the best horse, but he only has a 30 percent chance of winning." I was assigning my own odds to every horse, similar to a track handicapper making a morning line (assessment of how the public will bet), and I was only betting on animals with inflated prices. If I believed

Empire Maker had a 38 percent chance to win the Kentucky Derby (which I did), then his odds should be 8–5. He'd be a good investment at 2–1. At 7–5, he'd be a waste of money. It didn't matter whether he won that race, just as it didn't matter, over the span of a lifetime, whether the stock market rose or fell that day.

For guidance, I'd bought a book called *Money Secrets at the Racetrack,* by Barry Meadow, who assured his readers that this was the *only* way to make a profit at the track. As proof, he reproduced a $109,989 check from Santa Anita, made out to "Barry Joel Meadow."

"Picking winners is overrated," Meadow wrote. "You can make money at the racetrack even if you pick very few winners. You can lose money even if you pick plenty." (I was picking very few winners, so this was what I wanted to hear.) "Shopping for bargains, not picking winners, is the key to making money at racetrack betting. Seek overlays—those animals being sent away at more than their true odds."

The book even included a computer-generated chart telling you how much to bet on every race, depending on the odds. I copied it, trimmed it to four inches by four inches, and carried it in my wallet.

After watching Mary construct her Derby chart, I went home and drew up an odds line for the race. This is how it looked, in order of post position:

| Horse | Odds | Percent Chance |
|---|---|---|
| Supah Blitz | 100–1 | 1% |
| Brancusi | 100–1 | 1% |
| Sir Cherokee | 100–1 | 1% |
| Atswhatimtalkinbout | 20–1 | 4% |
| Peace Rules | 9–1 | 12% |
| Funny Cide | 12–1 | 8% |
| Offlee Wild | 100–1 | 1% |
| Buddy Gil | 8–1 | 11% |
| Indian Express | 25–1 | 4% |
| Lone Star Sky | 100–1 | 1% |
| Domestic Dispute | 100–1 | 1% |

| Horse | Odds | Percent Chance |
|---|---|---|
| Empire Maker | 8–5 | 38% |
| Eye of the Tiger | 100–1 | 1% |
| Ten Cents A Shine | 100–1 | 1% |
| Outta Here | 100–1 | 1% |
| Ten Most Wanted | 12–1 | 8% |
| Scrimshaw | 12–1 | 8% |

Empire Maker deserved to be the chalk. I'd watched him win the Wood Memorial on an April-muddy track at Aqueduct. In the stretch, he was running head-to-head with Funny Cide when his jockey, Jerry Bailey, cocked the whip. After a poised moment, Bailey's arm relaxed, as though he were thinking, "Nah, let's save something for Louisville." Empire Maker sprang away to win by half a length. He was the fastest horse, with the highest Beyer speed figure, but I was not willing to bet him blindly. For one thing, he'd bruised his hoof while training at Churchill Downs. For another, the Kentucky Derby foils good hand-icapping every year. In the past twenty-five runnings, only one favorite had won—the Japanese mercenary Fusaichi Pegasus. When seventeen horses gallop in a pack, it's hard to predict who'll pop out at the fin-ish line. You gotta get a price.

At my first Derby, I didn't get a price. It was 1997, and I'd fallen hard for Captain Bodgit after watching him race across the simulcast screens at Sportsman's Park, so I drove down to Louisville to see him in the flesh. I believed, and I still do, that it is every horseplayer's duty to visit Churchill Downs on the first Saturday in May. It rained that day. I stood by myself in the infield for five hours, a handicapping geek toting a pair of binoculars, a program, and a colored pen. I felt like a jazz snob in a mosh pit. While I huddled under the eave of a tempo-rary betting hut, trying to play the undercard, every frat brother in the Ohio Valley was sliding shirtless through the mud. Every sorority sis-ter was giggling off the plea to "show your tits!" (OK, every sorority sister except one. This should have made the five-hour drive worth-while, since, as a dedicated horseplayer, I hadn't seen a pair of real breasts in several months.)

Captain Bodgit was the favorite at 3–1. I bet him anyway. I was clinging to a fence in the homestretch when he ran by me on his final lap, a neck behind the unyielding Silver Charm.

I hadn't been back to Louisville since. I'd asked Rob if he wanted to make the trip that year—he'd be good company in the infield, since he, too, preferred horses to booze and breasts. But Rob had shaken his head no.

"I don't like crowds," he mumbled.

So on Derby Day, I was sitting at a wobbly picnic table on the Hawthorne apron with Soren the musician and Bob the bookseller, the only two friends I'd ever been able to drag along on my gambling expeditions. They'd each been to the track with me once and never returned, either due to my pleadings or their own itchy Thoroughbred jones. I'd taken Soren to Arlington during my first spell of gambling fever seven years before. After we'd both lost sixty dollars, he suddenly began moaning as though he'd locked his only child in a hot car.

"Oh my God, I can't believe I lost sixty dollars. I could have bought a new guitar case with that money!"

"People who think money is for buying stuff shouldn't be gambling," I told him.

I then bet fifty dollars on a turf race. After my horse finished eighth, Soren grabbed me by the shirt and dragged me out of the track.

It had taken me longer to get Bob to the track. We were high school friends, fellow refugees from Michigan, but the first time I invited him he was married, which meant the track was in the same no-fly zone as strip clubs and wet T-shirt contests. Eventually Bob graduated to bachelorhood, and I was able to talk him into a trip to Sportsman's during its final spring. Bob was a Rat Pack fan, mixing his own martinis and mourning for Sinatra, and he loved the cigar aroma of the grandstand, the sight of old white ethnics—Frank's people— sporting dapper hats and shouting phlegmy curses. He bet on a horse named Four Jacks, because there is a band named Four Jacks and a Jill in the movie *This Is Spinal Tap*. The races were called on account of snow, after a horse belly flopped in the mud to finish the sixth race, and Bob left without cashing a ticket.

"I just want to win one bet," he said. "I don't even know where to go if you win."

I badly wanted to win money on the Derby. Not just to show Bob and Soren that I wasn't wasting my life, but because Derby Day is to a horseplayer what St. Crispin's Day was to Henry V and his troops: "All shall be forgot/ But he'll remember, with advantages/ What feats he did that day." We forget the names, and eventually even the numbers, of the horses who won us our $1,200 exactas or our $7,500 trifectas, but a Derby wager is a boast that's good at all tracks, for all time, because everyone watches the race, and because the winner's name will be recorded in almanacs long after you've blown the money on lesser animals. (Almost all horseplayers. Creighton wasn't betting, and Scott was living up to his description in Steven Davidowitz's *Betting Thoroughbreds*: "Hardened professional players such as . . . Scott McMannis tend to disclaim any interest" in Triple Crown races.)

I started Derby Day by touting Bob and Soren onto two losers. That always happened when I brought friends to the track. The misdeeds of Cart's Forty Four and Alstott would be overshadowed by a bigger race, later in the day. But I would never forget them. They made me look like a blowhard.

By the third, Soren had stopped listening to me. He was doing his own handicapping.

"I like the name of this horse," he said. "Partywithavengeance."

Partywithavengeance won.

Now Soren was up $6.80 and I was down eighteen dollars. Nobody likes a winner at the track. A winner has your money. A racetrack is like a jail or a bar: you make more friends by being a loser. I wanted to get away from Soren. He wasn't supposed to be winning. I was supposed to be winning. If this continued, he'd think my charts and my odds lines were as worthless as lottery dream books, and that being a goof was as profitable as being a geek.

Peter Galassi saved me. Galassi had been calling horse races for twenty years, and most afternoons he recited the running order as prosaically as the four-thirty traffic report and read the payoffs as though they were stock quotes. But now his radio baritone became the call of a delighted friend, as he spotted an amply bosomed, hipped, and thighed woman waving from the winner's circle.

"It's Rrrrooosie," he crooned.

There was a time when it was common to see a four-inch pump step from the Cicero Avenue bus, followed by a silver lamé dress that could have contained all three Supremes, all under a hat so broad it could shade a summer's worth of suns. Racetrack Rosie only came to Hawthorne on holidays now, but Derby Day was the holiest, so there she was, wearing a homemade dress cut to form a window on her pressed cleavage and a floppy hat garnished with roses. A tiny plastic horse balanced on the brim. I ran over to introduce myself. Rosie had been here on St. Patrick's Day, wearing a green dress and invading the winner's circle to cozy up with startled owners. I'd missed my chance to talk to her then. I wasn't going to miss it now.

Racetrack Rosie was sixty-nine years old, a great-grandmother, but not a retired woman.

"I'm Chicago's oldest stripper," she said, her youthfully smooth face beaming. "I work for senior citizens, I work for birthday parties. I don't get totally nude. I wear pasties and a G-string. I can still do it better than the younger girls. I swirl a tassel on each of my titties. Young girls can't do that. They don't have the muscle control."

Rosie discovered the track in 1956, as a way to kill an afternoon before a nightclub gig in the Bahamas. She won forty dollars—"American money"—and when she returned to Chicago, she became a gregarious, brilliantly attired fixture at Sportsman's Park. She designed clothes to match the fluorescent silks of her favorite owners, so she wouldn't look out of place in the winner's circle photos. Rosie was so beloved that on August 17, 1991, Sportsman's Park held a Racetrack Rosie Day, putting her picture on the program cover. There were complaints. A few racetrack moralists believed her stripping was a come-on for more intimate performances, the sort of vice that could give gambling a bad name. Rosie was too sunny to let this embitter her. The backbiting was a compliment. It meant she wasn't following the crowd.

"I'm friendly," she said. "Everybody I'm kin to. Everybody that plays the horses is my family."

Rosie tilted her head, and the little horse toppled from her hat. I picked it up and replaced it.

"Your horse broke down," I said.

Rosie cackled.

"My horse broke down. Ahhhh, you're right! He did. You know, I went to the Kentucky Derby in '78 and I had a rose on my behind, and they took a picture of it and put it in the paper."

A fifty-dollar bill appeared between the fingers of Rosie's velvet glove. She had to go inside to make a bet.

"Every now and then, I might find a winner," she said. "But I'm a qualified loser."

The bustle that had once filled a page of the Louisville paper switched away. As soon as she walked through the door, Rosie stopped to smother a friend. Rosie was wrong. She wasn't a loser.

By five o'clock, Bob, Soren, and I had migrated to the third floor, so we could watch the Derby on a big-screen television. I'd lost almost $100, so Bob and Soren were ignoring my advice.

"Who do you like in the Derby?" Bob asked.

"Empire Maker."

"BORRRR-ING," Bob shouted, like a *Rocky Horror* fan heckling the movie's stuffy professor.

"Well, who do you like?" I challenged.

"Indian Express. He's owned by Phil Chess, of Chess Records."

Chess Records was the Chicago blues label that discovered Muddy Waters, back in the forties, when men wore real hats.

Soren liked Supah Blitz. His name was fun to say.

I didn't know whom I liked yet. The tote board would tell me. I'd lost my odds table somewhere on the first floor, but I'd memorized it by then, so I started comparing prices. The Kentucky Derby was a terrific race for a value bettor, because there were two pools to choose from: the pool at Churchill Downs and the pool at Hawthorne. The odds at Hawthorne were better. Ten Most Wanted had won the Illinois Derby here, so the bettors were treating him like a favorite son. At 5–1, he was ridiculously overbet. Which, of course, meant someone else must be underbet. Empire Maker was 3–1. Funny Cide was 16–1. Scrimshaw was 14–1. They were all overlays, according to my line, so I decided to bet on all three of them. ("Dutching" horses is a good strategy when an undeserving horse is eating up a lot of money, leaving overlays scattered across the board.) I also decided to sink $100 into the race. There was no risk involved. A friend had once assured me that "money bet on the Derby doesn't count against your bottom line." You can write it off as a charitable donation to the sport. (The reverse is not true, however: money won on the Derby counts toward your profits, and, as a bonus, you can brag about it to people who don't go to the track, because it's the only horse race they watch all year.)

I bet fifty dollars to win on Empire Maker, twelve dollars to win on Funny Cide, and fourteen dollars to win on Scrimshaw. Then I boxed them all in the exacta for two dollars and put an extra two dollars on the exactas involving Empire Maker. Soren watched over my shoulder.

"You bet fifty to win?"

"It's the Derby," I said.

The image of the Churchill Downs starting gate, painted a John Deere green, bridging the width of the track to contain seventeen fidgeting Thoroughbreds, was repeated on every television. Normally a dozen tracks ran at once, competing like carnival rides on a midway, and stretch calls barked from speakers on the minute. But now everyone's hopes were directed toward a single race, and for a rare moment, after Scrimshaw was led into the outermost stall, the grandstand was silent.

In Louisville, the starter punched his button, and then our room relaxed into a murmur. The horses tumbled forward, gathering into a dun mass. The broad crane shot miniaturized them to a tin-soldier cavalry.

When the camera focused on the leaders, the first horse I noticed was Funny Cide. He was on the rail, in a pocket behind the front-runners, Brancusi and Peace Rules. Ten Cents a Shine galloped alongside him.

"The Derby half in 46 and 1, *strong* fractions," the announcer barked. "On up front, Brancusi leads it a neck, pressed hard by Peace Rules as he sticks his nose in front. Two back to long shot Funny Cide in third."

Funny Cide is getting a beautiful trip, I thought. But I didn't want to get my hopes up over a 16–1 shot. I didn't want to jinx him. I stood with my *Racing Form* folded under my arm, anxiously stroking my chin.

Then the leaders sprinted around the turn, accelerating like speed skaters, and my dignified pose disintegrated. I'm a man in my mid-thirties. Only twice in my life have I been completely, ravingly out of my head with excitement. The first time was as a teenager, when I unthinkingly hugged my friend Al to celebrate a buzzer-beating shot at a college basketball game. I vowed to keep a lid on displays like that, and I didn't slip up again for twenty-three years—until the stretch run of the 2003 Kentucky Derby. Peace Rules shot away from the failing Brancusi. Funny Cide took up the chase, and then Empire Maker lunged into the screen, pursuing all three of them.

"Peace Rules ahead by a neck to Funny Cide," the announcer called, his pitch mounting. "Empire Maker makes his move on the far outside, and here he comes! Empire Maker digs in, set down by Bailey. Funny Cide has got a head in front!"

Peace Rules began to falter, and then I heard this magic phrase: "Funny Cide looking to upset the Derby!"

By mid-stretch, it was clear all the way from Louisville that Funny Cide was going to win. So it wasn't on his behalf that I was whipping my thigh with a folded-up *Daily Racing Form*. I was pleading with Empire Maker to complete my exacta.

"Six-twelve!" I screeched in a hoarse hurricane of supplication, as I flailed at my leg like a Kodo drummer. I was still lucid enough to realize that the exacta would pay more with Funny Cide on top. "SIX-TWELVE!"

Empire Maker's hoof was hurting him—his head was twisted to the side, as though he were gritting his teeth—but he ground through the dirt, and inches before the wire, his snout appeared to glide past Peace Rules.

The judges spent five minutes studying the photo, and then they put up the numbers I'd begged for: 6-12.

"That horse'll never win again," a losing gambler grumbled.

Once was enough. I raced outside to await the tale of the tote. Funny Cide paid $39.20 to win. The exacta paid $124. My tickets were worth $500, my biggest score of the year. I needed to brag to someone. My friend Terry was no use: back in February, he'd bought a two-dollar ticket on Funny Cide in the Derby Futures Pool, when the colt was 92–1, so he had even bigger bragging rights than I did. I looked in on Mary, who'd been so keen on Empire Maker. She folded her devotional and showed me three tickets: two dollars to win, place, and show on Empire Maker; two dollars to win, place, and show on the horse with the second most check marks, Buddy Gil; and two dollars to win, place, and show on her third choice, Funny Cide.

Mary is a cautious woman. She knows anything can happen in a horse race: "My chart is Utopia. It's how they should run."

Mary totaled her earnings on a sheet of notepaper. She'd wagered twenty-seven dollars and collected $88.20.

Mary's weekend was much more successful than Creighton's. Over the course of his three-day tournament, he bet eighteen races. His horses paid a total of $4.20.

"I was goin' for longies," he explained.

The tournament was won by Rudy Benes, who had been coming to the track every day for years, always wearing the same blue fishing hat. It was whispered that Rudy had gotten tips from his son, "Blond Jimmy" Benes, one of Chicago's most astute professional gamblers. Blond Jimmy always sat alone. He rarely talked to anybody. He rarely even looked at fellow members of his species. He didn't seem like the type to tell his father whom he liked, but I guess blood is thicker than money, even for horseplayers.

Once I'd finished talking to Mary, I ran back to find Soren and Bob. As soon as I spotted them, I paraded through the grandstand holding up five fingers, one for every bill. Horseplayers lose so often, we deserve the few shining moments of smugness.

Soren would write about his experience at the track on his blog later that day:

> Racetracks are something I can handle maybe once a year or so, maybe I've turned yuppie or something but the dark-sider lifestyle really doesn't appeal to me. The seediness and desperation really bother me. Ted kept talking to the regulars there (he's working on a book about horse racing so he's there every day. I think he'd be there every day anyway if he had a chance, but the book deal adds legitimacy). Mostly they seem to be a weird cross between statisticians and winos, very fringe-dwelling individuals. None of them seemed to drink much, but I suppose the track is their addiction of choice.
>
> For some reason, the track really wore me down. Chicago hot dogs and a cold, windy day spent outside mostly took its toll, and I've been feeling a head cold coming on ever since.

Bob, he still hadn't cashed a ticket at the track.

After the race, I took Soren and Bob out for drinks. Of course, I had to pay. I couldn't explain that, although I had won $500 that day, I was still down $1,800 for the season, and that I needed the 500 bucks for my vacation.

# 7

# Travels with McChump

"We need to be at Fairmount Park by three o'clock so we can play Arlington from there before the night races start," I was saying to Terry. "I want to start this trip with a full day of gambling."

"It's nine thirty," he said, guessing, because he never wore a watch. "We should make it there by then."

Terry Bjork and I were standing in front of a rental-car office in Evanston, Illinois. A cigarette smoldered in Terry's tight-lipped mouth, and he was dressed in his racetrack outfit: a Breeders' Cup baseball cap, a denim jacket, faded-to-sky jeans, and a souvenir T-shirt from one of the 110 tracks he's visited on his McChump Racing Tours. Every summer, Terry drove around the country, stopping at tracks with grandstands that were smaller than high school football stadiums, tracks with names that were mysterious abbreviations in the agate of the *Daily Racing Form*—Gil, for the Gillespie County Fair in Luckenbach, Texas; or FtP, for Fort Pierre, in Pierre, South Dakota—the bleakest Class D, minor league hamlets, where twelve-year-old Thoroughbreds who hadn't won in years galloped around half-mile bullrings.

When I'd stopped at his apartment that morning, his girlfriend, Jan, answered the door. She'd discovered him through his online travelogue, mcchump.com. They'd met at Lone Star Park, near her home in Dallas, and he'd lured her north.

"Mr. Bjork is *so* excited," she said, and I took her word for it. As a southern girl shacked up with a Norwegian, she handled most of the couple's emotional displays.

Mr. Bjork was indeed excited. As soon as our Pontiac Grand Am rolled up in front of the office, we would begin another McChump Tour: seven racetracks in nine days, culminating with a weekend at the Miles City Bucking Horse Sale in Miles City, Montana.

"Don't tell them we're taking the car all the way to Montana," Terry said. "They don't like it when you drive that far."

So we told them we were going to Collinsville, Illinois. It's a suburb of St. Louis and the home of Fairmount Park, the first stop on our 5,000-mile journey.

U

I'd first heard about Terry through mcchump.com, the anthology of his racetrack adventures. A mutual friend introduced us at Sportsman's Park, and on Derby Day 2002 we took an overnight McChump Tour to Great Lakes Downs. Great Lakes Downs is the second-biggest attraction in Muskegon, Michigan—after the giant waterslide. It's a track where starved horses with barrel-slat ribs race on a sandy oval, a track where seven-year-old children bawling for ice cream sprint across the apron in the evening lake breeze, a track where the only decorative touch is a model lighthouse that looks as though it were swiped from a miniature golf course. That weekend, I learned the McChump betting strategy: play every race, hope to win enough money for beer. I heard the McChump soundtrack, a mix tape that reminded Terry of his travels. I already knew "Rockaway Beach" by the Ramones, the unofficial theme song of Aqueduct Racetrack in Queens, but that three-and-a-half-hour road trip was my introduction to "That's What I Like About the North," a polka hit Terry heard on a North Dakota radio station's "Accordion Hour."

A McChump Tour sounded like my kind of travel. I'm a high-way dog. The autumn before, I'd made two trips from Chicago to New England—both by car. I've driven through all forty-eight states you can drive through. I refuse to take airplanes on intracontinental trips, not because I'm afraid to fly, but because I'm not an overnight package to be rushed from city to city. I want to find what's between here and there—even if it's North Dakota, to the sound of accordions. Most weekends, Terry can be found at a table by the Hawthorne bar-bershop, sitting behind an ashtray and a stack of computer-generated racing charts. But once a year, he has to hit the road. That spring, he invited me along.

$$\cup$$

Fairmount Park was a throwback to the days when racetracks cele-brated three of the major vices—drinking, smoking, and gambling—and were convenient to a motel that offered the fourth. Hawthorne and Arlington had risen from their ashes as family entertainment cen-ters, with bands, petting zoos, Sunday buffets, and all-star athletes sign-ing autographs. There was none of that crap at Fairmount. When we walked in, at ten minutes to three, the afternoon crowd was in full grumble. Wobbly tables were crowded with gamblers taking time off from work—like six months—to throw crumpled dollars at races from Churchill Downs and Aqueduct. The usual result was confettied all over the grandstand, a fluorescent cavern hidden under the bleachers. The mutuel clerks were sequestered behind barred windows, like bank tellers in an Edward G. Robinson movie. I bet twenty dollars on the first race at Arlington, lost, and didn't bet again until the ninth, which I also lost. I was a disciplined horseplayer.

Not Terry. Terry bet Pick Threes starting on every race. He had once tried to play the races like a professional. He'd subscribed to All-Ways, the same service that was helping Creighton Schoenfeldt lose his life savings. "It worked if you sat around and waited for the over-lays," Terry concluded. "But it was boring."

Since almost everyone loses in the long run, Terry decided he'd have fun going broke. He won $120 betting on Arlington that afternoon.

The real racing at Fairmount started after dark. The track was lit up like a stock-car oval, and young men and women huddled together in the bleachers. Evidently, Collinsville nightlife was so threadbare that Fairmont qualified as a wholesome date. It felt like a county fair: the silent, aimless walking of hand-holding couples, the chewy, sodden barbecue sandwiches served by "the Paddock," a fly-screened concession stand with a fan buzzing over the grill.

As I inspected the brochure-sized program, I recognized horses I'd seen at Hawthorne. They hadn't been able to win there, so now they were here in the minors. Almost every horse had a record of big-city failure. Uptown Brown, who'd run in the race I'd refused to bet with Glenn's money back in March, was entered in the third, a $3,200 claimer for horses who hadn't won in the last ten months. He was the favorite. In the same race was Uwana Prop, an eleven-year-old gelding running in his 110th race. His margin of defeat at Hawthorne reached twenty-three lengths before his trainer shipped him to Fairmount, where he'd finished as close as ten lengths behind a winner. Terry led me to the paddock, where he introduced me to Uwana Prop's groom, a woman he'd met on a horse racing message board.

"It's about the end of the road for Uwana Prop," she said, leaning against the chain-link fence that separated the paddock from the track. "It's almost time for him to go home. We're going to find a nice farm for him to live on. He's not too interested in racing anymore, but the owner's trying to wring the last dollar out of him."

The third race taught us everything we needed to know about handicapping at Fairmount—or at any small track. It was all about class. The winner, at 11–1, was Just a Runaway, who had last run in a $5,000 claiming race. An $1,800 drop made all the difference. Here, at the bottom of Thoroughbred society, was a caste system that would have baffled a Hindu. A handicapper who learned it could win a lot of money.

This was why Terry had hopes for Toy Tiger Jr. Terry had a fondness for futile racehorses, and few were more futile than Toy Tiger Jr. He was already five years old, two years beyond Secretariat's pension age, and in thirty races at Sportsman's and Hawthorne he had never won, although he had once come in second. Now, the horse who'd flunked every audition in Chicago was trying community theater, hoping to "break his maiden"—win his first race—here in the sticks. Terry planned to bet him.

"This is where you get all the quality horses," he said sarcastically. "These are all the accidents that happened out in the field. Oops!"

That night, Toy Tiger Jr. did something he'd never done before. He took the lead. It happened on the turn. By the top of the stretch, Toy Tiger Jr. headed a five-horse parade. Terry was thrilled. He pressed himself into the rail and shouted like a soccer dad cheering his son.

"You can do it, Toy Tiger! This could be the night. You're seeing history. Come on, Toy Tiger Jr. You can do it! He's lookin' at me."

But first was a disorienting place for Toy Tiger Jr. Unsure of what to do with the lead, he offered it to the favorite, Asa un Fuegos, another Hawthorne carpetbagger.

"No!" Terry moaned, as Asa un Fuegos swept past. "Stupid favorite."

Terry would have made a great campaign volunteer for Harold Stassen. He refused to lose faith in this thirty-one-time loser.

"It's only a matter of time before Toy Tiger Jr. breaks his maiden," he said. "He had the lead down the stretch, and he probably didn't know what it was. Moe Dickstein broke his maiden. Gifted Peter broke his maiden at Pimlico. Everyone's broken his maiden except Toy Tiger Jr."

In the next race, I finally made a score by combining two out-of-town horses in an exacta. Stop the Violins had been racing—unsuccessfully—at Mountaineer Park, in West Virginia. Lt. Austin was from Hawthorne. I'd bet him just before one of his second-place finishes, so he owed me money. He paid it back by running second to Stop the Violins. The exacta paid twenty-nine dollars, putting me ahead six dollars for the night. I felt like a two-legged version of Stop the Violins: a big-city gambler, taking money from rubes.

"I may play this track more often," I remarked to Dan, another of Terry's Internet friends. "Hawthorne shows it sometimes."

He sensed my smugness.

"It's hard to handicap this track," he said. "The best you can hope for is a string of low-priced horses. We've got some good handicappers down here, and they still have a tough time."

Amateur handicappers had it even tougher. I didn't cash another ticket at Fairmount Park.

The next day was a doubleheader.

We were due at Blue Ribbon Downs, a quarter-horse track in Sallisaw, Oklahoma, by one o'clock. Then we'd spend the evening at Fair Meadows in Tulsa. As Terry gunned the Grand Am through the Ozarks, trying to make post time, there were hours to talk, so he told me about the horse who had inspired the McChump Racing Tour. Every one of us racetrack loafers has a fondly remembered horse who launched the downward spiral. Terry's was named Layton Hill.

One spring, Terry went to Phoenix to see an old friend and to attend the Cactus League ballgames. After a few days, the Cactus League got old. Baseball has nine innings. The track has nine races. And ballgames get tedious: the same players come onto the field every inning, then you see them all again the next day.

"My friend Scott got tired of going to baseball, and one day he said, 'Let's go to Turf Paradise,'" Terry said. "In the last race, Scott told me a horse named Layton Hill was going to win, and he told me exactly how he was going to do it, and it was like a play unfolding. He was an out-of-the-clouds closer. He wasn't even in the race until the top of the stretch, and then he went 'zoom.' A light clicked on in my head: the races could be figured out."

Like a lot of other lucky novices, Terry bought a shelf of handicapping books. He squandered his summer at Arlington, and by Labor Day he was back in Arizona for an excursion to Prescott Downs.

"It was really a crummy track," he recalled, "but Scott knew a lot of people, and we slept on this woman's floor, and there'd be big breakfasts, and jockeys' agents would be hanging out there. It was go to the races all day and go to the bars all night. There were all sorts of conspiracy theories about jockeys hitting horses with buzzers."

Terry wrote up an account of his visit to Prescott Downs, and posted it on the "Derby List," a horse racing message board. A friend read the story and suggested that Terry collect his racetrack reviews into a book. A book seemed like too much work. A Web site sounded easier. Terry set up mcchump.com, he said—"And then I decided to visit as many racetracks as possible."

After that, Terry started touring like the Grateful Dead. He was divorced, so his weekends were free. When they weren't, it was because his employer, a pharmaceutical concern we'll call the Big Company, sent him on business trips to cities with racetracks. A few years into the project, after hitting Belmont, Santa Anita, Philadelphia Park, and Golden Gate Fields, he read a post on the "Derby List" from "one of these racing snob kind of people who was making fun of little tracks. I made the conscious decision that since he didn't like it, he was going to read about little tracks. I was going to put a story about a little track on the "Derby List" every week that fall. I grew up in Great Falls, Montana, and when I was a little kid, I used to go to the horse races at the fair, so I've always been of the opinion that little town people deserve horse racing as much as anybody. I take exception to these people who say all these little tracks should be closed, and they should just simulcast the big tracks. Nobody gets interested in horse racing by going to the OTB."

Every weekend, he set out in his Toyota Celica, with his rubber dinosaur, Kozno the Ultimate Monster, on the dashboard. At Detroit Race Course (since demolished, like so much else in Detroit), he was besieged by touts and "people swearing at jockeys." At Thistledown in Cleveland, the grandstand fit "a general Rust Belt theme: red brick architecture with small windows that made the whole place look like a typical upper Midwest factory."

From there, he descended to Stampede Park in Calgary, Alberta; to Arapahoe Park in Aurora, Colorado; to Yavapai Downs in Prescott, Arizona. But his greatest find, the discovery that made him feel like the horseplaying descendant of La Salle, de Soto, and Balboa, was Quarter Pole Downs in Rayne, Louisiana, deep in Cajun country. He was in Lafayette for a music festival when he heard a horse racing ad on the radio. It wasn't for Evangeline Downs, so Terry asked a Cajun at a nearby gas station if there was another racetrack in the area. He was directed to Rayne, a town of 8,500, where he found "a little building with a bar inside, and an apron outside. It was just the littlest, tiniest building."

The six-race program was a single mimeographed sheet, listing only the name of the horse and its owner. Only one of the jockeys owned nylon pants. The rest wore jeans. There was no tote board. There were "auction pools": one ticket on each horse, sold to the highest bidder.

"Guys were just walkin' around, taking wagers," Terry remembered. "Or guys were just bettin' with each other. They were walkin' around saying, 'Your horse is a pig.' 'Oh yeah? You wanna bet on it?' That was the dinkiest track I've ever been to. As far as I know, I'm the only one of my friends who's ever been there. I know a guy who's been to over 200 racetracks, and even he hadn't been there."

In 2001 the Big Company moved its offices to New Jersey and gave Terry a choice: a transfer or a layoff with eighteen months' pay. He wanted to spend as much of his life as possible at the track, and as little as possible in New Jersey, so he took the buyout. He spent it on the longest McChump Tour ever: twenty-five tracks in fifty-five days.

Terry hadn't set out to see America—he just wanted to gamble—but visiting racetracks gave him a better look than any tour of museums, battlefields, or national parks. Locals don't go to museums. They do go to the track.

"You get to see the people who live there," he said. "When I went to Rockingham Park in New Hampshire, it was just the quietest, grumpiest, sourest crowd I've ever been with at the racetrack. It was like they were in prison. The most fun was the Gillespie County Fair in Fredericksburg, Texas. Everybody there's having a good time. They're making up conspiracies about the races. They've got German tacos, German everything. After the races, you can go to Luckenbach and listen to people play guitars."

◡

Sallisaw, Oklahoma, lives in American literature as the hometown of the Joad family in John Steinbeck's *Grapes of Wrath*. Steinbeck is my favorite author, but I'd never had a reason to visit Sallisaw. Now I did: quarter-horse racing.

We were late to Blue Ribbon Downs. There were two minutes to the fourth race when we hustled into the grandstand. I speed-read the entries and picked out a 4–1 shot. This is the best way to handicap a strange track: bet on whatever catches your eye. We ran upstairs to watch our horses. Sallisaw had passed under a rain shower, so the track was as muddy as a river bottom and pocked with ankle-deep hoof-prints. It was a drag strip for horses. A dozen stocky animals jack-rabbited down the course, and in twenty seconds, I was twenty dollars richer. It would be my only winner at Blue Ribbon Downs. Quarter-horse racing, I quickly realized, was not the main attraction here. We sat down in the grill with two of Terry's "Derby List" friends. Our table-top television was tuned to Churchill Downs. Their *Racing Forms* were open to Lone Star Park, and they jawed about the Lone Star Derby later that afternoon. Every twenty minutes, they looked out the window to watch the horses dash past. They never bet two measly bucks on those equine sprinters. Blue Ribbon Downs was east-central Oklahoma's offtrack betting parlor: the quarter horses were paraded in front of the grandstand to persuade the state racing board that it was a race-track, too. Make money on the real live animals? Forget it. I bet a horse at 3–1; as I walked to my seat, he dropped to 5–2; when I sat down, he was 2–1. Terry pointed at the tote board.

"Uh-oh. Someone dropped a ten-dollar bill on your horse."

There was $500 in the win pool. I knew gamblers in Chicago who bet more than $500 by themselves. Fifty to win here would scramble the odds as severely as twenty grand at Saratoga. At Blue Ribbon Downs, the tote board was so volatile you couldn't count on an overlay—you just had to pick a horse you liked and hope no one else noticed. After two more races, I lost interest, as the rest of this crowd had done years before, and turned our nine-inch television to Arlington. The ninth race was coming up, and I decided to apply a lesson that had cost me ten dollars the night before at Fairmount Park. In the two allowance races—contests in which horses are not for sale, normally restricted to horses who have not won a certain number of races in their lifetimes—the horse with the shortest resume had won both times. It made sense. If you were building a basketball team, would you draft a twenty-one-year-old college kid or a twenty-eight-year-old who's been knocking around the CBA? You'd draft the twenty-one-year-old. He's got potential. He hasn't spent years playing with minor leaguers. So in the ninth at Arlington, I bet nine dollars on Gracious Humor. At three, he was the youngest horse in the race. He'd run once, winning his maiden race by a nose. His father was Distorted Humor, the equine sperm bank who'd sired Funny Cide. And he was 6–1. Gracious Humor squirted away from his elders to win by two. With my exacta bet, I collected eighty-five dollars. I knew nothing about quarter horses, but I was a winner at Blue Ribbon Downs.

It was clear that we'd crossed a cultural watershed since leaving Illinois. It had probably happened that morning, in the Ozarks, somewhere around Branson, Missouri. But it wasn't until Tulsa that I realized we were in the Southwest. At Fair Meadows, I saw a man in a cowboy hat and a David Allan Coe T-shirt. The concession stand sold snuff. The paddock was full of Native Americans, traveling in families of five or six, and all the whites, men and women, seemed to have been bred for the same coltish figure. They were lean and high-bottomed, and their stovepipe blue jeans made their horse-straddling legs look as long as stilts. As I walked under the bleachers, I overheard someone say, "I can just hear the headlines: One fat sumbitch gets killed by electric, the other fat sumbitch laughs hisself to death."

"Oklahoma has the best-looking women at racetracks, in my opinion," Terry said, as he carried a beer away from the bar. He always had a beer in his hand or between his feet. I never drank at the track, so he decided I must be a teetotaler. I'm not, but I don't mix my vices. A beer only costs four dollars, but it can inspire ten times that much in dumb bets, which is why taps flow on every floor of every track. I don't gamble in taverns, either.

Fair Meadows sat like a giant carnival booth between a minor league baseball stadium and a waterslide park. There was a screen above the far turn to prevent the Tulsa Drillers from beaning the horses with foul balls. The track shared Yale Avenue with miles of one-story pawn shops, dive bars, and windowless strip clubs. But it plays as big a role in the literature of horse racing as Saratoga, thanks to Jay Cronley, columnist for the *Tulsa World* and author of the novel *Good Vibes*. *Good Vibes* inspired the movie *Let It Ride*, which is to horseplayers what *The Godfather* is to wiseguys. It's the story of one card in the life of Trotter, a racetrack loser who parlays fifty dollars and a tip from a cabbie into something like forty grand.

*Let It Ride* was filmed at Hialeah Park, in Florida, but Fair Meadows is Cronley's home track, and it's where he picked up many of the stories for his book. We didn't see Jay at Fair Meadows, but months later, I called him up to talk about *Let It Ride* and gambling in the boondocks. Legend has it that Jay's story was inspired by the day he took down the entire trifecta pool at a country track in Oklahoma. That's not true. He wrote it after a big day at Oaklawn Park, in Hot Springs, Arkansas.

"Have you ever been to Oaklawn?" Jay asked me, in a good-ol'-boy growl.

I admitted I hadn't.

"Taaaiiid," he bellowed into the phone, as loudly as Lyndon Johnson. "Taid, Taid, Taid. You went on a racetrack tour and you didn't go to Oaklawn?"

"It wasn't open in May."

"Ah luuuve Oaklawn. There was one day, I stayed out on a lake, about twenty miles from the track. This was before simulcasting, and on Friday, I just got killed. On Saturday, though, there was a horse I just loved in the first race. I got in the car twenty minutes before post time, and it was like the Grand Prix—on the shoulder, in the ditch, and I ran in and dove at the window, and it came in. It paid maybe twenty dollars. There's some days you can't lose."

After he counted his money, it occurred to Jay that no one had ever written a novel about horseplayers. So he went home to Tulsa and did it himself.

"About the only thing that had ever been done was *Guys and Dolls*," he said. "There's an impression that that's about horseplayers, but it's really about gamblers. Other than that, nothing. *Seabiscuit* was the only horse racing movie with no gambling."

*Good Vibes* is so far out of print you can't even find it on the Internet, but *Let It Ride*, which stars Richard Dreyfuss, is on DVD. According to Rob Fasiang, it's "the greatest movie ever made." During his lucky streak, Dreyfuss's character drops to his knees and cries, "God likes me, he really, really likes me," which is even better than God loving you, because He loves everybody. On days when Rob was hot, he would declare, "I feel just like Trotter," and he once informed me of a trivial gaffe that only a fanatic would notice: "What's the date on the *Racing Form* that Trotter reads in the bar? It's Wednesday. But the movie's supposed to take place on a Saturday!"

A lot of horseplayers feel the same way as Rob. OK, it's not the *greatest* movie ever made, but it's our movie, because it depicts the fantasy so many of us harbor every time we walk into the track: *Today's the day that's going to change my life. Today's the day I'll get even and pull so far ahead I'll be a winner even if I live to be ninety.*

"You cannot believe what I hear," Jay said. "It's like a ritual. Somebody said that every year before Santa Anita opens, they light candles and watch *Let It Ride*."

U

I flipped through the Fair Meadows program. It appeared to have been photocopied at the library. The track had carded quarter horses, Appaloosas, paints, Thoroughbreds, and bastard offspring of all four. In Chicago, horses had disappeared from the streets generations ago. Only the fastest Thoroughbreds were allowed in the cities, and they were regarded as nothing more than betting units, like living roulette balls. In Oklahoma, the relationship between horse and man was still close. Horses worked on ranches, rode on trails. Fair Meadows honored every breed with a race. Terry and I bet on all of them. This was our one night in Tulsa, so if we wanted any money out of this place, we had to take it now. There was no getting even tomorrow. Terry attempted a trifecta in a five-and-a-half-furlong sprint, which was a little more than one lap around the half-mile oval. The favorite, Daylightin Dizzy, won the race. Terry gnashed his teeth.

"Stupid favorite," he growled.

"Did you have him on top in your tri?"

"No, I threw him out. Where'd my horse finish?"

"Second."

"Damn. I always get the second-place horse."

"You've been picking first-place horses all day," I said. "What are you whining about?"

But Terry got his money back in the ninth, a 350-yard sprint for Appaloosas and paints. The exacta paid $141.20, and he had a buck on it.

"I'm the king!" he shouted. "I'm way ahead now. Thank God for quarter horses."

I picked one winner that night. Ambition's End had lost his last race, at Sam Houston Park, by twelve-and-three-quarters lengths. But

he'd been near the lead, and now he was running for a lower claiming price. When he led all the way, I whooped and stuffed my ticket
in the losers pile accumulating in my pocket. I forgot to cash it before
I left. I still haven't cashed it. The next time I visit Tulsa, I'll have
twenty-six dollars waiting for me.

We spent the night at a Super 8 motel in an east Tulsa neighborhood that could have been the set for *The Outsiders*. Terry had stashed
a map of every Super 8 in North America in the glove compartment,
shunning all finer motor lodges, bed-and-breakfasts, or RV camps. In
the morning, I went for a run through an unmown park with a rusting Frisbee golf course, past hundreds of houses with Beware of Dog
placards hammered above the carport, through the miles of blue-col-
lar Potemkin streetscape you can't see from the ninth floor of the
Radisson. When I got back to the motel, Terry was standing in the
parking lot, smoking a cigarette. He was wearing his Breeders' Cup
cap, his denim jacket, his jeans, and his Top-Siders. I studied him closely.
He'd changed his T-shirt.

U

Terry had planned this tour around a festival that was taking place
1,200 miles to the northwest and a week in the future: the Miles City
Bucking Horse Sale, at the Eastern Montana Fairgrounds.

"They auction off all these rodeo horses, and on the night before,
there's a big street dance," he promised me. "The bars are all full of
cowboys. It's the biggest event of the year in Miles City."

So after a day at Eureka Downs, a tiny Kansas racetrack with its
own tack shop, we headed toward the Rockies and then followed them
to Montana. Gambling is everywhere in Montana. In most of the
United States, you can only risk your paycheck in undesirable locales:
Indian reservations, barges moored on rivers flowing through forlorn
Rust Belt ghettoes, the state of Nevada. But Montana had sanctioned
Keno, a video game resembling bingo. Banks of Keno machines had
muscled their way into every bar. In Terry's hometown of Great Falls,

there were even Keno parlors, one-story huts with smoked windows. From the outside, they looked like adult bookstores. The one saloon that lacked Keno made up for it with a three-screen OTB. We killed an afternoon there, playing Aqueduct and Churchill.

Terry's grandfather, Percy Wollaston, had achieved a posthumous fame. His family memoir of life on an eastern Montana farm had formed the basis for Jonathan Raban's *Bad Land*, a book about the futility of growing crops in the near-desert between the Mississippi and the Rocky Mountains. The old farm was on the way to Miles City, and Terry wanted me to see it.

The Montana of Percy Wollaston is not the lush, mountainous Montana that has been mythologized in so many books (*A River Runs Through It*), movies (*Legends of the Fall*), fly-fishing catalogs, and SUV ads. To see that Montana, you have to go to Missoula or Helena, along the backbone of the Rockies. As we made our descent from the foothills of the Rockies, on Interstate 94, the landscape paled. The hills were furred with a thin layer of felt, the faintest shade of green before it crisped to brown. The grass would be dead by summer. It looked like Mongolia, or the moon after a Turfmaster seeding. The car heaved over pebbled, corduroy roads, through the near-ghost town of Ismay, which once tried changing its name to Joe to attract a visit from the NFL quarterback. (He never came.) There were no road signs, only tires with "Cows on Road" painted on them dangling from fences. Propped up by the roadside was a car door marked "Leland Ranch— 2." We knew we were close when we passed the Whitney Creek School, which was no longer a school: exposed to every whim of weather the vast sky could throw down, its pitched roof was flaking shingles, its white paint fading to dinginess.

When we finally reached the Wollaston homestead, along a saddle in the rolling dirt roads, we stepped out into the unbroken wind. It blew through my jeans and ruffled my notebook until it hummed. The old farm had been in a coulee, a swale between two hills. We found a square foundation in the thin, rocky dirt, but that was all that remained of the cabin.

In Fallon, we passed the K&R Bar, a white building all alone by the roadside. It was long past noon, we hadn't seen a restaurant in miles, and we weren't likely to see one for miles more.

"Let's stop here," I suggested.

Hungry, and ignorant of western niceties, I swept through the door and shouted to the white-haired men behind the bar, "Do you have a menu?"

The old men froze. The lone drinker on his bar stool froze. Terry trailed behind me, mortified.

"Uh, can we still get some lunch?" he asked.

"Well you can get it from *him*," said one of the old men, pointing at his partner, who was wearing suspenders. "But I'm leaving."

He slipped through the kitchen door. Two menus flopped on the bar.

"We pretty much got hamburgers, hamburgers, and hamburgers," the man in suspenders said.

"That sounds OK to me," I said.

"What kind of potato you want?" he asked.

"Baked."

His pencil stopped dead and he stared at me, unable to comprehend how anyone with a lick of common sense could be unaware of the dining options in a rural Montana bar.

"You really don't know where you are, do you?" Terry said.

"Well, it says choice of potato."

"We've got fried wedges and spiced fried wedges," the bartender said.

"OK. Fried wedges."

He turned on Terry.

"I'll have the deluxe cheeseburger," he said.

"Deluxe is only pickles today. We're out of tomatoes and onions and everything else."

"Well, pickles is better than nothing, isn't it?"

"I suppose. Do you want ranch with that?"

Terry and I glanced at each other. We didn't know what ranch was. We weren't going to ask.

"Nope," he said.

"Nope," I said.

The bartender glared at me again.

"I suppose you're going to want your hamburger burnt all the way through," he accused.

"Medium rare."

"We can't cook it that way anymore," he snapped. "State law."

"Fine. Burnt."

Nonetheless, he was sure I was allied with those meddlers from Helena who would no longer let him serve bleeding hamburgers. So he hit me with the maximum western insult.

"You're not from this part of the world, are you?"

"Nope," I said, curtly and airily, no longer willing to quail before his surliness. This was a foreign landscape to me. I'd grown up among greenery: oaks, elms, and pines; rivers and lakes that generated brooding gray clouds. The treetops, the mackerel skies, they sheltered us from the unblinking blue eye of heaven. Here, in this arid Golgotha, the land was naked to the elements. Few people were from this part of the world, which may be why those who wandered in were treated with suspicion.

"I grew up in Great Falls," Terry offered.

The bartender was unappeased. An *Ausländer* was an *Ausländer*, whether he was from Great Falls or Chicago. Evidently, we had invaded the local social club. The wall before us was paneled with portraits of local ranchers, fitted together like yearbook photos. Neither of those pale, genial, pouchy faces was familiar to us, nor ours to them. A local woman sat down on a stool. The bartender set a can of Busch before her and sprang the tab.

"It always seems to rain on Bucking Horse weekend," she said.

A cowboy hat beside her tilted up and down slowly.

"Last year was nice," its owner offered.

"Yeah," she conceded. "I guess last year was OK."

The streets of downtown Miles City were closed to cars, but every neon cowboy bar was open. The crowds surged into the Montana Bar and the Six Hundred Lounge and backwashed onto the sidewalk. On a side street, a woman was singing "I Love That Country Music, But I Love Jesus More" to an oompah beat, while her listeners crouched on hay bales. But the action was on the main street, where dancing cowboys flung their dates as violently as you'd pull the string on a spinning top. A blond woman asked me to dance. I took her hand, but I didn't exactly dance with her. I sort of pushed her around the street, in an ellipsis. She had come to Miles City from North Dakota. It wasn't far, in western miles.

"My girlfriend told me it was a good time," she said. "So here we are."

U

There are a few things you can only find in a small town. The unironic display of Americanism is one of them. Terry and I saw it at the Saturday morning parade in Miles City, where the Custer band marched in the uniforms of the doomed Seventh Cavalry, where a high school marching band blatted a brassy rendition of "America the Beautiful," and where a plywood cutout of a steer, branded with the star-spangled letters B-E-E-F, rolled past on a flatbed. We heard it at the Bucking Horse Sale, which opened with a recording of John Wayne's paean to America. Then came Ray Charles's "America the Beautiful," while three rodeo queens cantered around the infield with the flags of three revered institutions: the United States, the state of Montana, and Coors beer. People listened with their hands over their hearts. It wasn't the national anthem, but the sentiment was the same.

The Eastern Montana Fairgrounds was a rusting grandstand, but it was distinguished by the presence of the governor, who wore a black cowboy hat over her gray bouffant. The Bucking Horse Sale was the biggest event in Montana that day. Every horse had a chance to prove its unruliness. Cowboys climbed on their backs, and straps were cinched around their bellies, as tight as a thirty-inch belt on Diamond Jim Brady. The moment the chute opened, the bidding began: "Hey, $200 gimme $225, got $200 $200 $200. $225! $225 $225 $225 $250! Gimme $300..." The stakes were high: if the irritated mustangs flailed around like dolphins on marlin tackle, they were on their way to the rodeo. If they made like the flower-sniffing Ferdinand the Bull, they were bound for the belly of a Golden Lab.

The Bucking Horse Sale dates back to the nineteenth century. When the U.S. Army was still buying horses for its cavalry, local ranchers rounded up mustangs and herded them to Miles City for sale. The ranchers complained because they weren't getting top dollar, so the army challenged them to prove the animals' worth.

The ranchers responded by holding an exhibition, which drew such a big crowd it became an annual event. After the army stopped buying horses, rodeos came to Miles City looking for stock.

"Some of them will be used in rodeos, some of them will be used as broodmares, some of them will become dog food," said Don Richard, a local radio executive who runs the event.

The most spirited sold for $800 and were trucked away to Oklahoma, or Wyoming, or another state where rodeo is as popular as hockey is in Minnesota.

In between the auctions, there were races. Horse racing was added to the Bucking Horse Sale in the 1950s. As Fair Meadows had done, Miles City invited any horse that could run. That's why the card included the $11,855 Dan Lockie Quarter Horse Derby, the $8,075 Paint Horse Derby, and a slate of races carded for Thoroughbreds, but open to paints and Appaloosas.

"In order to fill races here, we have to run what we call 'mixed-breed races,'" Richard explained. "We don't have as many horses as they have at Belmont. Your bigger tracks, Thoroughbreds are all they have on the grounds."

May 17, the day of the 2003 Miles City Bucking Horse Sale, was also the afternoon of the Preakness, and all the televisions in the grandstand were tuned to the local NBC station's broadcast of the big race from Baltimore. In the Horseman's Bar, where Jim Beam on ice was three dollars, someone had plugged in an old peg-legged set with sun-faded colors. I'd made my betting line in the Super 8 the night before, anointing Funny Cide my 9–5 favorite. Derby champs had won four of the last six Preaknesses. Miles City had its own betting pool, which presented me with an opportunity—and a dilemma. At Pimlico, Funny Cide was 9–5, too low for a bet. In Miles City, he was 5–2, but there was so little money on the board I was afraid to bet fifty dollars. I might knock down the odds. So I bet forty. Funny Cide won by nine lengths. At the finish line, his jockey, José Santos, held up an empty palm. After the Derby, he'd been accused of carrying an electric prod. Now, he wanted to show the world he was clean.

"You show 'em, José!" someone shouted.

"I had to bet on Funny Cide," I told the man standing next to me, "because I bet him in the Derby."

"Did you really?" he said. "Did you *really?*"

I really did. It was indeed a boast good for all tracks.

Funny Cide paid $6.80 to win at the Miles City Bucking Horse Sale, a dollar more than at Pimlico. I liked Montana. I took my winnings outside to the flea market behind the grandstand, where I tried on cowboy hats. Everyone in Miles City was wearing one, but I would have looked like an ass on the streets of Chicago. Instead, Funny Cide bought a pair of turquoise earrings for my girlfriend, Kate.

I was back in time for the final event of the day: the Wild Horse Race, a hybrid of rodeo and horse racing. Six horses were let loose in the rodeo ring. Four-man teams of cowboys chased after them, armed with ropes and saddles. The goal was to wrestle one into submission and ride it around the track, but the frightened stallions lunged from their pursuers like a flock of birds. The eight-legged teams tripped and lunged and jam-piled, but finally, one of them full-nelsoned a horse, cinched on a saddle, and raised a rider onto its back. The frightened animal threw its conqueror and fled through the open gate with the rest of the herd in pursuit. Only one horse remained in the pen. Two cowboys circled him. He reared and flailed at them with his front hooves, but they pinned him against the fence. One cowboy saddled him, one cowboy held him in a headlock, and two more pressed his rump to the fence. But the horse's strength and his will were those of five men. With a mighty back kick, he knocked his captors onto their backs and ran for freedom. He bolted around the track with a saddle dangling from his abdomen. The cowboys made one final rodeo clown pursuit, but he was free.

"Well," the announcer said, "I don't recall us not ever having a winner before."

I'm sure that horse disagreed.

Our final stop, Prairie Meadows, in the Des Moines suburb of Altoona, was a "racino," a combination racetrack and slot machine palace.

The Prairie Meadows grandstand was not built to evoke horse racing: it had the witch's-hat turrets and foam-stone appearance of a Disneyland castle, much like the Excalibur Hotel in Las Vegas. Inside, it seemed to be ruled by machines, which were serviced by humans who soothed them by pressing their spin buttons. There was no conversation. Only the machines communicated, blipping and pinging whenever they rewarded one of their attendants with a jackpot. The slots didn't pay out coins but rather dispensed paper vouchers redeemable at the cashier's window, so one never heard the chunking of quarters into metal trays. The bottom two floors were mazes of slots, which meant that Terry and I had to ascend several escalators to find our action.

Post time was four o'clock, but even at that hour, the clubhouse was as spotless and silent as a country club dining room during the doldrums between lunch and dinner. It was raining gently—one of those day-long spring rains—so the apron outside was deserted, except for the racetrack crew in yellow slickers. It probably would have been deserted on a clear day, too. Horse racing had been relegated to a floor show for the casino patrons. After Terry's first trip here in 1996, he'd written that Prairie Meadows "has positioned the casino so as to marginalize the horseplayers as far out to the front of the facility as possible . . . . it's a nice enough place, but the racin' is really incidental, chump."

On the other hand, admission was free, Pepsi was free, beer was a dollar, and there would have been no racin' without the casino.

Prairie Meadows opened in 1989 as Iowa's only Thoroughbred racetrack. That same year, Iowa became the first state to legalize riverboat gambling. Gamblers preferred driving all the way to Dubuque for spin-a-second slots to staying in Des Moines and waiting twenty-five minutes between horse races. By 1991 Prairie Meadows was bankrupt. Simulcasting allowed it to reopen in 1993, but two years later, it hit the real jackpot: the legislature approved the installation of 1,164 slot machines, making Prairie Meadows the first racino. In their first month, the slots took in $125 million. The purses increased tenfold, from $18,000 a day in 1994 to $190,000 in 2001. Prairie Meadows loses $20 million a year on its racing meet, which runs from April to October, but it's one of the most profitable tracks in the country, thanks to slots. In 2002 it took $7.1 million in bets on live racing, $64.7 million on simulcast races, and over $2 *billion* on slots.

Other states, including West Virginia and Delaware, have since approved racinos, and racetrack owners in Illinois and Maryland are begging for slots to bail out their horse racing industries. It's a defensible request. For decades, states granted racetracks a monopoly on legal gambling. Then came the lotteries and the riverboats to steal the racetracks' customers. Despite the smaller crowds, the tracks were still expected to put on nine races a day and support hundreds of trainers, jockeys, grooms, and breeders. We're gambling joints, too, they said, so let us in on the new action.

Terry was meeting some "Derby List" friends who had their own private table, with a nameplate and a television. Only one of them was winning. He was an elderly man, sunken into Alzheimer's. That disease steals the first memories last of all. The old man had owned racehorses, so he remembered how to handicap. He'd pick a horse from the program and bet it with one of the roving tellers who carried Bet Mates strapped to their waists, like steno machines. (The Bet Mate is an electronic keypad that is linked to the tote, so you can type in wagers without leaving your seat.) He watched the races on the little television, but either he didn't understand what he was seeing or he forgot instantly.

"When's the fourth race?" he asked his daughter.

"It's over, Dad," she said.

"Who won?"

"The 8."

"Is that my horse?"

"Yes."

"Oh." He looked proudly at his ticket, but a moment later he showed it around the table again, asking, "Is this a winner?"

The old man took my money that day. I lost forty dollars on the horses, and when I went downstairs to try the slots—just for research, although I really did want to play the Munsters machine—I lost another ten dollars. No wonder Prairie Meadows was doing so well.

U

I don't know exactly how much money I lost on the road. I was betting out of my pocket, out of the $500 in cash I'd brought along for travel expenses. There was a thick deposit of losing tickets in my slicker, but when I got home, I threw them into the closet without counting. The McChump Tour had been a respite from the pressure of making money, as all vacations should be. No one at the Miles City Bucking Horse Sale calculated win probabilities or worried about their return on investment per two dollars wagered. With $500 of your neighbors' money in the pool, it wasn't worth the effort. In the bleachers of small-town racetracks, playing the horses was a leisure activity, like watching the Fourth of July fireworks or inner-tubing with the family on the Red River. Me, I never did anything to relax. Everything was a self-improvement exercise. When I ran, I ran hard. When I gambled, I gambled to win. When I read a book, it was always something edifying, like Dickens or Flaubert. I'd once been told I was too uptight to enjoy myself—by a guy from Germany.

Terry and I got back to Chicago on a Tuesday in mid-May. I planned to take one day off before I started my summer at Arlington Park. The Thoroughbreds had been vanned over to Arlington on day one of my McChump Tour. They'd be running there until late September. The track changed each season, a rotation dictated by the Illinois Racing Board: Hawthorne in the spring, Arlington in the summer, Hawthorne again in the fall. (We all spent the winter at the OTB, betting on Gulfstream, Aqueduct, and the Fair Grounds. Sadly, Chicago is the largest American city without winter racing, and will probably remain so until global warming kicks in.) Half my bankroll was gone, lost at Hawthorne or out west. I had $2,000 left to get me through the next seven and a half months. I was going to have to figure out how to win—and soon.

# 8

## The Rebel Enclave

Scott McMannis didn't have an office at Arlington Park. He played the horses from an alcove on the third floor, at the far eastern end of the grandstand. It was hidden behind an escalator, so almost no one walked through, except for elderly widows descending from the Wednesday bingo games in the dining room above. Jim O'Donnell, the horse racing columnist for the *Chicago Sun-Times*, called it the Rebel Enclave. The acolytes who managed to find it he dubbed the McMinions.

At the old Arlington, Scott had commanded a 190-seat classroom. But the old Arlington burned in 1985, destroying the classroom and incinerating the notes for a book he'd planned to call *Comprehensive Handicapping*. The classroom was the bigger loss.

Many of his peers had published: Steven Davidowitz wrote *Betting Thoroughbreds*; Jim Quinn wrote *The Handicapper's Condition Book*; Dave Litfin wrote *Angle Handicapping*. But Scott could brag about students who'd turned pro: Tom Quigley, publisher of the *Horseplayer* magazine; Noel Michaels, a reporter for the *Daily Racing Form*. Scott was the type of professor who belonged in a classroom, not in a laboratory or behind a typewriter.

"I have an ABD degree," he liked to say. "All But Dissertation."

After the fire, he abandoned *Comprehensive Handicapping* and sat down with Arlington's architect to design a classroom for the new track. It was just off the tunnel between the paddock and the race-track. Today, it's a storage room for maintenance equipment. Scott last worked for Arlington in the mid-1990s, when he did pre-race analy-sis on a closed-circuit broadcast. By the time I knew him, that job belonged to the racing secretary's wife. Scott's relationship with Arling-ton was down to one perk: a press pass, because he wrote a column for the *Horseplayer*. It entitled him to free admission.

U

Arlington Park is posh. I'm not using that British term to be cute, but because Arlington models itself on the grandest English racetracks: Newmarket, Epsom, and Ascot. It wants to be a rural fair, with musi-cians and petting zoos. Upon its reopening in 1989, the track rechris-tened itself Arlington International Racecourse. It has since reverted to Arlington Park, but its owner, Richard L. Duchossois, still wants to persuade Chicago that horse racing is the most aristocratic sport, that *equestrian* can stand as a synonym for "patrician." Duchossois, who made his fortune in railroad cars and garage door openers, was once named to the Forbes 400 list of richest Americans. His racetrack is as socially superior to Hawthorne as a country club is to a plumbers' and pipe fitters' hall. In 2002 Arlington hosted the Breeders' Cup, the one-day, eight-race event that crowns the champion of every Thorough-bred division. A year later, that event's purple emblem was still visible everywhere: at the finish line, on the backs of mutuel tickets, on base-ball caps in the gift shop.

Like its English models, with their jacket-and-tie members' enclo-sures, Arlington believes in class. Anyone can eat a focaccia sandwich in the grill or drink in the Paddock Pub. But you must spend ten dol-lars in the Silks Lounge, where Duchossois displays the colors of Euro-pean noblemen who've raced their horses here. (The silks of Her Majesty Queen Elizabeth II, whose horse Unknown Quantity won the 1989 Arlington Handicap, are in a glass case by the gate, where every-one can see them.) The Gold Club Room is reserved for whales who wager $100,000 a year. The Turf Club's smoked-glass doors are barred by a Members Only sign on a gold-plated post. Above that, accessible only by elevator, are private boxes reserved for powers and principalities who are friends of Mr. D (a nickname that makes Duchossois sound like an informal guy, while still reminding people who's the boss).

I'd been up there once, on Belmont Day 2002. The editor of the *Reader* received an embossed invitation to sit in a skybox and passed it down to me. Jacket and tie required. My father was visiting for the weekend, so I lent him a suit coat, two sizes too small, and a stained yellow tie. We drank Mr. D's beer, ate pastries from his dessert trays, and mingled with his celebrities: George Ryan, Jr., son of the outgoing governor, and Richard Roeper, Roger Ebert's TV partner. There were no gawkable Chicago A-listers: no Jim Belushi, no George Wendt. I was used to gambling among the groundlings, so I made a skybox faux pas. I bet on a horse named Naperville and, as the gate opened, I leaned over the balcony and screamed, "Get him to the rail!" Well-dressed women gaped. If you need to win a bet, you don't belong on the upper level.

Arlington's turf course is as lush as a fairway at Augusta. Its infield is a Yeats-inspired grove of willows. In the paddock, a large clock—the type you'd see on a courthouse, overlooking a town square—marked off the minutes between races. I could go on and on with this Song of Solomon litany, but in sum, there is no more pleasant place to spend a summer afternoon in Chicago. Not Wrigley Field. Not the beach. Not the jazz festival.

The horseplayers hate it, of course. Horseplayers love to grouse ("Oh, goddamn it! My exacta paid $600, but if I'd played a trifecta, I coulda had $2,000"), but they really love to grouse about Arlington. Creighton Schoenfeldt, who could grouse longer and louder than anyone, announced a boycott of the track. Its offense: refusing him membership in the Gold Club. He'd bet only $96,000 the year before, but he thought he deserved to be in the $100,000 Gold Club Room, with the guys "who really fire." Instead, he got a Silver Club card, which entitled him only to a free program.

"I wrote 'em a letter and they never responded," he griped. "If they don't want my action, then the hell with 'em. I'll go somewhere else."

"Somewhere else" was Hawthorne, which simulcast races all summer. Every morning, Creighton boarded the El, stopped at an Arlington-owned OTB to pick up his free program, then continued the ninety-minute trip to Stickney. He figured he could make more money there, anyway. Because of simulcasting rules, the payoffs were 1.5 percent lower than they were at Arlington, but Hawthorne offered a 4 percent rebate on all bets. Arlington's rebate program gave back two-fifths of 1 percent. That put Hawthorne bettors half a percent ahead of their rivals at Arlington. If you bet $1 million over the course of the summer—which some people did—Hawthorne would give you forty grand, while Arlington would give you $4,000. The disparity reinforced the feeling that Arlington is more interested in luring suburban families to its face-painting booths than in hanging onto the gambling addicts who support the place. The horseplayers have never forgiven Duchossois for shutting down his track for two years to squeeze a share of casino profits from the state. (When the legislature caved, passing a law granting the racing industry 15 percent of the revenue from a casino planned for the vicinity of O'Hare Airport, Duchossois reopened Arlington.) Mr. D is greedy, they say, when they see him walking around his track, a short man in perfectly cut suits. Arlington is greedy. Admission is six bucks. A sandwich is $6.95.

"I can't even afford to eat lunch there!" moaned a parking attendant who worked at both Arlington and Hawthorne.

The biggest complaints are about the small fields. Arlington averaged 8.1 horses a race. Hawthorne averaged 9.1 at its fall meet. "A typical Arlington race," you'd hear, when the starting gate held five or six animals. Small fields mean shorter prices on the winners. A horse who would have paid seven dollars in a ten-horse field might pay five dollars in a six-horse field, since the bettors are spreading their action among fewer entries. The difference is even greater in the exactas. A six-horse field has thirty exacta combinations. A ten-horse field has ninety. Some handicappers just took the summer off. Blond Jimmy often disappeared between Mother's Day and Labor Day, showing up at the end of the Arlington meet to compile trip notes he could use during the fall season at Hawthorne.

Frank Gabriel, Arlington's racing secretary, didn't deny that he scheduled skimpy races. But it was unavoidable, given the time of year and the quality of horses Arlington wanted to attract.

"This place is always going to have short fields," he said. "We're a summer facility, and like all summer facilities, we have to run two-year-old races. As we get turf racing, the fields get bigger."

Arlington could have filled its starting gates with $5,000 claimers—the "cheaper brand of racing" that made Hawthorne so attractive to bettors—but that would not have been fair to stables trying to move young horses up the ladder to more lucrative stakes.

"That trainer and that owner have paid the money for that animal to run," Gabriel explained. "That's how we develop those horses."

Scott shook his head when I told him this.

"They're slowly strangling this place," he said.

U

Not all the McMinions followed Scott to Arlington. Creighton was sticking to his boycott, and Rob lived in Indiana, too far for commuting. He played the horses at an OTB or on his home computer. Some afternoons, when his wife, Wendy, was busy, Scott sat all alone in the Rebel Enclave. I stopped in to see him every day.

I'd come to think of Scott and his handicapping cronies as my coworkers. The Rebel Enclave was my watercooler, my local tavern. I'd only had one full-time job in my life, and I'd quit that almost a decade before, so this was one of the pleasures of going to the track, especially because the patrons were so colorful. Sometimes, we'd get a visit from a middle-aged man with thick glasses, pants sagging lower than a street thug's, and kinky russet hair that looked as though it had been cut by the stylist to the Romantic composers. During the race replays, he stood on a chair under a television set and scribbled notes on a stack of papers in the crook of his arm. The man looked like the quintessential broken-down horseplayer, so I finally asked Scott who he was.

"We call him Art Garfunkel," Scott said, "'cause of his hair. Some people call him Bob the Plumber, because his pants are always falling down. He's been coming out here for twenty years. He always has these charts that tell him how much he should bet on an exacta, and he'll say, 'That exacta should have paid twenty-six dollars, but it was only paying twenty-four dollars, so I didn't bet it!'"

From the looks of him, the system didn't seem to be working.

$$\cup$$

It wasn't long before Scott had a new pupil at Arlington. Warren Weaver was another stout, broad-shouldered man—he'd played full-back for the 1952 Austin High team that competed for the Chicago city championship at Soldier Field—but above the neck, the two men had nothing in common. All his life, Warren had been a hunch bettor. He'd learned to gamble from his mother, who placed bets at a newsstand in their West Side neighborhood. She never taught him to handicap, though, so when he went to the track, he hung around trainers, owners, and high-rolling gamblers. Guys who had tips.

"Once, I met a guy at bingo who said he won $500 or $600 at the track all the time," Warren related. "Then we went to the track together and he told me about this horse in the second race. The horse broke down in the stretch. There went my money. There went my hopes. Last summer, I hung around the paddock at Arlington and relied on trainers for tips. But the best guy I knew was the shoeshine guy, Big Red. He knew everybody. I was winning some money, but it was costing me too much, 'cause I had to pay for his bets. I figured there had to be a better way."

A friend told Warren about Scott's newsletter. He subscribed and started attending Scott's classes at Hawthorne, where he learned to use the speed figures.

"The first night I did it, it took me eight hours and I got two headaches," he said. "But sonofabitch, the next day I had a field day. I won three or four hundred dollars! It really paid off, but I couldn't do that every day. It's too hard on my physical being."

Warren didn't exactly match the psychograph of a professional gambler. He was the impulsive type. "When I was younger, I wanted to marry every woman I went out with," he told me.

Eventually, he married three—each one twice. One of his wives was a Gypsy. After their first divorce, he claimed, "She put a spell on me to lure me back." His current wife was a Filipina who worked in a beauty shop. Three or four days after they met, Warren asked her to marry him.

Warren was sixty-nine and retired from a job in City Hall, but he was as randy as a nineteen-year-old. In the paddock, he speculated on whether the female jockeys enjoyed their mounts. Once, when I mentioned that a passing gray horse was the son of Preakness winner Louis Quatorze, his free-associating mouth blurted, "Louis Clitoris?!" This is a healthy attitude, but as Andrew Beyer learned, women and horses don't mix. Handicapping is a jealous mistress. In the real game of life—procreation—Warren was beating Scott (and everyone else in the Rebel Enclave), eight–nil. But at the track, Scott was ahead by a few hundred thousand dollars.

"At first, I thought he was one of those guys who shouldn't be out here," Scott said. "Every race, he'd have this huge pile of tickets in front of him. I think he's one of those guys who would have been better off before exotic betting [multiple-horse betting], when you could only bet to win."

A real teacher doesn't give up that easily. Besides, Warren was paying for the speed figures. So one Thursday, they pushed together two tables in the Rebel Enclave and spread out their *Racing Forms*.

"Let me ask you a question," Warren said to Scott. "I knew a guy once, said you could make money if you just doubled your bet after every time you lost. You know, two dollars, four dollars. When you finally got a winner, you'd get all your money back."

(This is a strategy known as "due-column wagering." Suppose your goal is to generate $100 a day at the track. In the first race, you bet fifty dollars on a 2–1 horse. It loses. Now, you need to win $150 to meet your goal. So in the second race, you see another likely 2–1 and bet seventy-five dollars. If that horse loses, the next time you bet a 2–1 shot, you'll need to spend $113. And so on, to the limit of your bank account.)

"Warren." Scott paused.

"Yeah?" Warren asked, warily.

"Do you know what happened to the woman who backed into a propeller?"

"What?"

"DISASTER!"

Scott flipped over a sheet of paper and jotted a list of the powers of 2: 2, 4, 8, 16, 32, 64, 128, 256, 512, 1024, 2048.

"Where would you start to get uncomfortable?" Scott asked.

Warren pointed at $128.

"What would happen if you lost ten bets in a row? Then you'd have to bet $2,000. Think you could do that?"

"Uh-uh."

"You'd start affecting the odds then. You wouldn't get the price you needed to get even."

"Ah hah," Warren nodded his head.

Warren was paying fifty dollars a month for Scott's *Lookup Service*, a daily fax that spared its subscribers from digging through old newsletters for a speed figure or a trip note. A dozen pages long, it listed two years of races for every horse. Most handicappers set it side by side with the *Form*, copying Scott's speed figures into the past performances. It took two or three hours a day. Warren seldom found the time.

That Saturday, he trundled into the Rebel Enclave just before the first race, carrying a folder stuffed with papers. A bag of trail mix swung from his hand, and his satchel was packed with Nutter Butters and Cocoa Puffs cereal bars. The day before, he'd taken his daughter to the supermarket. The snack shelf caught his eye, so he bought everything on it.

Scott was already in his seat, under the television screens. He glared at Warren over the top of his reading glasses.

"Warren, did you do your homework?"

"I've done three horses in the first race."

"Three horses!" Scott feigned shock. "What are you even doing here?"

Warren bent over his program, frantically handicapping the race until the bugler blew "Call to Post."

"I don't have time to do this at home," he grumbled. "I got eight kids. Two are still at home, and the rest are a phone call away. I'd rather take a beating than do this stuff. I hate it. It's not for me."

But he finished the task. When he was done, he ran off to bet Golden Prophecy, who looked like a good thing at 3–1. Golden Prophecy finished third.

Scott had not moved since his arrival.

"That race was too close," he told Warren afterward. "All the horses' speed figures were about the same—Liberation was a 41, Golden Prophecy was a 40, Wild View was a 39."

Indeed, the field was so closely matched it produced a "flat board." There was no favorite, but four horses were 3–1. That's a sign that there's no standout in the race, no horse you can bet with confidence. Warren wanted to be disciplined. He really did. But he had a hard time staying away from the betting machines, even in situations like that.

"One of the first things Scott noticed about me was I bet every race," he told me. "He'd say, 'You want the number to Gamblers' Anonymous? You can't do that and win money at the racetrack.'"

Warren managed to sit still throughout the second race. (It was easier to resist. The horses were two-year-old maidens. Some of them had never run before.) But just before the third, he popped out of his seat. He had to bet the trifecta. Scott tried to stop him.

"Where you going, Warren?" His voice was half-bemused, half-demanding.

"I got a tip on this race from my friend Babe. He runs Babe's Tavern on Milwaukee. Babe said this was a good race, and when Babe comes to the track, he comes to win!"

Warren spent twelve dollars to box Babe's horses in the tri. His ticket hit—for $21.80, one of the smallest trifectas anyone in the Rebel Enclave could remember.

"Warren, you better cash your ticket before they run out of money," Scott taunted. "You know, the objective of this game is to make a little money, do a lot of work, not the other way around."

The rest of that afternoon, Warren fretted over his *Racing Form*, filling in numbers from the *Lookup* sheet. Scott was already handicapping Sunday's races.

"Let me copy your charts," Warren entreated. "I gotta spend time with my family!"

Scott waved a sheaf of papers.

"You know when I did this?" Scott said. "Today. You're not with your family when you're at the track."

Warren borrowed his put-upon delivery from Rodney Dangerfield. He loved to imitate the comedian. The sad-sack jokes sounded right coming out of Warren's broad, squashed face, his wide, comic mouth. Like Rodney, Warren was a city boy, born before the Second World War. "My family was so poor," Warren would bray, "that if I hadn't been a boy, I woulda had nothin' to play with." Watching Warren struggle with his handicapping reminded me of Rodney studying for his final exams in the movie *Back to School*. His character, Thornton Mellon, is an earthy, unlettered tycoon who made his fortune with street smarts. Faced with history, economics, Faulkner, and Joyce, he panics. "I can't do it," he moans. His family forces him to study. They hold books in front of his face. They push him through all-nighters with coffee and cold showers. It's a miserable week, but Thornton earns his degree. Scott was trying to force Warren through the same academic labors.

"You know," Warren whispered to me, "he's not really easy to get close to as a friend."

"Well, no," I said. "He's the teacher."

"I just hope he'll be friendly with me," he muttered. "Just give me the number. Sign language, anything. I'm sixty-nine years old. It's all I can do to be out here every day. I have trouble walking. I got pains in my knees! I wanna get one of my kids to come out here and place the bets for me. I'll give 'em a little cell phone so I can just sit here."

The next day, the professor and the pupil met an hour before post time. Patiently, Scott went over each race, showing Warren how he had used speed figures to predict the winners. Scott was a head taller than Warren, so sitting side by side, they looked like a teacher and schoolboy who'd been at the same lesson so long they'd grown old together.

"OK, who do we like in the fourth race?" Scott asked.

"This one," Warren blurted, stabbing a blunt finger at the name Doughty.

"Well, look at the numbers we wrote off to the side here. What's Doughty's fastest figure?"

Warren's eyes scanned, his mind calculated.

"Forty-one," he said at last.

"OK. Now, look at this one over here. Sweet Baby Jane. What's her best figure?"

"Forty-six."

"So do you think maybe Sweet Baby Jane is the fastest horse?"

Warren agreed that maybe Sweet Baby Jane was. It was a widely held opinion—Sweet Baby Jane was sent off to victory on a tide of cash, which she returned to her investors. Scott and Warren were not among them.

(I once asked Scott what was wrong with betting a horse at 4–5, if it had the best speed figures. I'd just passed up two short-priced winners, and I was getting blue balls.

"Most people bet on short-priced favorites," I pointed out.

"Most people lose money here!" he bellowed.)

Scott had shown Warren how to pick a winner. They were making progress, but Warren wanted to make money. By the middle of the following week, he still hadn't made a big score. He was getting antsy. He sat across the room from Scott, at a table scattered with programs, *Lookups*, Nutter Butters, his bag of trail mix, and a copy of the *Green Sheet*, the tip sheet sold at the gate for $1.50.

"What do you need a *Green Sheet* for?" Scott asked him.

"It's got this arrow next to the horse's name that tells whether he's going up and down in class," Warren explained.

"Can't you tell that from the *Racing Form*?"

"Yeah, but this is easier."

Double Audit was going to win the eighth race, and everyone knew it. Double Audit was 3–5. The only way to make money was to put him on top of an exacta. But the rest of the field looked evenly matched. Their figures were identical. It was impossible to single out a second-place horse.

"When you've got three who look like they can finish second, what do you do?" Scott asked.

Warren jumped at the question.

"Bet a ten-dollar exacta," he shouted.

Scott looked over at me with a slumped expression.

"It's like he didn't hear the question."

The correct answer, according to Scott, was put Double Audit in the Daily Double. Scott rose to play him with Mount Kilimanjaro, a good-looking long shot in the ninth.

"Oh, you're gonna bet, though," Warren roared. "Do as I say, not as I do."

Warren hustled after Scott. He bet five dollars to win and place on Double Audit and he bet a two–dollar exacta: Double Audit over a challenger named Anyplace Anytime.

Double Audit won, of course. He paid $3.40 to win and $2.20 to place. Anyplace Anytime finished third, wiping out Warren's exacta bet.

"I wanna see if you break even on this one," Scott mumbled.

Warren had wagered twelve dollars. He won fourteen dollars.

"It wasn't a total loss," he shrugged. "I made two dollars."

And twenty minutes later, he got to feel smarter than the teacher. In the ninth race, Mount Kilimanjaro finished last, flushing Scott's Daily Double down the drain.

The next day, Scott loved King of Chicago in the ninth. It was a turf race. Warren had done his homework and he, too, saw that King of Chicago's speed figures towered over the twelve-horse field. At three minutes to post time, King of Chicago was 5–2. The professor and his pupil stood up together and stumped off to the betting machines, two heavy-bellied men with identical rolling gaits. They returned with their tickets and watched King of Chicago spring down the stretch, gathering up rivals with long, grasping strokes until he saw nothing ahead of him but grass. A glint of satisfaction glittered across Scott's eyes. Warren was open-mouthed with exhilaration.

"There you go, Warren. You got your winner. You didn't bet a lot of goofy exactas and trifectas, did you?"

"No."

$$\cup$$

This all took place shortly after midsummer. It was the zenith of the year, and the zenith of Scott's tutelage with Warren. After Warren singled out King of Chicago by himself and bet him to win, Scott felt that maybe he'd sharpened that soft, pleasure-loving mind, that maybe Warren would stop mooning about food and sex, stop betting every race, and start playing the horses like a hard-assed investor.

It never happened. In his classes, Scott taunted out-of-control bettors by asking, "Are you here to have fun or are you here to make money?" Warren was there to have fun. Even after his private tutorials, he wanted to bet on every race. As Scott watched Warren piss away his education, two bucks at a time, his attitude soured from frustration to disgust to contempt.

"Warren, where you going?" he'd call, whenever his student strayed from the Rebel Enclave. After Warren disappeared behind the escalator, Scott would mutter, "I need to get a bungee cord and tie it to his waist to keep him from betting." When Warren returned, stack of tickets in hand, Scott would shout, "I've given up all hope for you, Warren. Do you have enough tickets there to play canasta?"

Scott finally concluded that Warren hadn't been born to beat the races.

Once, he followed Warren to a betting machine and stood a few inches behind him, smirking. When Warren turned to see who was crowding him, he looked sheepish. Then he finished punching in his bet.

"I'm beginning to wonder how bright he is," Scott said one day when Warren didn't show up. "From what I can gather about him, he got involved with his local political machine at a young age and sort of rose up through the ranks until he got his job at City Hall."

Warren was a ward-heeler, an organization man. A horseplayer had to be an individualist.

Warren was getting fed up with Scott, too. Looking pained and oppressed, he'd glare at his *Lookup* and declare, "You know, this shit's no good. This shit isn't helping me at all."

He stopped using the *Lookup*, and then he stopped coming to the Rebel Enclave altogether. One day, Scott spotted him in the paddock.

"He hid behind a pillar when he saw me," Scott reported.

I went down to the paddock to find Warren. He wasn't hiding behind a pillar. He was sitting on a bench, near the point where the walking ring empties into the tunnel. There was a bottle of water at his feet, and his lap was cluttered with papers. A few yards away, a bookie leaned over the railing, yakking on his cell phone. ("That's Phil Santori," Warren whispered. "He bets *big*.")

Warren was tired of the homework. He was tired of Scott's lecturing.

"What is it with that guy?" he asked me. "He's always gotta be going after somebody. He was always, 'Where you going?' He never leaves you alone."

In the paddock, Warren felt liberated. In mind, in body, in wallet. He had a new system: he was betting ten dollars to win, twenty dollars to place, and thirty dollars to show on his horses.

"That way, even if the horse comes in third, I get something back," he said.

He was about to use it, too, on the 3–5 favorite. I think our chat distracted him, though. When he checked the Diamond Vision screen that looms over the paddock like the Great Oz, the horses were being led to the gate. Warren scurried to a machine, but he couldn't punch in his bets before the gate opened. His horse won easily.

"Darn it. I coulda won twenty-five bucks there," he cursed. "Now I gotta start all over again."

Three floors up, Scott McMannis sat alone in his nook, patient as a spider, waiting for the next good price.

# 9

# The Stat Man

Scott liked to call his McMinions "my loyal band." None was more loyal than the Stat Man. Scott never had to worry about the Stat Man deserting him for the paddock. Every time the Stat Man came to the track, he set up his laptop computer in the Rebel Enclave. An electronic box of records, it held the winner of every race run in Chicago for the last dozen years, along with his "Scott figure," as the Stat Man called McMannis's speed ratings. He used the information to assemble the *Lookup* sheets that Warren had found so aggravating.

The Stat Man, whose real name was Steve Miller, was built like a logger who's spent the entire winter in front of the television set. He was six foot four, and his belly was so out of hand it had to be confined with suspenders. When I first met him, he wore a feral gray beard, striped polo shirts, blue jeans, and heavy leather boots. It was the outfit of a man who, after years of marriage and corporate labor, had slipped the restraints of maturity and was finding his way back toward boyhood.

Steve had grown up in Rock Island, Illinois, on the Mississippi River. There was a harness track outside Rock Island, but Steve never went. His favorite pastimes were electric football, a game played with little plastic men on a vibrating metal gridiron, and Strat-O-Matic baseball (that evil gateway to playing the horses). He organized leagues for his tabletop teams, keeping rushing statistics for his football players and batting statistics for his baseball players. Whenever he bought a pack of baseball cards, he recorded his acquisitions in a log organized by team, number, and alphabetical order.

Had Steve been a teenager in the 1920s, he would have built radios. In the 1950s he would have built rockets, like the boys in *October Sky*. But he was seventeen when protogeeks Steve Jobs and Steve Wozniak invented the personal computer; he looked into its screen, as though looking into a crystal ball, and saw his future.

"One of the reasons I really wanted to learn to program a computer is to sort out my baseball card collection," he remembered.

At Augustana College, a small Lutheran school in Rock Island, computers were seen as a purely academic pursuit, like linguistics or semiotics, so Steve had to major in math. As soon as he graduated, he moved to Chicago and found a job programming computers for a bank. Since he loved bowling (that other gambling gateway), he joined a league, and, of course, became its official scorer. One Saturday, a teammate invited Steve on a family trip to Arlington.

"The family got the *Green Sheet*, so I looked at the *Green Sheet* for tips. I lost every race. They suggested I bet to show, but I didn't like the prices that were being offered on the heavy favorites. I was picking the fifth- or sixth-rated horse, and I was mad. I thought to myself, 'I'm never going there again.'"

Three weeks later, his teammate Bill asked him to go again. Bill was bringing along his cute girlfriend, so Steve said yes. This time, he bet to win. He cashed four tickets, made forty dollars, and thought, "Where has this game been all my life?"

He no longer needed a pretty girl to entice him. The next week, he went alone, hit a $138 trifecta on the ninth race, and realized he'd found his calling. For a decade, he went to the track on weekends, dribbling away his paycheck. Finally, he broke down and visited the library, where he checked out Tom Ainslie's *Complete Guide to Thoroughbred Racing* and Davidowitz's *Betting Thoroughbreds*. He was going to learn to handicap. He was intrigued by a chapter in *Betting Thoroughbreds* entitled "The Trainer's Window," which argued that the best trainers have signature moves that produce winners. Some do well with horses running again after long layoffs; others win by claiming horses and dropping them in class. Steve began cutting the race results out of the paper, writing down the winning horse, the winning jockey, and the winning trainer in a notebook. That became too tedious, so he convinced his wife to let him buy a computer. Her mistake. They'd been married for five years, but now, at last, he fell in love.

That summer, the *Racing Times*, a short-lived rival to the *Form*, began publishing Arlington charts. Steve bought the paper at a convenience store every day.

"My handicapping evolved, so I hit my first Pick Three and I picked my first twelve-dollar-plus horse," he said. "I won $300. I had a friend I was with that day and he had never won that much money. I was on frickin' cloud nine. Grinning even bigger than normal. But once I started handicapping, my wife didn't like me, because I'd have my face buried in the *Racing Form* and I wouldn't talk to her. Sad but true."

Steve began to fantasize about life as a professional gambler. He'd live like Dean Martin, sitting in a Vegas sports bar while beautiful women bought him drinks. At the bank, where he spent seventy hours a week troubleshooting a balky computer system, he felt like an exploited chump. At home, he felt like a domestic irritant: his snoring had driven his wife into a separate bedroom, he said—"So I got to have sex once a year on my birthday, whether I needed it or not. And every time I talked about racing and being a professional at it, my wife would say, 'We have a mortgage.'"

Steve knew of only one pro: Scott McMannis. When he read that Scott was speaking at a handicapping conference in Las Vegas, Steve bought a plane ticket.

"You didn't need to fly all the way out here to see me," Scott told him. "Just come take my classes at Hawthorne."

He did. Scott became his guru. He added Steve's winning jockey/trainer combinations to his *Chicago Trainer Profiles*, a book he compiled and sold at the beginning of each racing year. In exchange, Steve got free speed figures. By age thirty-four, most men are living the lives that will carry them into old age. Steve didn't think he could make it that far as a henpecked computer troll. All he wanted to do was go to the track. All his wife and his bosses wanted him to do was fix computers. So he fired them both. In the spring, he asked for a divorce. In the fall, he quit the bank.

"I really hated that job," he said. "Loved the people; hated the work. And I did it for seventeen years. What a dumbass."

He was single, he had no job, and he had no kids. ("God blessed us with no children," he liked to say.) He was ready to turn pro. The next year, he went to the track every day, carpooling with Scott. He wanted to find out how good his game was. At first, it was awful. In two months, he lost $9,000. Panicked, because he had nothing to fall back on—he'd sold his stocks and his life insurance policy to amass a bankroll—he stayed home from the track and tried to figure out where he'd gone wrong. He'd been betting to win and place, looking for horses good enough to finish second. That's exactly what he found. He'd also neglected to write his "Scott figures" next to a horse's record in the *Racing Form*. After two weeks, he returned to the track, filled in his Scott figures, bet to win, and won back his $9,000.

"That was one of the most wonderful years of my life," Steve said. "Just to carpool with Scott and be able to talk about handicapping with Scott, that was a time I treasure."

Impressed with his protégé, Scott helped him land a job as a hand-icapper for the *Green Sheet*. Don't try to live off your bets, he told Steve. You've got to have something on the side. In the summers, Steve covered five tracks a day. He'd never been to Finger Lakes or Belmont or the Fair Grounds, but some handicapping principles work any-where. At the Fair Grounds, 30 percent of his top picks won. One day, he nailed five winners. There wasn't much time for a social life. On Sunday mornings, he was a reader at his Catholic Church, and twice a week he made it to the racetrack, where he had to sit close to a plug to keep his computer running. The rest of the time, he holed up in his house, handicapping.

(Steve's hit rate was outstanding, but he was not as good as the masses in the grandstand. Nobody is. The betting favorite generally wins between 33 and 36 percent of all races. The collective mind is more perceptive than the sharpest public handicapper.)

"I feel very lucky," he said, "because I have a job doing something I love."

"Would you say you beat the races now?" I asked him.

"Actually," he said, leaning over and cupping his hand to the side of his mouth, "I don't. I think I could if I had time to follow Arlington exclusively, but I have to keep up with all these other tracks."

That wasn't the only reason. When you're only at the track twice a week, it's hard to pass a race. The regular can tell himself, "The odds here don't look so good; maybe I'll wait 'til tomorrow." The weekend player has to make his bones today. That's how, one weekday in July, Steve ended up betting on Keys to Astro. We all liked Keys to Astro. Scott predicted he'd run two or three lengths faster than the rest of the field. I made him 3–2 on my line, which meant he'd be a great bet at 2–1. A horse that fine is liable to set off a bidding war. Keys to Astro opened at 6–5. He was still there when announcer John G. Dooley intoned, "You have five minutes to wager."

Steve folded his arms.

"I refuse," he shouted back at the speakers.

A moment later, he was on his feet.

"That's what happens when you don't go to the track very often," Scott murmured, as soon as Steve was past the escalators.

I got up to follow. If Keys to Astro ticked up to 2–1, I wanted a piece of it. I sort of hoped he wouldn't, though. Betting was nerve-racking, and I felt thrifty and self-disciplined when I passed a race. I played the horses with a Protestant work ethic: gambling wasn't a vice if you applied Puritan virtues to it. It was investing, the same as in those WASP casinos on Wall Street.

Steve studied the electronic board displaying the exacta prices. Modeled after the odds board in Vegas race books, they were on every floor at Arlington. He hated to throw away a good horse just because the win price was chintzy.

"I'm trying to find some value on Keys to Astro," he said. "I'm betting some exactas with him on top."

"Are you betting him straight, too?" I asked, meaning, are you betting him to win?

"Yes, but don't tell Scott."

I watched the tote board in suspense. At 9–5, I was tempted. The devil was dangling a $5.80 payoff in my face, and I wanted to snatch it. Then the odds dropped to 8–5. Betting is like voting: in the last minute, the undecideds break for the favorite. I stepped back and held up my hands.

"He's too low for me to bet," I said. "I'm going to have to root against him now. This'd be an easy game if it weren't for the odds."

I watched the race with my shoulders clenched. They didn't relax until two horses passed Keys to Astro in the stretch. Steve was a big bettor, anywhere from $80 to $500. He'd knocked down the odds with the size of his bet. I was grateful. He'd lost money, so I didn't have to.

◡

There was another distraction that kept Steve from winning. He was thrilled to be divorced, but he wasn't thrilled to be single. The solution, he thought, was to find a woman who loved horse racing. The track wasn't much of a meat market. There wasn't an Adelaide for every Nathan Detroit. You saw plenty of young women in shorts at Arlington, but most of them were with dates. The single ones were interested in owners and trainers, those who got to stand in the winner's circle and, usually, left the grounds with more money than they'd brought in.

As my (divorced) buddy Joe puts it, "If you want to do this full time, you're gonna have to forget about women. Women hate horse racing, man. They hate losing money. When I lived in Vegas, I knew all these guys who'd been divorced three or four times. Their wives hated 'em. All they wanted to do was play the horses."

But Steve thought he'd found his ideal woman at the racetrack. Bonnie was petite, dark-haired, and had her own horse racing Web site. It was an immediate crush. But Steve was boyishly wholesome, while Bonnie chain-smoked ladies' cigarettes and drank with the horsemen at the first-floor bar.

"Bonnie?" I asked, when he told me he was interested in her. "You know she's a smoker?"

He knew.

"And she lives in northwest Indiana."

It was less than an hour on the highway.

One night, he took her to Jimmy D's, an after-the-races tavern catty-corner from Arlington. This did not ignite a romance, so the next time Bonnie came to the track, Steve deserted his computer and lingered among her circle at the bar. That didn't work, either. Worse, it cost him money. When he sat back down behind the laptop, he was moaning about a missed bet in the fifth race.

"The odds were great," he said, "but I was too busy chasin' tail to notice."

Pittsburgh Phil was right.

"A man who wishes to be successful," wrote the early twentieth-century gambler, "cannot divide his attention between horses and women."

# 10

## The Late Great Eight

All summer long, I was a devoted speed handicapper. I snapped every issue of the *Speed and Trip Service* into the school portfolio I carried around Arlington. ("Poindexter at the track," a friend mocked.) Between races, I handicapped the next day's card, copying speed figures from the *Lookup* to the *Racing Form*. Scott did the same. So did Warren, and so did Steve, when he was there. The Rebel Enclave was usually as subdued as a college library on a spring Saturday, when the warm sunlight is glowing through the windows and only the dissertation-bound grad students are at the tables. I felt like Bartleby the Scrivener, myself. It was a dry task. We were trying to reduce a physical competition, a noisy, sweaty contest of dirt, muscle, and willpower, to a number. I'd never enjoyed math—I quit it my junior year of high school, surrendering before I had to face trigonometry. But the numbers worked for Scott, so I tried. When I was done and I'd projected how fast each horse would run, I made my odds line. This involved probability, an even more complicated mathematical concept, but it didn't take long before I could do it in my head. If I thought a horse had an 18 percent chance of winning, I knew, instantly, that his fair odds should be 9–2.

Some days, it all worked. Some days, I was Trotter. My first winning afternoon at Arlington was a Saturday. Scott was at Hawthorne—

his Handicapping Center was open on weekends during their summer harness meet—so I roamed the grandstand alone, just as I had in my early years at the track, when playing the horses was a private vice. All day long, I got inflated prices. Bay Raider, a maiden I'd pegged at 9–2, was sent off at 8–1. The odds made me nervous. Bay Raider seemed like a rank outsider, so I bet seven dollars, half the amount recommended by the betting chart I'd clipped from *Money Secrets at the Racetrack*. Bay Raider won. In the turf race, I liked a horse at 6–1. I bet five dollars. He won. And in the ninth, I bet three dollars on a wild proposition who won the race at 17–1. I was on fire! I flipped through the *Form* and added up my winnings for the day: ninety-six dollars. One of the great handicapping performances of my life, and I'd won ninety-six dollars. I felt like the biggest pussy in the history of gambling.

If I was going to be that responsible with my money, I should have stayed home and calculated the interest on my checking account. Betting like a eunuch had made me a loser at Hawthorne. Man, it was the flip side of the Protestant gambling ethic. I couldn't loosen my white-collar Anglo-Saxon fist enough to let go of $100. If I tried to lay out more than sixty bucks, my stomach rumbled and my temples ached. After a lifetime as a tightwad, living in rented rooms on less than twenty grand a year, frugality had become more than a personality trait. It was as much a part of my physical being as the gag reflex. My guts and my bones cried out when I tried to cross the line. I've always believed that a man's virtues are inseparable from his faults. Thanks to my cheapness, I was never going to blow $170,000 of the company's money like Matt Lovello. But I wasn't going to win $81,000 on the twin trifecta, either. I was treading water in the bland middle depths of the ocean, not powerful enough to swim up to the surface with the whales who breathed the air of victory, but strong enough to keep from sinking to the floor, where toothless bottom-feeders turned over tickets with their shoes. In the macho potlatch of the gambling culture, bragging rights don't just come from winning a lot of money, but from betting a lot of money. The Gold Club Room wasn't for big winners. It was for big players, guys who thought a hundred grand was such an insignificant sum that they could toss it into a mutuel pool, never knowing whether it would float back to the top.

To cure my fear of long shots, I decided to bet whatever *Money Secrets at the Racetrack* dictated. It would function as a set of auxiliary gonads, bound between covers, preventing me from bonking against the wall of my own miserliness. It was time to go from tightfisted to two-fisted.

For three wonderful days, the strategy worked. That week, there was a track bias at Arlington. There are times when one part of the track is unusually fast, due to weather, or track maintenance. Horses running there have a huge advantage over the rest of the field. In this case, horses departing from outside posts—nine, ten, eleven, and twelve—were winning most of the sprint races. This same situation had produced my $660 exacta at Hawthorne, so I took notice. On Friday, in the ninth, the obvious horse was Ranelagh, who had clocked a Scott McMannis speed figure of 49 in his last race. No one else looked faster. But down at the bottom of the sheet, breaking from post twelve, was Kid Diamond. Kid Diamond had run 45s in his past two races. On May 4 at Hawthorne, he'd scored a 48, a length shy of Ranelagh's best, while running with the leaders until the final 400 yards. If Kid Diamond got a fast start, he could win. Ranelagh was 7–2. Kid Diamond was 8–1. I'm ashamed to say I bet most of my money on Ranelagh—thirty dollars, to eight dollars for Kid Diamond. (Don't blame me. I was just following the betting chart's orders.) But when Kid Diamond wheeled around the turn and found the sweet spot in the middle of the stretch, I saw that the track bias was the most important factor in handicapping Arlington that week.

The next day's card also ended in a cheap race (a race full of slow horses), this one for fillies. My eye ran down to the number 13 horse, Stop That Dancer. In her last race, five weeks before, Stop That Dancer had run head-to-head with the winner for half a mile, then pooped out and lost by eleven and a half lengths. To prepare for her comeback, she'd trained three furlongs in thirty-six seconds. It was a "bullet work-out," so named for the black dot beside the time in the *Racing Form*, indicating it was the fastest of the day at that distance. Also, her trainer was fitting her with blinkers, which help horses concentrate on the track ahead of them, rather than the herd around them. Stop That Dancer was the likely winner. I made her 9–5. Her main competition looked to be Baltic City, who had the fattest speed figures.

The money poured down on Baltic City: orts, cataracts, and deluges. It was like the Jerry Lewis telethon, with every timpani heralding another odds drop: 2–1, 9–5, 8–5. Meanwhile, Stop That Dancer marched unnoticed through the post parade. She was an astonishing 10–1 when I went to a betting machine and laid down thirty dollars. But it got even better. Arlington's computers were still tabulating the bidding frenzy on Baltic City after the gate opened. At the track, luck isn't your horse winning. Luck is getting a good price. As Stop That Dancer sprinted around the turn, her odds jumped to 12–1. Illiterate, blinkered, she couldn't read the crowd's indifference. Stop That Dancer ran like a rabbit down the middle of the track. Even before she took the lead, her momentum told me she was the winner, and she carried my spirit down the stretch at forty miles an hour.

I pulled out my pocket calculator (Poindexter again), because I couldn't wait to get to a window to find out how much I'd won. It was $402. Champagne ran through my blood. When I cashed out, the teller chirped, "Congratulations!" I wasn't quite a whale, but I was Somebody at Arlington.

Earlier that month, my girlfriend, Kate, and I had moved into an apartment overlooking Lake Michigan. Most evenings, I shut myself in the office, where I handicapped until bedtime. My desk was piled with books and *Racing Forms*. Soon, my operations spilled over to her desk, too. She tolerated the mess, and my absorption with horses, because I was working on a book. It was my job. (Most guys can't get away with going to the track every day. I won't either, once this is published.) The night of Stop That Dancer's victory, we finally spent some time as a couple.

"Kate, you gotta see the replay of this race I won!" I shouted, calling her into the office. "This horse came in at 12–1!"

Kate watched the race on my computer once. I watched it four times, savoring John G. Dooley's staccato call of the winner's name: "Stop . . . That . . . Dancer!"

Sometimes, a big win can cost you more than a big loss. Stop That Dancer almost got me even for the Arlington meet, but she also convinced me to follow Barry Meadow's betting chart as obediently as an Orthodox Jew follows Leviticus. I kept my four $500 betting vouchers in my desk drawer; this was my entire stake for the summer. But, following Meadow's system, over the next month, the vouchers all slipped out of my desk, into my wallet, and into the mouths of betting machines.

If you follow Meadow's *Money Secrets at the Racetrack* to the letter, you'll be betting on a lot of long shots. Suppose you think the best horse in a race should be 7–5, while the third or fourth best should be 9–2. If the favorite goes off at 2–1 and the outsider at 8–1, both are overlays. Meadow recommends betting the long shot, because it's a bigger overlay. But it's also less likely to win. The win pool is an extremely efficient market. In theory, a long-shot player will cash fewer tickets than a chalk player, but he'll make more money. This is one of those financial assumptions, like supply-side economics, that makes sense on paper, but doesn't quite work in real life. Stop That Dancer's victory was followed immediately by the longest losing streak of my life. Those 12–1 odds were a peak from which I leapt, and I didn't stop falling for a long time.

That weekend, I was at Hawthorne. I'd written an article about Glenn for a newspaper assignment, and I needed to track him down to follow up on some editors' questions. He was nowhere to be found, so I spent the afternoon in the Handicapping Center. In the fourth race, Unlock the Vault had an outside post and, therefore, a middling chance. A 4–1 chance. As he loaded into the gate, his odds were 5–1. My chart demanded 6–1. I clenched my fists. I put down roots in the tiled floor. I would not be tempted. I would not surge toward a window like a loser chalk-eater who had to bet nine times a day. Midway through the race, Unlock the Vault zoomed to 7–1. He won.

"I got screwed!" I complained to John Walsh, Hawthorne's computer technician. "I got screwed by a late odds change!"

"The odds on the TV monitors are usually a little behind," he said. "The odds on the betting machines are about thirty seconds ahead of the TVs."

I related my bad beat story across the sill of the program booth, stacked with *Chicago Tribunes*, *Chicago Sun-Times*, simulcast books, and *Racing Forms*.

"I needed 6–1 to bet that winner last race, and the monitor said 5–1. Then he won and paid seventeen dollars."

"What's wrong with 5–1?" John asked.

I would have felt foolish explaining about odds lines and overlay percentages.

"You're one of those guys who bets for value," John said. "I don't worry about that. Just bet on who you like. The value will take care of itself."

At the moment, John was flush. He'd bet on Empire Maker to win the Belmont at 2–1. I'd passed the race, partly because I didn't want to root against Funny Cide to win the Triple Crown, partly because, well, 2–1 seemed a little low on Empire Maker. At 5–2 I might have taken it.

"I bet all the money I could get my hands on that horse," John boasted. "I knew that trainer would have him ready. There was no way he was gonna lose that race."

In the sixth race, I bet another "overlay"—Great Eight at 16–1. Like Kid Diamond, like Stop That Dancer, Great Eight had a history of rushing from the gate, then faltering at the finish. This time, he dawdled in third or fourth place before giving up.

Scott promised the Fourth of July would be better. Holidays were always windfalls, because Arlington was overrun with once-a-year amateurs, the families with strollers who came for the post-race fireworks show. It would be like hustling pool, or playing poker against a table full of fish.

"The Fourth of July was one of my biggest days last year," Scott told me. "I won $8,500. I hit a big exacta, and then I hit the Daily Double. On Father's Day last year, I won $7,500."

It didn't happen again. Arlington brought in high-quality horses for their holiday card, and the winners were obvious even to the soccer dads. I played an exacta in the fifth: the favorite, Red Wildcat, on top of three lesser animals. Then one of my second-place horses reared in the gate, tossed his jockey, and was sent off to the paddock for unruly behavior. The late scratch reduced the field to five, depressing the payoffs.

"Is this race even worth betting on now?" I asked Scott, who was holding an identical ticket.

"Not really."

The Buddha had spoken. I sprinted down an escalator and cashed in my ticket just before the bell rang. Scott—with a tender ankle, a full belly, and the surety that, however this bet turned out, he was going to turn a profit at Arlington—remained in his seat. Red Wildcat won. The exacta paid only twelve dollars, but that was twelve dollars I wouldn't be taking home.

It was always frustrating to bet in the presence of Scott McMannis. There were days I thought he fixed the races. Once, in a turf mile for maidens, we had to choose between two horses who'd run nearly identical figures. Highland Facts had earned a 29, Grand Jete a 28. I bet Highland Facts. Scott bet Grand Jete. When Grand Jete pulled away in the stretch, he grinned cattishly and shouted, "There she goes! She was just toying with 'em."

"How'd you know that horse was going to win?" I asked him.

"Well, that last race was her first race on the turf," he explained. "Horses usually improve three to five lengths their second race on the turf."

If you intercepted Scott on his way to the window, he was usually willing to reveal how he was betting. "It's the 3," he'd mumble, or, "I'm betting the Pick Three." I didn't always heed him, though. Someday, I would have to bet without Scott, so I wanted to learn how to do it on my own. The point of playing the horses is to be smarter than the masses, so what's the use of winning with another man's picks?

The few times I did bet with Scott, I lost. And I found a way to blame it on the teacher.

"Need to get away from Scott McMannis," I wrote in my notebook. "I don't have stone ears. He played a Pick Three; I played a Pick Three. He got excited about Pushed at 9–2. I'd been planning to pass the race, but I bet Pushed. Pushed lost."

When my shutout streak reached nine days, when I'd lost nearly $1,000, I asked the Stat Man to go over my bets with me. I couldn't ask Scott. Scott had no patience for bad beat stories. Winning gamblers didn't look back. If you told him about a losing bet, he might grunt—not out of commiseration, but as an acknowledgment you'd made a noise—or he might ignore you, studying his program in silence. Steve, who'd suffered losing years, was more sympathetic.

"You're picking winners, but they're short-priced winners," he told me, after looking over my betting records. "Your handicapping is sound. It could be that you're too fussy about the odds you'll take. Or it could be you're just noticing the same things as everyone else."

I complained to Kate, too.

"I used to be a lot better at this," I told her. "My first year at the track, I only lost thirteen dollars for the entire Hawthorne meet."

"You've got too much mental flak," she said. "You're trying out too many angles at once."

"I can't seem to win when I'm sitting around Scott McMannis, either."

"It's the anxiety of influence," Kate explained.

◡

"The anxiety of influence" is a term coined by literary theorist Harold Bloom to describe an artist's oedipal struggle to outdo his idols. Every poet, painter, musician, and author must, as one music critic put it, "find his or her own voice through an ambivalent, anxiety-ridden relation precisely with those precursors whom they most admire."

George Bernard Shaw expressed his agon with Shakespeare by writing *Shakes v. Shav*, a skit portraying both playwrights as puppets in a boxing match. I tried to work out my struggle with Scott by hiding out in the Mud Bug, miles away from his gravitational pull. "The Bug" is an OTB on the Near North Side of Chicago, around the corner from a dance club once frequented by Dennis Rodman and a titty bar once patronized by Michael Jordan and the rest of the Chicago Bulls.

It was the day Great Eight returned to the races. When I got there, twenty minutes before post time, most of the chairs and stools were taken, so I sat down at a table next to Primus Anthony. I'd met Anthony back in April, at Hawthorne's spring handicapping contest. He was a 400-pound foghorn in a picnic-table shirt, which billowed around his bell-shaped torso. Whenever he had a winner, the whole room knew it. His deep-as-the-ocean voice poured from his lungs, heaved forth from a formidable belly. "Oh, yeah," he'd boom. "Oh, yeah! Come on! Come on!" It was like playing the horses with a bass from the Lyric Opera. People paid him a dollar to cheer their horses, because it was so entertaining, and because it might actually be heard on the track.

Anthony wasn't just a loudmouth. He was a studious gambler. He had finished tenth in that contest. Now, during the run-up to the first race, he was recording the odds in a graph-paper notebook, noting every change, just as a broker charts the rolling fortunes of a stock.

"I'm playing the board today," he explained, after I introduced myself. "Look at the 5. He goes from 9–1 to 6–1. That's a trainer hit. I got to put two and two on the 5. [That's two dollars to win and two dollars to place on the 5.] Anytime a horse drops more than two points, it's live. And then I've got to play a 1–7 exacta. 1 and 7 are live, too."

His *Form* was lined with squiggles like cartoon waves. They were his "freshness marks." If a horse hadn't run for forty-five days, he drew a red line above its last race—to indicate "major freshness." If it had been laid off only thirty days, he drew a black line—for "minor fresh-ness." Anthony had paid a man in California $200 to learn that sys-tem. He offered to retail the secret for much less.

Opening his wallet, Anthony removed a much-folded, much-scribbled sheet of paper. Unwinding its creases, he spread it out on the table. Across the top, he'd written "Trainer Maneuver Handicapping Method." "This'll make you a professional horseplayer," he rumbled. "This has got everything you need to know to beat the horses. I'll sell it to you for fifty bucks. It's worth 300 bucks. It's worth a million."

I tried to get a look at it. There were three lists, dated May, June, and July. Each was longer than the one before. The method was under constant revision, like the Baltimore Catechism. I spied a few handi-capping factors—"45 days off," "won last race"—followed by point values. Evidently, it worked like Mary Schoenfeldt's Derby chart, with every horse assigned a score. When Anthony snapped it shut, I could see it was written on the back of a Social Security benefits statement.

"You can't write none of this down in your notebook," he said. "You gotta *buy* it."

"I don't have fifty bucks in cash," I told him, because I was feel-ing skeptical—and broke. "All I've got are betting vouchers. When are you going to be down here again?"

"I'm usually here at the beginning and the middle of the month. That's when my check comes in. If I win, I might be down here a lit-tle more often. A lot of times I'll be at the OTB at State and Lake."

Anthony's 5 horse, the horse who'd taken the "trainer hit," was Great Eight. Great Eight had let me down last time, but I decided to give him one final chance, since this time he'd be running with blink-ers. That equipment change had worked for Stop That Dancer. No one else trusted Great Eight. After that sudden drop, his odds floated away like a balloon. When they hit 19–1, I had to bet five dollars to win and five dollars to place.

The blinkers worked for Great Eight. He went to the lead and stayed there, all the way around the track. With 100 yards to run, he had one rival to put away: Mister Fox, a career quitter whose record was full of second-place finishes. This race was in the bag. I jumped to my feet, blocking the screen from all the Middle Eastern guys sitting at the counter behind me.

"Nineteen-to-one!" I shouted, whirling my fist. "Nineteen-to-one! That's a forty-dollar horse! A forty-dollar horse!"

Anthony had bet two and two on Great Eight. He pounded our table, bellowing at a jockey thirty miles away: "Come on, Jesse!" he boomed. "Come on, Jesse!"

Then, seventy yards from the wire, Great Eight broke his leg. Seventy yards from turning my $10 into $140, he stumbled, as though he'd stepped into a post hole. Coming up short, at forty miles an hour, he pitched his rider over the pommel. Jesse Campbell rolled toward the rail to avoid a stampede. Great Eight limped forward, pricking at the ground with his shattered leg. Mister Fox galloped by for a lucky victory: no one else was close enough to pass him. When Great Eight broke down, all the cheers in my throat clustered at a bottleneck. Then, after a dazed moment, they burst out as bitter laments.

"He was gonna win!" I cried. "Nineteen-to-one! He was gonna win and he broke his fucking leg!"

Anthony shook his head. Right then, I wondered whether horse racing had been invented by a mischievous god for the sole purpose of making a fool out of me. I had bet the right horse, at the right price, and I'd still lost. Maybe my dead grandmother ("You can't win gambling!"), my ex-girlfriend ("It's a mug's game"), and all those hustlers on the first floor at Hawthorne ("You ain't gonna win money by handicapping"), maybe they were all right about playing the horses. Maybe it was just luck.

(Several months later, I would read the story of a gambler who'd suffered far worse from a breakdown in the stretch. In March 2004 the Pick Six carryover at Santa Anita reached $4.7 million. Thousands chased after the pot, but going into the final race, there were four tickets left alive. Only one of them included the 75–1 shot who took the lead in the deep stretch, then snapped his leg 100 yards from the wire. If that horse had managed to keep all four legs intact, one bettor would have collected the entire pool, for the biggest score in the history of pari-mutuel wagering, a life-changing payout. But since he didn't have the eventual winner on his ticket, he got nothing but a consolation prize. The agony, the agony.)

That night, Kate and I went to see *Stone Reader*, a documentary about an Iowa writer who produced one great novel, then disappeared from the face of literature. It was a frightening and fascinating study of the one-book wonder, but afterward, I was still too traumatized to talk about the film or anything else but Great Eight.

"I'm sure he's dead now," I said, as we walked out of the theater. "They always put 'em down after they break their legs."

"That's too bad," she said. She made a sympathetic face—for the horse, not for me.

"It is too bad. It's also too bad about my ten dollars. I gotta look on the bright side, though: this is the second time I've lost a bet on that horse. He'll never take my money again."

I know my words sound callous, but after months of handicapping, I'd come to think of horses as betting units, the way a poker player thinks of playing cards. To me, they came alive as individuals in the *Racing Form* far more than they did in a post parade with eleven identical-looking chestnut colts. Maybe it was because I'd grown up reading baseball box scores instead of riding horses. But Scott was the same way. He never went to the paddock. He could tell you whether Tee Wee was likely to improve her speed figure in her second race off a layoff, but he couldn't describe the shape of her fetlock. In his book *The Wrong Horse*, William Murray observed the same attitude in the hard-bitten gamblers he met at the Southern California tracks: "I don't know a single professional horseplayer who enjoys the sport for its own sake or feels any sense of identification with the animals and the riders," he wrote.

We gamblers are no less sentimental than the owners and trainers, who sometimes saddle injured racehorses, hoping to grind out one last win, or sell them to slaughterhouses when they become too gimpy for the track. Part of handicapping, in fact, is guessing whether a horse suddenly running at a lower level is suffering from an injury. That's an agrarian outlook alien to most modern city-dwellers, but it's the same practical attitude once held by a farmer who needed his field plowed, or a teamster who was running a stagecoach and couldn't afford to feed a lame horse. Horse racing is a business, and horses are the product.

Although I'd vowed to escape the orbit of Scott McMannis, the next afternoon I marched straight up to the Rebel Enclave. I had to share my bad beat story with someone. Scott would have to do.

"Did you see that horse that broke its leg in the third race yesterday?" I asked him. "That horse was going to win, wasn't it?"

"I thought so," Scott murmured.

That was as much as we talked about Great Eight, but Scott's assent made it official: I'd been screwed. The Racing Gods had fired a bolt of lightning right at my wallet. It had burned up $140 there, but it had also zapped my frontal lobe, where most gambling decisions are made.

In Shakespeare's *Julius Caesar*, when Brutus berates Cassius for losing all their money at the track, Cassius replies, "The fault, dear Brutus, is not in our stars, but in ourselves." In other words, it wasn't bad luck. Cassius was a terrible gambler. That was my failing as well.

Great Eight's defeat and death *were* bad luck. They were in my stars. Yet after that race, I changed the way I bet and handicapped. Maybe it was because I'd broken into my final $500 voucher to play the horse. Maybe it was because I'd deserved to win, and because of that, I could no longer tolerate losing. Whatever the reason, I threw away Barry Meadow's betting chart and I stopped printing out Scott McMannis's speed figures. I was going to find my own way to beat the races.

# 11

## Omar and Lucky

On the day Deep Roots was entered in a turf race at Arlington, Omar Razvi had the flu. But some horses are worth getting out of bed for. That morning, Omar drove his taxicab to the track and got a big bet down. He was feeling cocky. The week before, he'd won two grand, so he laid out $250 to win and put Deep Roots in a bunch of exactas and trifectas.

Deep Roots was born to run on the grass. Her mother, Grass Roots, had also foaled Lemon Grass, winner of six stakes races (the most prestigious type of race, with the biggest purse) on the turf. Omar had been playing the horses for half of his twenty-nine years, so he knew their family stories.

After collecting his tickets, Omar drove back to his apartment and went to bed until three o'clock, post time for the sixth. Then he moved to the couch and turned on TVG, a satellite horse racing network that broadcast the races from Arlington. Most horseplayers aren't into breeding, so Deep Roots left the gate at 16–1. A few steps out, she was bumped hard by a horse from a neighboring stall. Knocked off stride, she let the field fly past. Deep Roots recovered some ground on the backstretch, as the pack jogged along to save wind for a finishing kick, but turning into the stretch, she still trailed the leader, Highland Facts, by four lengths. Then the long-shot filly started sprinting as though she were on high-speed film. Suddenly, Omar didn't feel so sick anymore. As Deep Roots drew eyeball-to-eyeball with Highland Facts, he bounded from the cushions and hopped across the living room floor, screaming, "Commmme onnn! Goooo!"

Deep Roots paid $35.40. The exacta paid $240.80. The trifecta paid $2,014.80. When Omar made it back to Arlington that afternoon, the track paid him $10,000.

Omar needed the money. He was a small-time horse owner, and his stable hadn't been winning a thing.

For over a decade, Omar had done his betting at the windows— he made small wagers, because he was trying to save enough money for a cab. Once he started his own taxi service, Omar became a real gambler: he bought a racehorse, a filly named Sassiness. Sassiness was such a loser that her owners let her go for $3,000, which is midway between the highest canning price and the lowest claiming price. (Again, in a claiming race, every entrant in a race is on sale for a specified price tag.)

"Nobody wants to get rid of a horse that is going to win," Omar explained. "They had given up on this horse. The principal owner was ready to send it to the killers"—that is, to the slaughterhouse.

You couldn't blame them. Sassiness had an 0-for-15 record at Arlington. In her first few months as the sole possession of Razvi Ltd., Sassiness added three notches to that streak. She finished fourth in a mile race, fifth in another mile race, then ninth in a race at a mile and an eighth. Sassiness didn't like running. On the morning of each race, her trainer, Mike Dini, injected her with Lasix, a drug that improves a horse's endurance by suppressing internal bleeding. Lasix is also a diuretic. When Sassiness began peeing uncontrollably, she knew the bridle, the saddle, the gate, and the bell were coming soon, and she spun anxiously around her stall. Omar tried to calm her by visiting the barn each night with peppermints. But, he said, "She's a real nervous filly. She goes into heat a lot, too. She's a horny horse. She sweats a lot in the paddock, too."

If Sassiness didn't win soon, Dini planned to ship her to Great Lakes Downs, which is like a ballplayer being dropped by the Chicago White Sox and catching on with the Lansing Lugnuts.

Sassiness was costing Omar $250 a week in trainer bills. He also owed $4,500 to the Illinois Tollway Authority, and he'd just made a down payment on a new pickup truck. So what did he do after he won that ten grand on Deep Roots? The very next day, he bought another horse.

Northern Catch had begun his career with much promise. The colt, who belonged to Brereton C. Jones, the former governor of Kentucky, won a maiden race at Gulfstream Park under the ridership of Pat Day, one of the United States' leading jockeys. After that, though, Northern Catch tanked. By the summer of his three-year-old year, he was running in $12,500 claiming races at Churchill Downs. Omar's friend Mike Melcher—a $1,000-a-day gambler who kept a private box at Arlington—thought Northern Catch was a steal at that price.

"I had some money saved up, but I was near bust," Omar said. "I went ahead and gave Mike everything I had."

As soon as Northern Catch arrived at Arlington, Omar asked a friend who grooms horses to take him for a gallop.

"This horse is bad, real bad," the friend said, as soon as he hopped off. "His knees buckled. I think he's got bone chips. Get out of this horse as soon as possible."

That's why Brereton C. Jones is a wealthy horseman. He was already out of the horse.

Omar tried running Northern Catch for his old claiming tag, hoping no one would notice the colt's infirmity. The horse finished last in a turf race. The next time out, Omar entered Northern Catch for $7,500. Minutes before post time, as the horses were warming up on the track, Northern Catch's jockey called the veterinarian over. He said he wouldn't risk his life on the wobbly-legged animal. No one else would mount him, either, not even the 2-percent riders who hang around the jocks' room, hoping to be named to the nags the winning riders won't touch. Northern Catch now had a ninth-place finish and a vet scratch to show for his month at Arlington. Omar took to calling him Northern Crutch.

"Right then, I was at break even," Omar said. "I had to win a race."

That's how it is when you're a cabdriver supporting a string of cheap claimers. You always have to win a race. Horse racing is called the Sport of Kings because it requires a royal treasury to support a stable. Northern Catch ate just as much hay as Funny Cide. But Funny Cide earned his owners $800,000 for winning the Kentucky Derby. Two weeks later, he won another $650,000 at the Preakness. The Triple Crown gets the television coverage, but nearly two-thirds of all horse races are claimers. In a $5,000 race, anyone can buy a horse by putting up the money with the racing secretary before post time. The $5,000 claimer is the bottom of the barrel at Arlington. The purse is $11,000 divided among the top four finishers. Since the winner gets 60 percent, Northern Catch would have to win 220 consecutive races to gather as much scratch (cash) as Funny Cide did that May. Claimers rarely win twice in a row. You can see the economic imperative. The only way to make money off a claiming horse is to win right away and hope somebody buys it. Chicago's top trainers, Michael Reavis and Wayne Catalano, did this all the time. They claimed a horse for $10,000, ran him for "the nickel" ($5,000) and made a bare profit by collecting the winner's share, plus the claiming price.

Northern Catch was not going to rescue Razvi Ltd. But Omar's friend Lucky had a bright idea. Lucky is a short, wiry, speed-walking, quick-rapping racetrack knockabout who earned his nickname due to his misfortunes at the betting windows. I once saw him fly into a rage after a horse named Serai lost by a nose.

"I had a sixty-dollar exacta, Serai on top of the horse who just beat him, and fifty dollars to win on Serai," he fumed. "That just cost me $2,500!"

"Did you bet the exacta the other way?" I asked him. "With the winner on top of Serai?"

"No!" he shouted. "I don't bet like Scott McMannis! I bet to win!"

I relayed this to Scott.

"That's why they call him Lucky," Scott said. "He does that all the time."

Lucky had worked as a groom, so he knew horses. He'd noticed that Sassiness was tiring in her mile runs, so he suggested that Omar enter her in a shorter race—six furlongs.

"I figured this was her last chance to be a come-from-behind sprinter," Omar said. "That's what she was bred for."

Sassiness rallied from eighth place to finish two lengths behind the winner. The owner gets 20 percent of the purse for second, and $2,200 was enough to keep Sassiness eating for two months. Omar thought his filly had found her niche.

On the first of August, Omar entered Sassiness in a six-and-a-half-furlong race, hoping the extra 110 yards would give her more room to run down the leader. Before the race, he stood in the paddock with Mike Dini, Mike Melcher, and Lucky, watching Sassiness parade around the walking ring. Omar was not optimistic. He drew a finger across his throat when he saw me coming.

"It doesn't look good today," he said.

I told him I'd figured that out. I was betting on Minister Lake. Lucky nearly hopped down my throat when he heard that.

"Don't ever say that in the paddock!" he snapped. "You should never talk about someone else's horse!"

"But she's 0-for-18 at Arlington," I countered.

Lucky looked at me in disgust.

"You and your statistics," he sneered.

Sassiness's jockey, Eddie Perez, Jr., strode into the ring, wearing the silks of Razvi Ltd. Omar had designed them himself. They were black with crossed silver scimitars and a crescent moon, emblems of his Islamic heritage. (Omar's parents are from Pakistan, but he is as Muslim as Creighton Schoenfeldt is Catholic; Creighton goes to the track on Good Friday, Omar drinks beer and eats pepperoni pizza at Jimmy D's.) The four-foot-ten-inch jockey shook hands with Omar and his friends, and then Dini cradled Eddie's boot in his hands, boosting him onto Sassiness.

Everyone went inside to bet. Omar and Lucky had told me to meet them down by the rail, but I couldn't find them in the Friday afternoon crowd, so I sat down on a bench just as the gate opened. The favorite, Just a Sheila, bolted out of the gate and ran the first quarter mile in twenty-one and four-fifths seconds. Her sixteen-year-old jockey, Timothy Thornton, had not yet learned how to pace a horse, so he rode every mount like a rocket, hoping it could still breathe at the finish line. Thornton pushed Just a Sheila through the half mile in forty-five seconds. That's a killing pace even for good horses. These were cheap claimers. The rest of the field strained to keep up. By the stretch, almost every filly was exhausted . . . except for one who'd saved some energy by starting in tenth place.

I spotted Lucky and Omar jumping up and down and screaming, just as John G. Dooley was calling, "Sassiness in the black now, coming with a blitzing run! It's Sassiness to win!" They were the only ones celebrating. A 7–1 long shot doesn't have a lot of fans. I ran down to the rail to meet them, then followed them to the winner's circle.

"Who was it who told you to run that horse in a sprint?" Lucky badgered Omar. "Huh?"

Looking up into the stands, Omar formed an X with his arms. Crossed swords. The gesture was aimed at a friend who'd told him Sassiness couldn't win.

"We did it, Lucky!" Omar exulted. "We did it!"

"Calm down!" someone told him.

Lucky wheeled on the killjoy.

"Hey!" he barked. "You have no idea how much this means to this man!"

As the winning owner, Omar received a pewter cup and a check for $6,600. He posed for a photograph with his horse, his jockey, his trainer, and a girl in tight pants whom no one could identify after the picture was developed. It didn't matter. Owners are in a generous mood after a victory. They'll let anyone stand next to the horse.

"It's a real high addiction, getting into the winner's circle at Arlington," Omar said a few days later, while drinking Miller Lite at Jimmy

D's. "But I would never attempt to support a family while I do this. It's just me, a truck, and three horses."

U

Owning claimers is not a sentimental pastime. You claim horses the way a cattleman claims cows, so you can't treat the stock like pets.

Omar treated them like pets. There were the nightly visits to Sassiness, bearing peppermints in the palm of his hand. And there was his affection for Fleet Boss, the third horse in his stable. A week and a half after Sassiness won, Omar entered Fleet Boss in a race. He'd bought the horse for $7,500. Now he was trying to sell him for the same price. A win would mean a big profit. But in the paddock, Omar looked glum. Wayne Catalano, the winningest trainer at Arlington, was inspecting Fleet Boss.

"The Cat Man couldn't follow that horse fast enough," Dini reported to Omar. "He wants to claim him and run him for the nickel. He's trying to win the trainer title."

"It's been good to know you, buddy," Omar muttered, as Fleet Boss joined the parade of horses cantering toward the track. Then he said, "I kind of got attached to that horse."

Horseplayers who play the board, like Primus Anthony, might have been enthusiastic about Fleet Boss. He opened as the 9–5 favorite.

"Save your money," Omar advised his friends. "If it was 10–1, I might tell you to bet it. But not 9–5."

As post time approached, Fleet Boss's odds grew longer and longer: 3–1, 4–1, 9–2, and finally 5–1. The crowd had a low opinion of Fleet Boss, which suggested his early favoritism had been the result of one very big bet.

The crowd was shrewd. Fleet Boss's race was a disaster. The moment the gate sprang open, he reared up, costing him a jump on the rest of the field. Then the horse in the next stall slammed into Fleet Boss's flank, shoving him off stride. Fleet Boss never passed a single horse. Omar watched gloomily from a friend's private box, his mouth tightening with each furlong. His face suggested he was losing more than a beloved animal.

After Fleet Boss crossed the line last of all, John G. Dooley announced, "We have a claim in this race. Number 5, Fleet Boss, to the Mike Reavis barn."

A cell phone call to Dini revealed that Fleet Boss had torn off a chunk of his hoof. But that was the problem of the Reavis barn.

Omar went to the bar and ordered a screwdriver. When he returned to the box, he pulled a stack of worthless tickets from his pocket and pitched them to the Astroturf carpet.

"I fuckin' lost money on this horse," he griped. "I bought him for $7,500, I paid his feed bill, and he didn't pick up a check. Sassiness is running on Thursday. She'll probably get claimed. That'll be the end of my stable. I need to go back to my taxi."

That was the last time I saw Omar. I continued to follow his horses, though. Northern Catch was claimed by some sucker for $5,000. The horse finished third in his last race for Razvi Ltd., so Omar lost a lot of money on him. Sassiness returned to losing. No one would buy her, even for the nickel. Eventually, Omar gave up on his filly, retired her to a breeding farm in southern Illinois, down by the Kentucky border, and made a date for her to mate with Cartwright, a stud who had already sired several winning Thoroughbreds. He hoped that motherhood would make her happier than racing.

Then, during a $5,000 claiming race one humid afternoon, I watched a horse named Go Go Hasty stagger under the wire, victorious, but so exhausted that her jockey reined her to a halt, rather than cooling her down with a short jog.

"They're going to have to give that horse a looong rest," remarked Scott, who was sitting next to me.

"We have a claim in this race," John G. Dooley intoned. "Number 6, Go Go Hasty, for $5,000 to Razvi Limited."

# 12

## Men Betting Badly

It wasn't easy finding the Pro. I wanted to know whether there was anyone—*anyone*—who made a living just betting on horses. If there was, I wanted him to teach me how to do it, too. So I did an Internet search for professional handicappers. Amazingly, a name popped up. It was an Irish name. We have a lot of those in Chicago, so I had to call five numbers before I got the Pro's son on the line.

"Is this the home of the professional handicapper?" I asked.

"I think my dad does something like that," the son said.

"Ask him to call me. I'm writing a book about horse racing, and I want to talk to a pro."

Three days later, my phone rang. The Pro apologized for not calling back sooner. He'd been in Vegas. I said I understood.

"I'm not sure I should even talk to you, but if I do, don't use my name, OK?"

I said I wouldn't.

"Why don't you meet me out at Arlington? I'm usually in the paddock."

The Pro wanted to check me out. Maybe he thought I worked for the Internal Revenue Service or racetrack security, two organizations that might take issue with the way he earned his living. He described himself to me—a description I can't pass on, because you might see him at the track someday—and told me to look for him before the fifth race the following Saturday.

The Pro was big and wary, a city guy with a bored, thrusting lower lip. He looked tough, but as the saying goes in poker, "the nicer the guy, the worse the gambler." We chatted for a minute about an online handicapping contest he was competing in, and then he proposed a rendezvous.

"I gotta go down to Mississippi for a poker tournament on Wednesday, but I'll be at the Mud Bug Monday and Tuesday. I've got my own table in the dining room. Meet me there and we can talk."

Despite the invitation, he seemed surprised, even flustered, when I walked into the Bug two days later and sat down at his private table.

"Oh, hey, you made it," he said, looking up sheepishly from his *Form*.

The Pro was sitting with a gambling buddy, a Pakistani whose brown eyes flicked resentfully in my direction as he called in a $200 exacta bet on his cell phone.

"This guy's a writer," the Pro explained to his friend.

The Pakistani stood up to leave.

"Maybe we better get another table," the Pro suggested.

We sat down under a television tuned to Saratoga. The Pro had a Pick Six going—three races in the bank, three to go. "But it ain't gonna pay shit," he grumbled. "It's been all chalks so far."

The Pro had a small pension from "Streets and San"—the Chicago Department of Streets and Sanitation, a municipal operation that provides patronage jobs for guys whose uncles went to seminary with the alderman—but he made most of his money betting on horses and playing poker. He wrote "professional gambler" on his tax forms, along with enough of his winnings—"twenty, thirty thousand a year"—to make himself look honest to the IRS.

The Pro explained how he'd gotten his start in gambling, and how he made a living at it.

"I started out bowling for money"—another one!—"then a friend took me out to the track. If you've got the kind of personality where you can sort things out, you become curious as to how things work. You've got to be able to retain knowledge. You've got to be able to picture a race. You've got to know whether a horse ran with or against the bias. I have a friend who tracks biases. I keep trip notes, and I know which jockeys ride to the wire, and which ones ride horses outside. When it comes down to betting, a big part of this is having the bankroll. You've got to know when it's time to box horses. I have a special system for betting trifectas and superfectas. Everything is done by ear. You've got to be able to process a lot of information with six minutes to post time, all your information you picked up in your hand-icapping, whether this is a good bet for you."

This made playing the horses sound like one of those sorcerous arts, such as improvisational jazz, but I knew exactly what the Pro meant. The most important skill a bettor can possess is a fine sense of what the odds should be. It has to be developed by watching thousands of races and losing thousands of dollars, until, eventually, you have a feel for the tote board, the way a guitarist has a feel for the next note, the way a carpenter has a feel for just how hard he should press his chisel against the lathe to winnow a perfect table leg. I knew this because I'd won more money when I'd followed my emotions than when I'd tried to apply a book-taught system. When I'd looked at a tote board, felt a giddy flutter from stomach to sternum, and thought, "3–1 is a gift!" I'd often cashed. When I heard the sirens singing from the tote board, I would have run through gang crossfire to get to a betting window before the bell. I'd felt the opposite, too: a sinking, blah feeling as a Bet of the Day was bet down to 9–5, 8–5, 3–2—it was like staring at a date who got homelier and homelier as the beer goggles wore off. But all summer, I'd gagged my Inner Gambler and shackled him to my now-discarded betting chart. (In the final chapter of *Money Secrets at the Racetrack*, a master gambler tests the system. He wins, of course. However, the book points out that the man doesn't normally make a betting line. He relies on a "feeling." Scott was the same way. At the start of his career, he'd written acceptable odds on his program, but he abandoned the practice as he refined his appreciation for a good price. You couldn't be rigid. Too many things can happen between the evening's handicapping and the afternoon's race—a scratched rival, a track bias, a horse who'd looked brilliant on paper sweating and hanging his head like Eeyore in the post parade.)

The Pro's faith in his "ear" was one reason he was ahead $35,000 for the year. He'd hit a $70,000 Pick Six at Gulfstream, which accounted for all of his annual profits. There was another reason, though. Like every other Pro I'd met, this Pro had Something on the Side: he was a representative for a phone betting service.

Phone services are the most controversial dodge in horse racing. They offer big hitters a chance to beat the takeout by refunding a piece of their action. Say you bet through a service with a 10 percent rebate. Bet $500,000 a year, and the service will kick back $50,000. If you've been breaking even at the track, suddenly you're winning enough money to live on. Phone services can afford to do this because, as simulcast outlets, they pay 3 percent of their handle to the host track and keep 17 percent for themselves. But unlike most simulcast outlets, phone betting services—some of them headquartered in Third World countries like Bermuda and Costa Rica—are not affiliated with a racetrack, so they don't need to pay out purse money, maintain a grandstand, or build a backstretch housing project for the grooms. They can give almost all their profits to the customers. Some kick back as much as 18 percent on trifecta bets, which have a 25 percent takeout at most tracks.

Arlington's reward system, by contrast, returned a measly two-fifths of 1 percent. Officially, the track discourages phone betting. There are signs in the Gold Cup Room prohibiting the use of cell phones for wagering. Most guys honored this by stepping outside to the grandstand to call in their bets. On the other hand, Arlington didn't stop phone betting operations from feeding their money into its pools. And who could blame them? Phone bettors put down enormous sums of money—$1.5 billion a year, according to a study by the National Thoroughbred Racing Association. The study found that the average phone bettor, who tends to be smarter, better financed, and better informed than the two-dollar patzer at the track, loses at a 7 or 8 percent rate—but rebates turn the loss into a 2 percent profit. Instead of betting less as their bankrolls are eroded by losses, some gamblers have started betting far more money. If they were betting $3 million a year before phone accounts, now they were betting $30 million. (They could have gotten a better return from the Pegasus Fund, but where would be the fun in that?)

"It's a huge source of competition," an Arlington executive complained. "We can't compete with 10 percent. We can't compete with offshore operations. They are not helping the game, because there's less money that's going back into the purse structure."

Officially, Arlington groused. Unofficially, its attitude was, "We'd prefer you bet through our tote, but if you bet by phone, we'll take your money." Most racetracks took this stance, but it caused some hard feelings among the loyal gamblers. Throughout the season, there were a series of odds drops after the races started. Favorites who left the gate at 5–2 were coming down the stretch at 9–5. On a $200 bet, that could be the difference between $780 and $560. Jim O'Donnell, always looking for a scandal, kept a tally of odds drops in his *Chicago Sun-Times* column. Players howled that someone was "past-posting"—betting after the bell rang. The odds drops came up at a dinner for Gold Club members organized by track management. Cliff Goodrich, the track president, explained that they were due to late money flowing in from a phone betting hub in North Dakota. It was smart money, too. Most of the heavily bet horses won, which made people even more suspicious.

"The system is hardly a fair one for the majority of a track's customers," Andrew Beyer wrote in the *Washington Post*. "The gamblers getting rebates have a huge competitive advantage over the long-suffering souls in the grandstand betting at a 20 percent takeout rate. Peter Berube, general manager of Tampa Bay Downs, examined last season's wagers from rebate-shop customers and saw that these sophisticated players . . . were winning at an astonishing rate relative to everybody else. 'They're fleecing the rest of our customers,' Berube said, 'and this season we decided not to allow them access to our pools.'"

Soon after, Arkansas's Oaklawn Park joined the revolt, banning services that use "batch technology" from feeding into their pools. Batch technology allows computers to place a large number of wagers in the last seconds before the gate opens. Well-funded, technologically savvy players had been beating the races with sophisticated programs that analyzed the pools, identified overlays, and recommended bets.

"Essentially, this technology allows them to bet last, after they have seen and analyzed how everyone else has bet," said Bobby Geiger, the track's director of mutuels and simulcasting. "We don't think this is a level playing field, and we don't think this is fair to the 99.9 percent of racing fans who don't have access to this technology."

Phone betting was the most regressive form of taxation: the rich paid a *lower* rate than everyone else. Even worse, their money was depressing payoffs for the rest of us, as Steven Crist pointed out in the *Daily Racing Form* when he wrote:

> Imagine a betting pool with $100 in it. After $20 in takeout, the remaining $80 is distributed among the holders of winning tickets. Now add another $100 to the pool from a group that over time gets back $90 out of every $100 it invests. The total pool is now $200, with $160 paid back after takeout. If the new group is getting back $90, that now leaves only $70, rather than the original $80, for the first group of bettors. So even while losing, the new group is taking money from the old one. Someone who loses 10 percent is really doing two different things: losing 20 percent to takeout but winning 10 percent from the other players.

The Pro thought rebates were good for horse racing. Part of his job was handing out cash at the track. Sometimes he passed $20,000 to a single player. It was the only way to beat greedy racetracks that took twenty cents of a gambler's dollar, then charged him for parking, admission, programs, and food. Casinos took less and treated their big players as lavishly as college football recruits. That was why gamblers were abandoning the tracks for riverboats and Vegas junkets.

"You go into a casino and you play blackjack to perfection, you can almost make the game even-money," the Pro said. "They pick you up at the airport, they comp your meals. I've been going to the race-tracks for thirty years. I've never gotten a free program. Think about your average senior citizen. His wife gives him $100 to go to the track. He has to pay a six-dollar admission, five dollars for the *Form*, two dollars for a program. Now, he wants to get something to eat, and all of a sudden he's down twenty dollars, and he hasn't even made a bet. At a casino, there's a free bus, a free buffet lunch, a player's card that gives him rebates. At the track, he's gotta hear all the stories about how Chicago racing is fixed. Why doesn't he go to the boat every week?"

Why didn't the Pro take his money to the riverboats? He might have, but his rebates were keeping him in business. He'd already wagered $500,000, and it was only August. That was $50,000 in his bank account. Since he was only up thirty-five grand, it was the difference between winning and losing. And far from stealing Arlington's profits, he was enhancing them. The track only got 3 percent of his action, but since he was betting $40,000 a week, that amounted to $1,200, and, as he pointed out, "How many people walk in the door and bet $1,200? Until I started getting rebates, I would bet maybe $2,000 a week, period" (which translated to a $400 profit for the track).

"I don't think anybody can win without rebates," he declared.

We'd been talking for half an hour, and the Pro was getting anxious. He didn't like my notebook.

"I'm gonna have to let you go," he told me. "I've said too much already. One thing in life you can count on: people who know don't say and people who say don't know."

◡

My undercover confab with the Pro left me feeling cynical about the whole beating the races thing. With all his advantages, the Pro was winning because of a single Pick Six ticket. Suppose one of the horses on that ticket had broken his leg, like Great Eight. It would have made the difference between earning a living and taking out a second mortgage. It would have put the Pro $35,000 down, instead of $35,000 ahead. And he only won because of rebates. My last remaining voucher was down to less than $500. I didn't have enough money to buy expensive Pick Six tickets or to qualify for rebates. You had to fire $1,000 a week to get back your 10 percent. How was I supposed to survive?

I'd always known that horseplayers were the lowest form of life at a racetrack. Even the illegal immigrants who lived on the backstretch, rising at three in the morning to feed the horses, got to compete for a Groom of the Week plaque. There was no Gambler of the Week. But our bets, our foolishness, and our false hopes paid for their minimum wages, not to mention the six-figure salaries of Mr. D's neck-tied chorus line and the million-dollar carrot he dangled before the crowned horses of Europe once a year. I was still the muck at the bottom of the stable, but now a new breed of horseplayer had evolved past me on the food chain, equipped with a Maxwell Smart array of cell phones, computers, and cameras. I had to admire the whales. They'd found the wormhole that led to victory in a game that was bankrupting the rest of us. But I admired them the way I admired John Dillinger, and I had to resent track management for letting them walk into the vault. It upset the whole competitive balance of playing the horses. Arlington brayed that it wanted every gambler to bet through the tote. Yet if you wanted to see the races live on the Internet, you had to buy a subscription to youbet.com, the online wagering service. It was just for the convenience of the customer, of course. They didn't want people to *bet* online. Sure. And video poker machines are for "amusement purposes only."

The well funded also ruled the exotic-wagering pools, where the monster payoffs lurked. The superfectas often paid $20,000 and the Pick Six $500,000, but a two-dollar ticket was a lottery chance. A twelve-horse field contained over 10,000 superfecta combinations, so you had to spend hundreds, even thousands, to cover every plausible outcome. Playing the horses was turning into a battle of the titans, and most of us were paying two dollars for a ticket on the sidelines.

U

Creighton Schoenfeldt was down almost as far as the Pro was up. No one really knew where Creighton got his cash, but we could all see where it was going. All winter, Creighton had waited for Hawthorne's turf course to thaw. Once it did, he shoveled money into races. In April he hit a stupendous 35–1 long shot, Ave de Rapina.

"How'd he get that horse?" an awed onlooker asked Scott McMannis, after Creighton skipped off to cash his tickets.

"He stabbed," Scott murmured, suggesting Creighton had taken a wild guess at a longshot.

Ave de Rapina kept Creighton's bankroll afloat for a month, and it kept his ego afloat even longer. He won nearly $2,000 on the race. A few weeks after the big score, I was on the phone with Mary, discussing her Derby Day bets. Creighton seized the receiver.

"Aren't you gonna write about Ave de Rapina?" he demanded.

Ave de Rapina was Creighton's last big winner for months. Because of his boycott, I rarely saw him at Arlington, but in August he called and asked me to spend a day with him at the Jackson and State OTB. It was downtown, in the shadow of the Sears Tower. Creighton knew the manager, so we could eat a free lunch. By then, Ave de Rapina was $30,000 in the past.

"I'm tellin' you, Ted, I can't pick my ass anymore," he complained. "I'm gettin' desperate. I've been tryin' to scrape money together by not buyin' my medicine. I know that's not good but, Jesus, I can't play on a string. You know that saying, don't you? Scared money never wins."

Jackson and State, the oldest offtrack betting parlor in the state of Illinois, had been placed in the financial district, because the Racing

Board figured that guys who bet on soybean futures at the Board of Trade might bet on horses, too. On its inaugural day in 1988, Creighton was waiting outside the door at eight in the morning. He'd arranged to be late for his job at the county building. Creighton claims to have placed the first wager at an Illinois OTB. It didn't win. Since then, he and Mary had spent every wedding anniversary in the plush, sedate dining room on the third floor.

"We have a nice lunch," he said, describing his annual treat to his bride, "then I give her half of whatever I win. One year, I won $800 here, and she got $400."

I met Creighton in the dining room. It used to be coat-and-tie only, but in this era of casual Fridays, the dress code has been relaxed to a clean shirt. The carpeted room was so quiet I could hear the hissing of the air conditioners. At this stratum, the gamblers suffered with dignity. An angry drunk once urinated on the bar at this OTB, but that had happened a few floors down. As we speared a cold, limp salad— the opening course of our nice, free lunch—Creighton detailed the frustrations of his summer. He was thinking of canceling his subscription to All-Ways. It was worthless, he said. It never gave him a winner. He only hesitated because he'd written an article entitled "All-Ways and Me on the Turf" for the company's newsletter, and it might not be published if its author stopped using the software. But All-Ways was too expensive to keep.

"I've been betting trifectas and superfectas in turf races, and I haven't hit one all meet," he said. "I'm starting to get discouraged, and I don't get discouraged easily. Mary always tells me if I got paid for all the time I put into this game, I'd be a millionaire. When I come home at night, I've got to update my records. Then in the morning, I read *Handicapper's Edge* and *DRF News and Notes* while I drink my coffee and orange juice and take my pills. It doesn't leave a lot of time for Mary. Once in a while, there'll be a program we both want to watch, so I'll take time out for that. When I started doing this, I thought I could make a living at it, but now I'm starting to think I can't."

To give himself one last shot, Creighton had devised his own handicapping strategy. It was almost as complicated as Anthony's point system. These were the basics: Look at the last five races for horses entered in routes (races of one mile or longer) and the last ten races for horses entered in sprints (races under one mile). From those races, take the two highest speed figures and add them together. Bet on the horse with the highest result.

"But I'm not going to bet on any horses who've been gone more than ninety days," he said, shaking his finger. "Unless they've got a trainer who's really good at bringin' 'em back off a long layoff."

Creighton had brought along a directory of turf sires. He planned to pay closer attention to breeding. Racing on grass is a specialized skill. Good turf horses have broad, plate-shaped hooves, and their legs swing forward with long, skimming strides. These are hereditary qualities. Sires pass them down the way the Daleys pass down power.

(Creighton and Scott disagreed on breeding. Scott believed it was important the first time a horse tried a new distance or a new surface. After that, only its record counted. They'd had some loud disagreements in the Handicapping Center, which usually ended with Scott shaking his head at Creighton's stubbornness and Creighton muttering about the Professor's know-it-all attitude.)

Creighton's book ranked sires the way Mary had ranked her students—with letter grades. The turf races were clustered in the latter half of the card, so he had a few hours to study. When he found a horse with a B sire in the seventh race, he decided to make it the centerpiece—the "key horse"—of a trifecta bet.

Creighton's well-bred horse finished out of the money. Creighton started swearing as only he could swear, taking the name of the Father and the Son in vain. Had he been a Hindu, with a thousand gods, he would have cursed for hours. Eventually he settled back into his cushioned bench, opened his wallet, and drew out a business card. It belonged to the manager of an OTB in Sonoma, California. He couldn't pick a winner, but he still had tales of winning days.

Creighton's sister lived in northern California, and during his visits, he had played the horses every afternoon.

"I would just go in there and sit by myself, but after a few days, this guy"—he tapped the card—"he saw how I played, so he started giving me a free program, and he said, 'Hey, tell me if you need anything.' So pretty soon, he set me and a friend up with our own room. I'll tell you, one day there, we took down nine out of twelve turf races."

Creighton lost $300 at Jackson and State, digging the hole 1 percent deeper. I lost forty dollars. You see, I'd been thinking about betting this 13–1 shot, but—but I won't bore you with a bad beat story. In the First National Bank of Missed Opportunities, there was a five-figure account containing the proceeds of bets I shoulda made, and every day it got bigger.

Downstairs, Jackson and State isn't so genteel. The floors are tiled, not carpeted. There's no table service. You have to walk up to the grill and ask for a hot dog. The first floor has the hostile ambience of a crowded Currency Exchange in which the tellers have just run out of money and stamps and are grateful to be working behind bulletproof glass. I ran into Eli there.

"My man!" he shouted.

As Eli gave me dap, I tried to think of a reason not to lend him money.

"I haven't seen you in a long time," I said.

"I got kicked out over at Hawthorne," he said, pulling a sad face and speaking in a deep, confidential voice.

"What happened?"

"One of the security guards caught me with a rocket in my pocket. A crack pipe. So I've been hanging out here ever since."

I didn't respond. I looked at the floor. I was giving him an opening, so we could get this over with.

"Hey, man, can you spot me enough for a bet?"

"Eli, I lost forty dollars today."

Why didn't I just say yes and get it over with? I always gave in to Eli. Whenever a beggar approached me on the street, I handed him a quarter, no matter what his story was. I should have done the same to Eli. But I always had to string him along, to remind him he was a dead-beat. For two bucks, I should get to feel superior, shouldn't I?

"Come on, two dollars for Papa," he wheedled. "Just bet this exacta for me at Arlington. If it comes in, we can split the money."

"We tried that before," I reminded him. "You still owe me a nickel."

I gave Eli a dollar, which made neither of us happy. I was a chump for the ninth or tenth time, and he was only halfway to his next bet.

# 14

## Eureka?

Leo Szilard, the Hungarian physicist, was crossing a street in London when he came upon the insight that led to the splitting of the atom and, eventually, the atomic bomb. My great handicapping insight—the revelation that enabled me to beat Arlington the rest of that summer, and led to my greatest betting triumph—came to me while I was lying in bed, reading. There was always a pile of horse racing literature on the bedroom floor, and every night I read a few pages before going to sleep. On the first Saturday in August, it was Andrew Beyer's *The Winning Horseplayer*.

"To develop race-watching skills is not easy," Beyer wrote, in a chapter on trip handicapping. "For me, I suspect, it is practically impossible. I do not possess naturally good powers of observation. When I meet someone, I won't be able to remember five minutes later what color tie he was wearing or whether he was wearing a tie."

Well, I thought, I'm an observant person. As a journalist, observing was my job. Ever since college, when I'd carried a notebook and a pen for the campus newspaper, I had trained myself to notice: the way a chess grandmaster caged his face in his hands during a match, as though building a cell to isolate himself from his audience; the accent of a New York–born politician who gave away her origins by referring to her position as "awl-duh-min." I had tried to turn my eyes into a Richard Avedon camera, seeing every hair, every blemish, every wrinkle on a subject.

Scott McMannis had brought his old career to the racetrack, applying the principles of statistics and business to horse racing. I was neither a statistician nor a businessman. That's why his methods weren't working for me. But I thought I had skills that Scott lacked. Scott never watched a race live on the track. The horses running 200 feet from his table could have been at Santa Anita or Dubai. It was easier to take trip notes off a two-dimensional television screen. "If I notice a horse got into trouble as he was passing a certain tree in the infield, I'll be able to look for it in the same spot on the replay," he explained.

The next day, I brought my binoculars to the track. I hadn't used them much lately. (A magnifying glass would have been better suited to my scholarly task of analyzing speed figures.)

It rained that Sunday, but I took a seat outdoors, in the second tier of the grandstand. From there, I could see the tote board—not just the odds, but the place and show pools, too. Up in the second tier, I could see over the crowns of the infield willows to the distant backstretch. My binoculars brought the entire grounds into grainy intimacy, like a movie close-up, so I could even see down the one-mile chute, a long, alley-narrow tail that protruded from the oval, making the track resemble a giant lowercase *q* laid out by crop-circle aliens. (Arlington's track was a mile and one-eighth in circumference. If the mile races had started on the first turn, horses in outside posts would have been forced to run wide.)

Raindrops dribbled through the seams in the metal roof, and an autumnal chill pulled the mercury down into the sixties. I zipped my jacket. I wasn't going back inside. The upper deck was my new place of business.

I didn't bet until the third race. It was a one-mile run for very cheap claimers. In the post parade, most of them seem distressed by the mud. With every step they plucked their hooves from the goo, as though thinking, "What's this muck I'm walking in?" Only one seemed to enjoy it: Cooky Joe Fletcher skimmed through the slop, with his snout ascendant. I made a note in my program (all good reporters take notes): "lively PP," meaning lively in the post parade. Cooky Joe Fletcher was my horse, but he was only 2–1. Back when I'd carried my betting chart in my wallet and bet only to win, I probably would have passed the race. But now I was free of that. I bet an exacta wheel: Cooky Joe Fletcher on top of five horses who had run respectable figures in the mud. It was a dollar bet—if I was going to be a horseplayer reborn, I was going to start at the bottom of the financial scale. Cooky Joe Fletcher won by six and a half lengths. A few seconds later, Jamoke finished second. I not only had half of the exacta, I had a new strategy.

An hour later, it worked again. The fifth was a baby race, meaning it was for two-year-old maidens who were being thrown onto the track for the first time since being wrestled away from a mare's teats. These were the flight-school wannabes. This race was a proving ground. Some of them would wash out of this race and never see a starting gate again. I'd seen it happen. Terry Bjork had owned, in syndicate with some Internet friends, a colt named Franksgonhollywood. On the day of his debut, Terry and his partners gathered in the owner's enclosure, a canopied booth on the apron. Franksgonhollywood had drawn the one post, an intimidating spot for a rookie. When the gate opened, Franksgonhollywood banged into the side of his stall. Today, he lives on a farm.

Most of the horses in the fifth race had no records in the *Form*. So I studied their strides. Kemp and Elite looked comfortable in the mud, taking to it like piglets. I bet two dollars on each and was exhilarated when Kemp, a 6–1 long shot, swung around the leaders on the turn and splashed down the stretch, alone. Elite followed six lengths behind.

Scott was not impressed with my coup. When I stepped into the Rebel Enclave to brag, he chewed me out for using my money inefficiently.

"You turned a 6–1 horse into a 3–1 horse!" he scolded.

Hadn't he heard of dutching?

"I couldn't decide between them," I said. "If I'd only bet one, I might have ended up with nothing. What's wrong with a 3–1 horse?"

I was having a winning day. It had been a while, so I wasn't going to let Scott kill my buzz.

All day long I scribbled trip notes on my *Racing Form*, first as I watched the races through my binoculars, then as I watched the replays on the Diamond Vision screen across the track from my seat. I quickly developed a personal shorthand. In the second race, the number 8 horse, Spring Dip, was bumped coming out of the gate, ran along the rail on the backstretch, and was forced three wide around the turn, all while racing behind two dueling front-runners. I boiled this down to "bump G, R, 3pt, 2d flt." (That is, bumped at the gate, rail, three-path on the turn, second flight.) It was a second-place performance and, considering she was 20–1, one that suggested she was capable of beating her next field. At home that night, I printed out the charts from the *Daily Racing Form*'s Web site, as usual, but this time I copied my trip notes in red ink under each horse's running line. That added another ten or fifteen minutes to my workday, but it was private, exclusive information. I might have seen something everyone else had missed—something I could use to cash a bet when these horses ran again.

On my next day at the track, a Wednesday, I used a turf–breeding angle. Pleasant Sands was making her first start against a field of twelve maidens. None of them had ever run a decent turf race, and Pleasant Sands was a daughter of the Brazilian stud Sandpit, who had finished in the money in three runnings of the Arlington Million, the track's premier race. I bet two dollars to win and two dollars to place on Pleasant Sands—at 9–1, she was worth four bucks, so I wouldn't have to kick myself if she won.

Pleasant Sands had not yet learned how to run from a starting gate. My notes say "stumbled G, outrun," which means she nearly fell to her knees at the start and then was left behind by the pack. By the first turn, Pleasant Sands was fifteen lengths out of twelfth place, looking like a tugboat chasing a fleet of cruisers.

There's a herd instinct in horses. They race in a pack, even when their abilities are very different. In the wild, a horse that's left behind will be eaten by wolves. Thousands of years of instinct told Pleasant Sands to catch the herd or die. And a gene passed down from Sandpit told her that running on grass was delightful. Halfway up the backstretch, Pleasant Sands began to rally. And rally. And rally. She cornered the tight turn like a speedboat, catching every horse but the winner, Echo Jo. The faster she ran, the harder my fist pounded the air. I gave it the last pump when the payoffs lit up: $8.80 to place doubled my money.

If Wednesday was exhilarating, then Friday was—well, it was a cross between the film *Let It Ride* and the pilot of the television show *Early Edition*, when the hero gets a copy of the next day's *Chicago Sun-Times* and takes the racing page to the Mud Bug. Claudio's Type won the first race, which was worth $16.80 if you'd bet two dollars to win and place, and Virtue Ohso won the second, completing a $25.40 Daily Double. After that killing, I was confident enough to make a prime bet. I'd learned the prime bet/action bet system from Andrew Beyer and used it in my early days as a horseplayer. You divided your wagers into two categories: prime bets were horses you believed had a 50 percent chance of winning and were going off at odds of 7–5 or greater. These bets received, at most, 5 percent of your betting capital. Action bets, 1 or 2 percent of your bankroll, were for horses like Pleasant Sands, long shots with intriguing angles.

"These bets exist because nothing would upset my concentration more than a $40 winner or a $300 longshot that I liked well enough to think about but didn't bet a dime," wrote Steven Davidowitz, one of Beyer's racetrack buddies, in *Betting Thoroughbreds*. "I expect to lose some money on action bets, but they keep me in the race and provide peace of mind."

Scott, of course, disdained action bets.

"You mean 'fun bets' or 'play bets'?" he said, when I asked about them. "I did that when I first started, but I quit pretty soon. They lead to what I call 'the dripping faucet' effect. You say, 'Oh, it's just a two-dollar bet,' but over time, those add up."

Scott, however, had conquered his Fear of Regret. I hadn't. It was a struggle for me not to bet a long shot I loved. I would linger in front of a betting machine, while temptation warred with all my lessons about thrift, self-discipline, and speed figures, until the battleground of my brain began to ache. Playing the horses is not just a mental exercise, like crossword puzzles. There's also what one expert calls "the emotional work." Scott, so staid and phlegmatic, never seemed to suffer the storms that raced like lightning between the poles of exhilaration and despair. Whereas Lucky, who was wiry and high-strung, sometimes fell into a self-pitying rage after a tough beat. It's hard to concentrate on the next race when you can't stop reliving the last.

Action bets may have seemed like a leaking faucet to Scott, but to me, they were a pressure valve, releasing two bucks' worth of the angst I endured while deciding whether to bet or pass. They relaxed me, and that, I thought, was one of the reasons I was suddenly winning. When a batter is in a slump, his coaches sometimes tell him to "stop thinking and start hitting." I had stopped thinking and started betting. I'd thrown out all my charts, all my books, and now I was responding directly to what I was seeing on the track. My central nervous system was wired to the tote board. I was one with the odds.

My prime bet was Arbitrate. A three-year-old running an allowance race against older horses, Arbitrate had recently arrived at Arlington from Churchill Downs, where he'd been trained by D. Wayne Lukas, whose horses have won twenty-one Eclipse awards, racing's answer to the Oscars. Today, he was running a mile and an eighth, one lap around the track, and breaking from the two post, which meant he wouldn't have to run wide around either turn. Arbitrate looked like a great horse, but I wasn't looking for great horses. I was looking for great bets. In gambling, a horse and his odds are an inseparable unit. Cigar was a great horse, but he usually went off at 1–5, making him next to worthless as a moneymaking proposition. At 8–5, I thought Arbitrate was a fair bet, but a few more dollars in his wagering pan would yaw the scales out of balance.

With a few minutes to go, I rose from my seat. Bounding up the steps, I burst through the glass doors, passing from bright hot summer to the air-conditioned fluorescence of the grandstand. A crisp white voucher was poised in my fingers as I stood under a television screen, completely still, as though the odds were a trophy buck that would not stir as long as I stayed frozen in place. At zero minutes to post, Arbitrate was still 8–5. I plunged my voucher into the machine and punched in twenty dollars, win, number 2.

Arbitrate ran the perfect race. He stalked the leader for three-quarters of a mile, until his jockey decided to end the suspense and galloped off to a four-length win. I didn't even mind that the odds dropped from 8–5 to 3–2. For twenty dollars, I got back fifty dollars. God liked me. He really, really liked me.

◡

The second deck at Arlington was not just a good place to win money. It was a summer resort. Every afternoon, I showed up at the track in a T-shirt and cutoff jeans—toting a backpack over my shoulders as though I were a thirty-six-year-old college student—and found a seat in the shade of the awninglike roof. On brilliant days, one could see the Chicago skyline twenty-five miles away. It looked like a faint set of battlements poking up above the suburban treetops. Between races, I would swing my binoculars back and forth, picking out the John Hancock Center, the Stone Container Building, and the Sears Tower. On Fridays, I could hear the reverb, washing through the heavy air, of the bar bands who played at the racetrack's Party in the Park. I hadn't spent this much time outdoors since I was twelve, when all summer long I played softball at the junior high school playground and rode my bike on dirt trails through the woods. But this was even better than being a boy, because now I was old enough to gamble.

Most afternoons, I was almost alone in the grandstand. It was me, a few other degenerates, and an old woman in a red coat who shooed us out of the premium section, exiling us to seats far from the finish line. She had the body of a high school secretary, inhabited by the soul of a hallway narc.

"These seats are reserved," she would tell us.

"Reserved for *who*?" I asked, looking over long banks of empty green seats that never fetched their two-dollar price.

"Sir, don't ask me that. I don't make the rules."

Whiling away a summer at the track was a family tradition. It was the same life my Uncle Johnny led thirty years before at Monticello Raceway. Johnny died before I was old enough to bet legally, but I think he would have been pleased that I took after him, instead of his practical sister-in-law Sidele, my grandmother. I got hooked on the horses during the last year of her life, but even at age eighty-seven, she was still authoritative enough to lecture me, "You can't win gambling!"

She was right, of course. But that's no reason not to try.

U

"Have you met Bob the Brain?"

Bill Matthews, disc jockey, precinct captain, and horseplayer, did not appear at Arlington often. He lived near Hawthorne, which is where I'd first seen him, bending his lanky body to bring his squinting eyes close to a tiny television beaming in harness races from Dover Downs, a track in Delaware. Bill preferred the harness horses, the "jugheads," to the live Thoroughbreds in Chicago. I thought that watching harness horses was like watching Olympic sprinters run with their pants around their ankles. But Bill had a number of other tinfoil-hat opinions. He thought that Bill Clinton was a mass murderer and that the Jewish-run media was covering up the Armenian genocide of 1915.

This day, Bill was passionate about two things. The first was an essay on the dangers of aspartame, which he'd printed off the Internet and was urging Scott McMannis and everyone else in the Rebel Enclave to read. The second was a man he called Bob the Brain.

"If you're writing a book about horse racing, you've got to meet Bob the Brain," Bill insisted. "He's a genius. He's usually down by the replay center on the first floor. I'll take you to meet him."

The races were over for the day, so I followed Bill down the escalators. When we reached the bottom, he hurried toward a man standing in front of a bank of televisions, scribbling notes on a sheaf of papers. It was Art Garfunkel. Bob the Plumber. The broken-down horseplayer I'd seen in the Rebel Enclave. His head was tilted backward, so he could watch the races through the thick plastic glasses sliding toward the tip of his nose, and he held himself in a sagging, question-mark posture, inside clothes that were themselves sagging. His sport shirt was untucked, and his waistband drooped below a middle-aged potbelly.

Bill introduced us, and Bob turned away from the televisions. He engaged me immediately, not in the facile, handshaking style of a salesman or a pol, but like a man who's been sitting in a locked study carrel reading math textbooks for six weeks and finally has company. Was I a gambler? How long had I been coming to the track? What were my favorite handicapping methods? He spat words as propulsively as Dick Vitale rapped basketball, his Chicago accent snapping consonants and stretching his vowels.

"I've got to meet my ride," Bob finally said. He hastened out the door and crossed the paddock in a pigeon-toed scurry. "I don't have a car, so Blond Jimmy's giving me a lift home today."

I had to follow him out the gate before I could finally ask a question.

"When are you going to be at the track again?"

"Well, for the last six months, I've been engaged in an intensive speed-figure study, so that's been taking up a lot of my time."

Blond Jimmy was waiting outside his maroon sedan.

"This is Ted," Bob told him.

Wary as always, Blond Jimmy turned just far enough to admit me into his field of vision. Even in making that bare acknowledgment, he looked as though someone had wrenched his head in my direction. Before Bob climbed into the car, I wrote down his phone number on the back of a losing ticket. When I got home, I stapled it into my Rolodex, under Bob the Brain.

We met two weeks later, at a Chinese buffet, where I learned the real story of Bob the Brain.

Bob grew up in Skokie, Illinois, when it was still *the* Jewish suburb of Chicago. In high school he bet on baseball games with his friends and had a little bit of success, because, he said, "even then, I had a statistical bent." In the mid-1960s he tried studying journalism at the University of Illinois–Chicago Circle, but "I dropped out to join the revolution. I suppose I went to the racetrack as a rejection of mainstream society."

For ten years, he was a casual racegoer, but in 1978 he read *Picking Winners* and started calculating his own speed figures. One day, when he found long-priced standouts in the first and second races, he decided to go to the track and play a Daily Double. It came in for $450.

"I thought, 'This is interesting,'" he said. "'I'm going to bring this money to the track and keep playing until it runs out.'"

It didn't run out for twenty years. In the 1970s a horseplayer with good speed figures could make a living wage at the track. Gambling was a good career for Bob. He was mild-tempered, so he didn't fly into a rage after losing a photo finish, and he wasn't terribly social, so he didn't allow chitchat to distract him from the business of reading the *Racing Form* and studying the tote board.

"In a decent year, I was able to make thirty to sixty thousand," he said. "I've never held a steady job. Back in the nineties, I had a good streak of three or four years without having to do any outside work. But playing the horses is harder work than any work I know. It's a seventy-hour-a-week job."

Bob's winning streak began to peter out when "the information flow hit." In 1992 the *Form* began publishing Beyer speed figures in every horse's past performance line, giving the masses a tool once monopolized by the studious elite. Around the same time, riverboat casinos opened, luring away gamblers who liked to bet on cute names and lucky numbers. That meant less "dumb money" to drive up the odds on the real contenders. In addition, full-card simulcasting was allowing well-capitalized, well-informed gamblers from New York and Las Vegas to bet on Chicago races.

Mass-marketed speed figures "made a lot of terrible players average players," Bob said. "They made winners out of a few players who couldn't possibly have won before. The odds on figure standouts in the seventies and eighties were quite attractive, especially on horses going up in class off a win. Suddenly, you couldn't get overlays on figure horses. You had to find other ways to win—you had to make a betting line or bet Pick Threes."

The competition was "sharks against sharks." Bob's edge began to diminish, and, he said, winning became "more difficult than it's ever been in the history of horse racing. I had OK years in '96 and '98. Since the new millennium, I've been struggling to make money every year."

During all those years at the track, Bob was caring for his ailing father. When his father died in 1999, Bob moved out of their house on the northwest side of Chicago and into a friend's apartment in Barrington, the horsy suburb where Mr. D owned a farm.

(After I'd known Bob for a while, I heard him sing a ditty that went: "I am the Beast of Barrington/ I have a tail I wear/ I keep it tucked inside my pants/ So I don't give folks a scare." I assumed it was about Dick Duchossois, every horseplayer's personal Satan. It was about Bob.)

"My friend's good about the rent," Bob said. "He knows sometimes he has to wait until I make a big score."

But making a big score is impossible without big money, so Bob canceled his health insurance—a big risk for a fifty-six-year-old man—and started driving a cab on weekends to pay his bills and build up a bankroll.

"I'm undercapitalized," he said, finishing his third plate of chicken. "I need to get a stake together. It's not easy. I don't know if I'd recommend playing the horses to someone starting out today."

But it was all he knew how to do.

Bob would be the first to admit that he wasn't the best role model for a career in gambling, but other horseplayers shared Bill's admiration. He sold his speed figures, or traded them for trip notes, to a small circle that included Blond Jimmy and David the Owl, another lifelong gambler struggling to rebound from two straight losing years. David saw Bob as one of horseplaying's thwarted talents, a scholar without a chair, a man who just needed a MacArthur Foundation Genius Grant to show the world how the game should be played.

"If Bob ever gets a bankroll again," David said, "he'll be one of the best players out here."

# 15

# "'Seabiscuit' Jockey Nearly Trampled"

The finish of the first Arlington Million is preserved in bronze behind the grandstand, on the porch overlooking the paddock. It was such a good race they couldn't just take a photo. They had to cast a statue, too. The work, entitled *Against All Odds*, depicts John Henry—the gelding who ran into his second decade to become the wealthiest horse in history—lunging past The Bart, in a by-a-nostril victory that some fans are still disputing twenty-two years later. That finish didn't make the front page of the *Chicago Sun-Times*, though. The finish of the 2003 Arlington Million did. It was the most frightening stretch run of the year, and it happened at the end of the richest, most important race.

The Arlington Million always falls in mid-August, on the hottest Saturday of the summer. It's the track's signature race. Horsy tycoons fly in from all over the world to chase the purse. At my first Million, in 1996, I saw His Royal Highness the Aga Khan in the paddock, alongside Jenny Craig. Neither of their horses won, but in 2001 the German horse Silvano took the Million; the year after, it was Beat Hollow, from Great Britain. This year, I had the hots for Sulamani, a truly cosmopolitan animal. He'd been bred in Ireland but was trained by

Saeed bin Suroor, an ex-cop from the United Arab Emirates, and owned by Sheik Mohammed bin Rashid al Maktoum, Crown Prince of Dubai. The founding sires of the Thoroughbred breed—the Godolphin Barb, the Darley Arabian, and the Byerly Turk—were imported to Britain from the Middle East, so winning big races is a matter of Arab pride. Sulamani had already won the one-and-a-half-mile King George VI and Queen Elizabeth Diamond Stakes at Ascot, Britain's most prestigious race. If he could beat their best, he could beat our best.

A supporting player made the race even more glamorous: Gary Stevens, who'd played jockey George Woolf in the movie *Seabiscuit*, was riding the morning-line favorite, Storming Home.

(I'd seen *Seabiscuit* a few weeks earlier. The race scenes were so exciting that my crossed leg bobbed up and down as though I had money on the horse. It was like being at an IMAX OTB. But there was no mention of gambling. Maybe they thought it would give the sport a bad name or endanger the PG rating. During Seabiscuit's match race with War Admiral, he was portrayed as the crowd's darling. In fact, War Admiral was the chalk that day. It was typical. After the race is over, everyone has the winner.)

My press pass, which had gotten me in free all summer, was no good on Million Day. NBC was coming. Important turf scribes were coming. That meant I had to buy a ticket. I bought four: one for myself, one for my father, one for Soren the musician, and one for his wife, Tam.

The Million Day crowd was not as big a throng as the subway crush at the 2002 Breeders' Cup, but there were 20,000 in the stands, a decent Saturday crowd at Sox Park. One summer, Arlington was so empty it piped crowd noise over its race calls, like a laugh track for an unfunny sitcom. They wouldn't need artificial cheers on Million Day.

In a turf race, the real running doesn't start until the field rounds the second turn. Up to that point, the horses jog in a pack, and the final 440 yards becomes a contest to see who can sprint hardest after running a mile in under a minute forty. That's exactly how the Million unfolded. An 89–1 rabbit, Beauchamp Pilot, went to the lead.

When the field reached the one-mile mark, at the crest of the second turn, all the main characters were at least two lengths behind him. Storming Home, who'd started the race next to last, had snaked his way up to fourth and was wheeling four-wide (four horse-widths from the rail) around the elbow-macaroni bend. Sulamani was also trying to rally, but his jockey had to steer him wide to find a route around the rumps of the masses in front of him. Paolini and Kaieteur were trapped even farther back.

Near the head of the lane, where the dogleg straightened out, an exhausted Beauchamp Pilot surrendered the lead to an onrushing Storming Home. Sulamani gave chase to both down the fairway-green stretch, past the beer tents, past the Diamond Vision screen, past the shrieking grandstand, where fans were leaping up and down, thousands of bobbing shirts in a confetti of colors. When Sulamani zoomed past the sixteenth pole, at freeway speed, he was still a length behind. The finish was only yards away. Sulamani was too much a distance runner to win at a mile and a quarter. I'd been a fool to bet him at 5–2. Meanwhile, Paolini and Kaieteur were steaming into the gap between Storming Home and his wide-running pursuer.

Gary Stevens began to slip down Storming Home's flank just as the horse reached the Arlington Park signboard that filled the final ten yards of the rail. By the time they passed between the glittering photo-finish mirrors and tripped the brilliant camera flash, Stevens was hanging from his mount by a bridle grip. For a moment, he swung there, like a man clinging to the gunwale of an out-of-control cigarette boat. Then his fingers loosened and he was on the ground.

Cue the sound effects: forty-eight hooves trampling the grass behind him. The horses run at forty miles an hour, and they're trained to pound toward the finish, so they can't avoid him, and he can't get out of their way. He's stunned by his fall, and there's nowhere to go. As Storming Home speeds up the track in a panic, Kaieteur stomps on Stevens's shoulder.

It takes a moment for the cheering to stop, and then the half circle of shouts softens to murmurs as we all stare at the white-clothed figure lying very still on Arlington's green lawn. At first, nobody knows who it is. The runaway horse is wearing the yellow saddle towel—number 4. I look in my program and shout to Soren and Tam, "It's Gary Stevens! It's the guy from *Seabiscuit!*"

After the photo is developed, the winning numbers flash on the tote board: 4-1-3-9. Storming Home, Sulamani, Paolini, Kaieteur. Then they begin to blink, and the Inquiry sign lights up.

On the track, the ambulance that trails every race pulls up behind Stevens. He is sitting now, he is conscious, but the paramedics ease him back down, shift him onto a stretcher, and load him into their van, which spins away to a local hospital.

The tape of the final yards is played and replayed on the screen. The horses surge past the finish, recede on the rewind, surge again at "Play." It seems the stewards are trying to determine whether Stevens was aboard Storming Home at the wire. A riderless horse can't win a race. How can the stewards disqualify Storming Home? It wouldn't be fair to Stevens, who's been hurt so badly. Rules are rules, though. After eleven minutes of whispers, rumors, arguments, and puzzled faces in the grandstand—you don't snatch away a $600,000 purse without careful deliberation—John G. Dooley returns to the microphone.

"Ladies and gentlemen, may I have your attention please?" he says solemnly. It sounds not like a question, but a warning of bad news. "After reviewing the stretch run, the stewards have disqualified number 4, Storming Home, and placed him fourth."

The winner is number 1, Sulamani. The booing lasts ten minutes. Storming Home is the 2–1 favorite, with a third of the crowd's money. Gary Stevens is a movie star. And Sulamani is owned and trained by . . . Arabs. Arabs who'd blown up the World Trade Center and were blowing up our soldiers in Iraq. Amid the hooting, the head-on replay shows the real reason for the disqualification: Storming Home had freaked out just before the wire, swerved off course, and crashed into Paolini, who collided with Kaieteur. Sulamani had avoided the entire pileup. Without it, he might have finished fourth. Instead, he is the winner. It was an undeniable foul, but that doesn't stop the bitching. It grows even worse when Saeed bin Suroor appears in the winner's circle to accept the Million trophy on behalf of his desert prince. He is obviously embarrassed to be there, but the decision of the stewards is final.

"This is not the way we wanted to win," the trainer says, his voice nearly swept away by a tornado of whistling and anti-Arab slurs. "But he raced a big race. It was just a little too short for him."

The tote board shuffles the numbers and deals out 1-3-9-4. Tam and I are holding winning tickets on Sulamani. We run inside to cash them before the stewards change their minds again.

U

Gary Stevens spent three days in the hospital with a punctured lung and a broken vertebra. He was visited there by Dick Duchossois and received a phone call from Laura Hillenbrand, author of the book *Seabiscuit.* The accident cost him $55,000—the difference between the jockey's share of first-place and fourth-place money in the Million.

The next day, the *Chicago Sun-Times* ran a front-page photograph of Stevens slipping off Storming Home, under the headline "'Seabiscuit' Jockey Nearly Trampled." Horse racing never makes the front page. It's a niche sport, like bowling or marathon running, but this race had two elements newspapers love: celebrity and "tragedy." Inside, Jim O'Donnell's story quoted an anonymous trainer who offered a theory on why Storming Home had bolted:

> Instant speculation arose that Storming Home might have been spooked by a reflection of the late-afternoon sun as he approached the finish line. But more likely, said one senior turf trainer at Arlington, was the sudden appearance in the horse's vision of ground-level promotional signs on the inside of the turf course at the track, immediately adjacent to the mirror that helps to serve as the faux finish line.
>
> Said the trainer: "A horse can be clipping along in that stretch [at Arlington] and see nothing to his left but rail and

green, rail and green, rail and green. Then suddenly, as he gets two or three strides from the finish, he sees those signs. They can be very scary, especially to a horse who is new to the course.

Gary Stevens never complained about the money he lost as a result of Storming Home's spill.

Creighton complained, though. I saw him the day after the Million in the Rebel Enclave. He was in full rant.

"There's a red line at the finish, and Storming Home was across that line when he ran into those other horses," Creighton shouted.

Everyone was reading their programs, or pretending to. Bob the Brain was standing on a chair to get a closer look at a replay of the first race.

"Bob, you know if you stack two of those on top of the other, you can get a closer look," Scott called.

Creighton turned to me. A writer is a guaranteed audience.

"That horse cost me the Pick Four," he said. This was a bet, covering the winners of races eight, nine, ten, and eleven, that had paid $1,752.80. Creighton showed me a sheet of paper listing eighty-one dollars' worth of combinations he'd played. Storming Home's number was there; Sulamani's was not. It was obvious he'd brought it to the track to bolster his complaint. His grievance was so powerful that he'd suspended his Arlington boycott for a day, just so he could vent it to an audience.

"Let me tell you something about these stewards," he said, pointing a finger at me, as though it were a pin, and I a butterfly. "Here, why don't you sit down?"

I was copying the first-race payoffs off a television monitor, so I stayed on my feet. Creighton steamed forward with his story, his thin voice strained to a rasp by his outrage.

"Last week, I was playing in a handicapping contest in North Aurora. There was a race where the 3 horse ran into the 1 and 2 horses at the start, then he won the race, which messed me up in the contest.

So I called Eddie Arroyo [the head steward at Arlington] and said, 'This is Creighton Schoenfeldt,' 'cause he knows who I am. 'I'm playing in a contest in North Aurora. How come that horse wasn't disqualified?' He said, 'Well, the kids on the 1 and the 2 didn't want to lodge an objection, because it didn't affect the outcome of the race.' Those stewards should be cleaning up behind the horses, not judging races."

"Creighton, I watched that replay four or five times," I said. "Storming Home ran into those horses before the wire."

"Well, that's not what I saw."

"Listen," I said, because I knew Creighton was a member of a small group of contrarians known as the Chicago Republican Party. "Sulamani is the winner of the Arlington Million the way George W. Bush is President of the United States. He didn't finish first, but the judges named him the winner. So if I have to live with George W. Bush as president, you have to live with Sulamani as winner of the Arlington Million."

Creighton laughed and patted me on the shoulder. After that, we never talked about the Arlington Million.

# 16

## The Gold Club

For all his bad intentions, Creighton could not carry a grudge. A week after the Million, he suspended his boycott again, this time to watch a friend's horse make his maiden debut. Mary came along. When Creighton found me in the Rebel Enclave, he insisted I come downstairs to see her. She was in the Gold Club Room, the private lounge of the high rollers.

"Creighton, my Bet of the Day is coming up," I protested.

"Well, we'll go watch him together," he said, jerking his head toward the escalator to urge me along. "Then we'll go see Mary."

My Bet of the Day was Gonna Gidder. He'd shipped in from Churchill Downs, where he'd run a bafflingly slow time in his last race. After keeping pace with the leaders for half a mile, he'd faded to last. The race intrigued me. A horse who fought for the lead and collapsed was better than a horse who raced in the middle of the pack and finished a respectable fourth. At least he was trying to win.

I wanted to know why Gonna Gidder had sucked wind, so I looked up his last outing on racereplays.com, a ten-dollar-a-month Internet video library. Gonna Gidder had been the 10 horse in a ten-horse field, so he'd been led into the gate last of all. Before he could settle into his stall, the starter tripped the doors. Caught unaware, Gonna Gidder's jockey had to rush him to the front of the pack. By the time he hit the stretch, Gonna Gidder was exhausted. This was the best trip note ever: no one at Arlington had seen it, except for geeks with DSL lines. Gonna Gidder was 7–1. He would never have been 7–1 in Louisville.

I was so proud of my research that before Creighton dragged me away, I stood up in the Rebel Enclave and touted the horse to a few of Scott's drowsy followers.

"It's the 5 in this race," I announced. "Everyone bet the 5. He had a bad race at Churchill Downs last time, but this time *he's going to win.*"

Creighton and I sat down in the two-dollar seats. The old woman in the red blazer was harassing deadbeats in another section of the grandstand. Creighton started telling a story about a trainer who'd performed a scandalous gesture in front of the winner's circle camera. Most trainers celebrated victory by waving, flashing the V sign, or blowing a kiss. This miscreant flipped the bird. Outraged, Creighton stepped in to restore decency. Horse racing's wholesome image was at stake.

"I saw it at the OTB and I called the stewards right away," he said. "Yeah. That kind of thing makes racing look bad. A friend of mine in California saw it. He called me and said, 'What kind of racing you got in Chicago, anyway?' The guy got a $2,500 fine."

Only the starter's bell silenced Creighton's all-American spiel. Gonna Gidder took the lead, as I'd expected, but as he passed in front of the grandstand, a fast-closing rival was racing along his flank.

"Aaah!" I moaned. "Dammit. I should *not* have bet on this horse."

Creighton squeezed my forearm.

"Relax, guy," he said. "You got it."

And I did. Gonna Gidder hung on, covering my subscription to racereplays.com.

After I cashed, Creighton took me inside the Gold Club Room. The entrance was marked with a brass plaque beside heavy swinging doors.

Nobody challenged Creighton, even though he was a Silver Club member who'd fallen $4,000 short of this company. In years past, he'd qualified, so perhaps they recognized him. We walked by a room with a round conference table, where a man in a safari vest was chatting with two confidants.

"That's Paul Volkman," Creighton whispered, as reverently as if he were identifying a saint on a stained-glass window. "He really fires. He'll bet two or three million dollars a meet."

The Gold Cup Room was scarcely more luxurious than the rest of the track—there were bowls of pretzels and peanuts in the carrels, and the mutuel clerks stood behind lecterns, like maitre d's, but most of the gamblers wore the same Dockers, the same sport shirts I saw in the long betting lines on the first floor. Luxury was not the point of the Gold Club Room. It was about fraternity. Here, the true gamblers were insulated from the nickel-and-dime masses. They got to partake in that great Chicago tradition: clout. Clout meant not having to follow the same rules as everyone else. Clout meant never having to stand in line. In politics, clout meant going straight from law school to the state senate, because your dad was a ward boss. In the Gold Club Room, clout meant a clerk would deliver a Bet Mate to your carrel.

Mary was sitting alone in a carrel facing a wall of monitors that looked like a television director's control room. As always, she stood up to hug me. We'd been good friends ever since I'd written an article about her Kentucky Derby chart for a local newspaper.

"Put 'er there," Mary said, patting my back.

Mary's devotionals were spread across the tabletop. While Creighton had been outdoors, Mary had been imploring God to convert the Muslims to Christianity.

"Their religion teaches them to kill us," she said, with a puzzled, sorrowful look. "I pray every day that God will reach into their hearts and convert them."

Creighton, as far as I knew, had not been to Mass that morning. He was mainly interested in impressing on me that he belonged in the Gold Club Room.

"I know you're new to this game," he said, leaning his elbow against the wall of the carrel. "Just wait'll the day you bet $5,000 on a horse. Then you'll know you've arrived."

"When did you do *that*?" I asked. I knew Creighton threw a lot of money around, but not that much.

"It was at Sportsman's Park," he said. "Pat Day was riding the horse. I went and cashed in a CD."

"Did you win?"

"Ah, no," he said. "The horse pulled up on the first turn."

For weeks, I bugged track management to let me hang out in the Gold Club Room. They refused. Big players are a wary, secretive lot. They might have stopped gambling at the sight of my pencil, and that would have imperiled the entire Illinois Thoroughbred industry. Thwarted at the threshold, I started bugging Arlington's public relations director for the name of a Gold Club member. Finally, he gave me the cell phone number of Mike Melcher, the same Mike Melcher who'd told Omar to buy Northern Catch. When I called, Mike was sitting in his private box, which overlooked the finish line.

"Why don't you meet me after the races at Jimmy D's?" he suggested. "I'm easy to spot. I got gray hair and I weigh about 300 pounds."

Jimmy D's, just across the railroad tracks from Arlington, shares a two-story brick building with a barbershop and a few apartments. It's dark, like a neighborhood tavern, and its rectangular bar is usually ringed with gamblers, trainers, jockeys, owners, and other tight-mouthed horsy types who like to keep their words among themselves. The Mexican grooms don't come into Jimmy D's. They can't afford draft beer. They buy a case at the liquor store and drink in their barracks behind the stables.

Mike banged through the screen door, stepping from the bright summer evening into the saloon dusk from behind a beer belly that could have cushioned a headlong run into a brick wall. His entourage trailed behind—Omar was with him, and so was a lady racing writer from England. He stopped at the bar for a Miller, then headed toward my table in the back room. Balancing his bulk on a chair, he gulped his beer and explained that he'd stayed late at the track to pick up films of that week's races. He analyzed them for the *Sheets*. A service founded by Len Ragozin, an ex-Communist and professional gambler from New York City, the *Sheets* attempted to improve on speed figures by taking into account wind resistance, the weight a horse carried, and the ground it lost on the turns. It was, supposedly, one step closer to a unified field theory of handicapping, which would express every aspect of a horse's race in a single number. In the *Sheets*, a horse's record consists only of his figures, graphed in a ladder so handicappers can detect patterns of improvement or decline. Ragozin pioneered the concept of the bounce, which says that the stress of a harder-than-normal race will cause a horse to run poorly the next time out.

The *Sheets* was Mike's Something on the Side. He charted every horse's trip, collected wind readings from O'Hare Airport, and reported his findings to New York. When the *Sheets* came back, in a thick packet with a page for every horse, he made sure they were in the program booths and the liquor store across the street. The *Sheets* cost thirty dollars a day, six times as much as the *Form*, so he only had fifteen customers—but they bet with the strength of fifteen hundred.

Mike himself had bet $1,000 that afternoon, but "I only won a few hundred," he said, in a rough, wheezy voice. "It was aggravating. I lost a Pick Three. I bet the favorite in the sixth race, I used four horses in the middle part, and I singled a horse in the last race. Then Mike Dini's horse jumped up at the wire, got me out of $3,000."

It's been said that *Sheets* players are so devoted to their numbers that they'll hold up a slip of paper and declare, "This is a horse." Mike didn't do that, but he did have the serious gambler's disdain for real live animals.

"I hate horses," he said. "I don't like 'em. When I gotta get up in the morning to watch one of these horses, I hate it. I never even look at 'em before I bet. I remember one time I decided I was gonna be a wiseguy and look at 'em. I remember one trainer, Buddy Delp, he dumped a bucket of water over a horse, so it looked all sweaty. I didn't bet it, and it won. That's the last time I looked at a horse."

And of course, like any real horseplayer, he hated racetracks, too. Because he did business with Arlington, he still put his money through the tote—there was a Bet Mate in his box—but most of the serious players he knew used phone services, and he didn't blame them.

"Everybody in the world uses 'em," he shouted. "I'm a fool. I bet through the windows. Guys in New York, they wouldn't bet that way if you put a gun to their head. The tracks have gotten rid of all the big bettors. Everybody's gone. Nobody wants to go here. I was at Churchill, some guy sees me with tickets, he just laughed at me. There's only one guy left here that bets big money. In a place like this, why wouldn't you have phone accounts?"

Mike excused himself to drink with his cronies, but not before promising me a free set of *Sheets* for that Saturday's races. We met the next day at one of the program booths, where he slipped the package off a bottom shelf. They reminded me of All-Ways, Creighton's computer program: reducing a horse's record to a string of numbers seemed too simple. Whatever insights the *Sheets* have to offer, they were too fine for my eye. I lost money that day.

# 17

# The Twenty-Five-Dollar Horse

I always knew I'd found a good bet when I felt the Tingle. It was a lighter-than-air sensation that originated near the bottom of my stomach and spread northward through my chest. The Tingle had to be heeded. It was more accurate than any computer analysis. I only felt it once or twice a month, but when I did, I was like the old man who doesn't need a weatherman to tell him the rain is coming because he feels it by the ache in his knees.

It was a Tuesday night when the Tingle visited me. I was alone in the apartment, handicapping in my office, with the door shut to keep the dog out. The third race was a $25,000 maiden claimer for two-year-olds at six furlongs. I loved maiden claiming races. Since the day I'd stepped out the doors and started sitting alone in the grandstand, I'd been keeping a record of my wagers, broken down by type of bet, class, distance, and surface. Maiden claimers were the most lucrative category, by far. For every two dollars I bet on them, I won $6.54.

Like the minor leagues in baseball, the maiden claiming division consisted of numerous levels: $10,000, $12,500, $15,000, $20,000, and $25,000. A washout in one might become a star in another, like a backup third baseman for the Tigers who gets demoted to the Mud Hens and tears up the International League. The bust-down from a maiden special weight race to a maiden claiming race was called "the biggest drop in racing," but the divisions between maiden claimers were significant, too. I once saw a horse who'd been hopelessly out-distanced in a $20,000 race drop down to $10,000—and win at 59–1.

The magic of class drops was well established, so why were maiden claimers so lucrative? Because most bettors simply could not believe that a horse who'd been beaten fifteen lengths in a $20,000 race was better than a horse who'd lost by a neck for $10,000. It happened over and over and over again: maidens who had made small careers out of almost winning would go off as favorites, because the bettors figured they were "due." They'd be pipped at the post as usual. My favorite sucker horse was Three Punch Louie. A son of Preakness winner Louis Quatorze, he had inherited his sire's pearl-gray coat but none of his stamina. Three Punch Louie caused a run at the betting windows when he made his public debut in a maiden special weight race at Hawthorne in April. Bursting from the gate at even money, he raced to a three-length lead, then began gasping for air as three pursuers thundered past in the stretch. Three Punch Louie had a breathing problem. But in his next race, he was the chalk. Once again, he sucked wind. This happened seven times in a row. Eventually, his trainer put him into claiming races, but he still couldn't hold a lead. The public never lost faith in Three Punch Louie. He was the favorite in every race he ran. After eight months, he finally rewarded his investors by winning a $10,000 maiden claiming race at Hawthorne—and paying something like $3.20.

I started puzzling out the third race by paging through my hand-written records and calculating the average split times of maiden win-ners in the last two weeks: twenty-two and three-fifths seconds to the quarter mile and forty-six and one-fifth seconds to the half mile. (I'd learned this trick from Dick Mitchell's *Commonsense Handicapping*.) Then I wrote down every horse's splits from his last race, looking for someone who could match those times. Only one horse came close: number 8, Beamer'n Glick. He'd run his first quarter mile in twenty-two and three-fifths seconds, hadn't been able to keep up that pace, and finished ninth. Beamer'n Glick had chased an extremely fast pace:

twenty-one and four-fifths seconds, which was so taxing that the horse who'd set it, Ilya Balos, had faded to eleventh, while the horses running twelfth, eighth, and ninth finished 1-2-3. Furthermore, Beamer'n Glick had broken from the one post, which meant he'd been running on the rail, which was the slowest part of the track. And all this had happened in a maiden special weight race. I looked up Beamer'n Glick's morning-line odds on the Arlington Web site: 8–1. The Tingle fizzed through my chest. My pencil whipped a circle around Beamer'n Glick's number—an *O* that felt like Zorro's *Z*—and wrote "PRIME BET ON 8" at the bottom of the page. It wouldn't be a twenty-dollar prime bet, either. Wednesday was the first day of a new week, and, since I'd been winning, I'd decided to step up my maximum bet up to fifty dollars. I was still a nit compared to Scott, who never bet less than $200 a race, but someday soon, I'd match him.

Kate didn't get home from work until after I'd gone to bed, so I showed her the *Form* the next morning. She wasn't interested in horse racing, but she tolerated my project, and that was all the enthusiasm I needed. I had to tell someone about Beamer'n Glick.

"This is it," I told her, catching her in the hallway as she walked past my office. I'd risen early to do more handicapping. I flipped open the *Form* to the third race and jabbed at the number 8. "This is the bet of the day!"

"I hope he wins," she said, smiling sweetly. And she meant it, not because of the money—Kate knew I'd never win enough to buy a car or blow enough to miss the rent—but because I moped like a frustrated artist when I was losing at the track. After Great Eight broke his leg, I'd asked her, in a voice plaintive with doubt, "Do you think I'm a good handicapper?"

"You're just getting bad breaks," she said, and I loved her for having that faith in me.

Now that I was winning, I was less moody, more relaxed. One Saturday I even stayed home from the track so we could see a play together. The card was lousy that day, anyway.

When I walked through the clubhouse gate the next day, I was determined to lay it all on the line for Beamer'n Glick. ("Had a feeling of destiny," I later wrote in my notebook.) I had made up my mind, and nothing would dissuade me except low odds—3–1 or under. I fidgeted through the first two races, psyching myself up to bet fifty dollars. "Don't wimp out," I whispered to myself. Then, through gritted teeth, I quoted Lady Macbeth: "Screw your courage to the sticking place."

When the opening odds were posted for the third race, Beamer'n Glick was 18–1. Common Ground, who had recently finished second in another $25,000 race, was the favorite at a foolishly low 3–2. For twenty minutes, I sat very still in my chair, watching my horse's odds tick downward, feeling numb as I tried to stifle my nervousness. At five minutes to post time, the PA system always played a sample from Moby's dreamy song "Porcelain." That was my cue. Beamer'n Glick was 11–1. I got up to bet. At the machine, I had a moment of doubt as I recalled Dick Mitchell's dictum that "we must be apprehensive about maidens that aren't bet down from their morning-line odds." Silently, I told Mitchell, and every other handicapping author, to stuff it. Don't believe anything you read in horse racing books, including this one. Go out and learn for yourself. I punched in twenty-five dollars to win and twenty-five dollars to place on 8. (This was wimping out. I should have bet it all to win. At a lower price, say 5–1, I would have. But I couldn't bear the prospect of losing by a neck and leaving the track empty-handed.)

I slipped the ticket into my wallet, as though it were already money.

My arms were buzzing now. On my way across the grandstand, I ran into Mike Melcher.

"I just made a big bet and I need to calm down," I told him. "Did you see that Omar claimed Go Go Hasty?"

"Omar claimed that horse?" Mike asked, rolling his eyes.

After this, I really don't remember anything until the stretch run. It was difficult to watch the race. On the backstretch, Beamer'n Glick was running in the "garden spot"—just off the leader's shoulder, on the outside part of the track. I tried not to get my hopes up, but as the horses wheeled out of the turn, Beamer'n Glick took the lead, and I was lifted from my seat. Stone Rain was chasing him a length behind, and by the top of the top of the stretch they were racing stride for stride, with Beamer'n Glick on the inside and Stone Rain on the outside. Both animals strained forward, trying to run out of their hides, in a dirt-spraying duel, ten yards clear of the pack. All around me, women were screeching. I stood in lip-biting suspense. Stone Rain, running his guts out, took a neck's lead. "Thank God I bet to place," I thought. But Beamer'n Glick would not give up. Bearing down, he cut into Stone Rain's advantage, an inch every stride. I had a bad angle on the wire, but even from behind, I could see him pulling away. At first, his nose plunged ahead only when he dipped his head forward. But by the wire, he was half a length free. "Beamer'n Glick REFUSED to lose!" John G. Dooley shouted, as my prime bet passed between the pillars into the country of victory.

Those are the moments that sports fans live and suffer and spend for, when the feeling of triumph is transferred from the playing field to the stands. Beamer'n Glick's victory was my Miracle on Ice, my Immaculate Reception. I raised my arms to signal a touchdown and screeched "Yeahhhh." In the section next to me, I saw another man whooping and dancing.

"I bet fifty bucks on that horse!" I shouted to my new brother.

"So did I," he said.

We ran toward each and high-fived, then I called Kate on my cell phone.

"Today, I am the King," I told her. "Maybe I should quit now."

Beamer'n Glick paid $25.80 to win and $11.40 to place, so my ticket was worth $465. If I'd just bet to win, I would have made . . . well, let's not think about that. Playing the horses wasn't about the money, at least not for me. It was an intellectual game, like chess. It was about being smarter than the rest of the world, and when your best bet is everyone else's 11–1 shot, you are smarter (at least you're smarter than anyone who spends his afternoons at the track). One of my racetrack friends once told me, "You're more interested in being right than making money," but in that race, at least, I'd done both. After I cashed my ticket, I presented myself in the Rebel Enclave.

"I feel like I became a real horseplayer today," I told Scott.

U

Beamer'n Glick was my handicapping masterpiece. That Sunday, I had another big win, betting sixty dollars on a horse I'd picked using Scott's speed figures, but Premium Saltine was a 2–1 chalk. When the meet ended in late September, I totaled up all my bets since I'd become a loner. Over those seven weeks, I'd won $150.

"Twenty-one forty a week!" I thought. I had spent four hours a day gambling, two hours commuting, an hour keeping records, and three hours handicapping. I had ignored my girlfriend, blown off my fantasy football Sundays at my local tavern, never gone to the movies, never read a book that wasn't about horses, and refused to visit my parents on Labor Day, because it was a big racing day. All for $21.40 a week. That's even less than I'm getting paid to write this book.

From an investment point of view, I hadn't done that badly. I'd wagered $2,000 and collected $2,150, for a 7 percent profit. In that same period, the Dow Jones industrial average went up 4.2 percent, so I'd outperformed several Wall Street fund managers. But to make a middle-class income with that edge—say, fifty grand—I would have had to bet $700,000 a year. Hitting the windows twice a day, which was as often as I could hope to find a good bet, I would have had to lay out $1,700 a race, which is so far above my freak-out level that my tongue feels like cork just thinking about it. Betting that much would knock down the odds, so my 7 percent advantage might become a 6 percent advantage or a 5 percent advantage. There's no health plan for horseplayers; there's no pension. And, of course, when I figured my profit, I didn't include the money I'd spent on *Racing Forms*, the *M. Scott McMannis Speed and Trip Service*, racereplays.com, my handicapping books, and gas to the track. Factor all that in, and it probably cost me money to win.

You can make a life at the track, but you can't make a living.

# 18

# True Adventures in Gambling

When Hawthorne reopened in the fall, all the hustlers were gone: the blind man wasn't begging at the foot of the ramp, Eli was cadging dollars downtown, and Glenn had disappeared, barred for stooping.

Scott McMannis had his own handicapping center again, and one of the first things he did was ban Warren. Scott had continued their feud by taping a cartoon from the *Horseplayer* on the wall. It showed a sloppily dressed gambler standing at a window marked "Dumb Bets You Shouldn't Make." Scott wrote in "Warren's Window" and captioned the drawing: "Warren says, 'Ah, go ahead . . . It's only $12 in fun bets.'"

Scott also refused to renew Warren's subscription to the *Speed and Trip Service*. It wasn't the first time he'd cut someone off. He believed it was unethical to enable a lousy gambler.

"I told him, 'You don't know how to use it, you bet too much, you sit here and blame the service and everyone else when you lose,'" Scott told me during his first week back in his duchy. To tell the story, he got up out of his desk chair, ambled over to where I'd spread out my papers, sat down across from me, and leaned across the table. "I said, 'I'm not going to let you buy it again unless you sign up for the classes.'"

Then Scott put on a crabby voice, trying to imitate Warren: "'Why do I have to go to these classes? Why can't a guy make a bet around here without everybody picking on him?' I said, 'Fine, you don't want to go to the classes, I won't sign you up.'"

Scott shook his head.

"He won't do the work," he said. "He's like students I used to have who wanted me to lift off the top of their heads and pour the knowledge in."

Warren took his banishment cheerfully, spending his afternoons in a little dining nook behind the banquet room. It had been set aside for some of the track's heaviest gamblers, but they didn't mind Warren hanging around, and they didn't mind him betting on every race, since most of them were doing it, too.

Scott punished students who refused to do their homework, but he rewarded apple polishers. The day before the meet began, this item appeared in Jim O'Donnell's column: "Rob Fasiang has been hired as the video librarian at the Hawthorne Handicapping and Business Center."

It was Rob's dream job. Hawthorne had just installed a DVD system, so all he had to do was load a blank disk into the player before every race, press "record" to capture the replay, then file it on a bookshelf. Anyone could ask to see a replay, but Rob only had two regular customers: Liz Morris, a twenty-four-year-old apprentice jockey from Texas, and Blond Jimmy, who sat in front of the monitors, taking notes in his private code.

Rob was getting paid to go to the track, and he had plenty of free time for gambling. He used it. Over the summer, Rob spent two days at Arlington. It was too far to drive from Indiana, so one weekend, when Kate was out of town, he crashed on my couch. The rest of the time, he played Arlington on youbet.com, drove to the OTB in Merrillville, Indiana, or just blew off horse racing and sat on his couch watching *Seinfeld* reruns. By September he'd pissed away the two grand he'd won that spring, and he was in danger of going bankrupt—or getting a full-time job. So, when the Hawthorne meet started, Rob did what any real gambler would have: he pushed all his chips to the middle of the table.

With the year dwindling, a deadline coming, and all the colorful folks purged from the grandstand, I was spending most of my time in the clubhouse, writing in a study carrel. It was almost as cloistered as the Harlan Hatcher Library back at the University of Michigan, but here I could take a break every thirty minutes to bet on a horse race. When I wanted even more solitude, I worked at a table on the west end of the warehouselike second floor, in an alcove with a view of the After the Races tavern, just across Laramie Avenue. Nobody sat there except a few phone betting gamblers, who always used their cells at a whisper. Lucky, who liked the company of big shooters, fetched them coffee and soup. He was always looking for a hustle.

Scott noticed my aloofness. One weekday afternoon, I heard my name over the public address system, followed by the command "Please report to the Handicapping Center." When I made it upstairs, just before the eighth race, the room was almost empty. Scott was in his teacher's chair, while Rob was sitting in the back of the room by his A/V system. The Professor missed his loyal band.

"You can always write in here," he offered, when I explained where I'd been.

"I can't concentrate in here," I said. "You guys are always telling dirty jokes."

Rob had stepped out of the room, leaving us alone. A minute later, he returned with $400 worth of tickets. "I got $100 to win and place on the 8, and I got him in a bunch of exactas and trifectas," he explained, shuffling through his stack as matter-of-factly as a secretary of state clerk searching a sheaf of parking violations.

I was in awe. The man was a blown head gasket from bankruptcy, and he was betting a month's rent on a horse race. Damn, I was a pussy. After Arlington, I still had $600 left in my bankroll, but I hadn't brought it to Hawthorne. I'd cashed it in and put it in the bank. It seemed foolish to bet a lot of money in the first week of a meet, so I started the fall the same way I'd started the spring: with fifty dollars in pocket money. I understood, though, how Rob could plunge so boldly. Once I'd been so broke I knew the location of an ATM that dispensed five-dollar bills. But that didn't stop me from betting fifty to win whenever I got a check. Money didn't mean much then, because as soon as I got any, I had to give it to some bill collector. It wasn't much of an incentive to thrift.

For Rob, it was death or glory. And when his 8 horse led a parade of numbers that matched every one of his exactas and trifectas, he spun in a tight half circle, pumping his fist, hissing "Yesss." He'd won nearly $2,800. He was going to eat. He wasn't going to have to drive a delivery van or guard a factory, at least not this fall.

A week later, he scored again. I'd left the track early that afternoon, because I had to buy a book. As I was walking into a Borders bookstore, my cell phone rang. It was Rob, and he was over the moon.

"You left before the best race of the day," he shouted. "I won two grand on the ninth!"

At the track now, he would stand in a pose resembling the marines whose discipline he so admired: hands clasped behind his back, feet apart, chest out, shaven head cocked back. He was betting with a jarhead's discipline, too. Some days, he couldn't get the odds he wanted, so he passed every race.

"I don't need to bet just for fun," he said. "I don't need to smoke the crack. There's only a few good races a week, and the thing to do is wait until they come around, then hammer them." (Hammer is to place a big bet.)

The Stat Man was cashing in, too. Behind his unfolded laptop, his Peanuts'-kid-grown-up face grinned more broadly than usual.

"I . . . have . . . been . . . on . . . fire," he said, with huge satisfaction. "A week ago, I had $400 on my voucher, and now it's up to almost $2,000."

Rob and Steve both knew how to squeeze the cash out of Scott's speed figures. It was the right system for men with mathematical minds. In an October newsletter, Scott included this note:

"HAWTHORNE IS BETTER FOR BETTORS: Don't just take my word for it. The two subscribers I am in contact with most often are Steve Miller and Rob Fasiang. Both are off to great starts at this meet. I always preach that Arlington is prettier but Hawthorne is better for the bettor."

The three of them had started the meet with a 50–1 winner on opening day. Scott picked it based on the stats in his *Trainer Patterns* book. It was a first-time starter, and its trainer was 1-for-2 with unraced animals, so they all bet it to win and place. When the horse took the lead down the stretch, Scott actually got excited, stirring for once from his St. Bernard dignity to flick on his microphone and shout, "Heeeee's gonnnna win!" Hey, it paid over $100. Even Joe Friday would have danced a jig for that kind of money.

There was a reason the early fall was like a tilted roulette wheel for guys in the know. Hawthorne ran fuller fields than Arlington ("We card races for horses that are here, not horses we want to come here," was their response to Arlington's sniffy "It's a cheaper brand of racing"). Inevitably, this meant bigger payoffs on the winners, because you could put a Belgian draft horse in the starting gate, and the lottery dreamers would bet their two dollars on it. Even I'd been winning: by late October, the portrait of General Grant I had stashed in my pocket had multiplied ninefold.

U

The Breeders' Cup fell on October 25, a month into the Hawthorne meet. In 2002, the Cup had been run at Arlington Park, where I'd watched the races from temporary bleachers at the head of the homestretch. That Breeders' Cup was Mr. D's reward for reopening his track, but Arlington was too small for the honor. Forty-five thousand was a playoff-sized crowd at Sox Park. At Arlington, it became a humanitarian crisis. Overcrowded buses ferried gamblers from parking lots miles away. The horseplayers were grumpy before they even started betting.

When they did, they were grumpier still: the windows were in tents, staffed by day-labor clerks. The queues were thirty deep, so the line for the second race started as soon as the first was official. Those of us in the cheap seats—they cost forty-five dollars—were barred from the grandstand, and it was too cold outside to enjoy a beer. I sat at the top of the stretch, which gave me a good view of only one of the day's big events: Landseer breaking his leg in the Mile. On the buses out, the New Yorkers swore never to return. They'd been spoiled by Belmont, which was as spacious as Grand Central Station.

But that Breeders' Cup won't be remembered for transforming Arlington into a refugee camp. It will be remembered for a scandal that didn't even happen at the track: the Pick Six Fix, the hinkiest wager in the history of horse racing. A pair of ex-fraternity brothers from Drexel University was responsible for the caper. Christopher Harn was a computer programmer for Autotote, which processes telephone wagers on the East Coast. The bright young spark figured out how to create a phony winning ticket after the races were over, and he enlisted his stoner buddy Derrick Davis as a mule. On the morning of the Cup, Davis placed a Pick Six bet through a phone account he'd opened earlier that week. The bets weren't reported to Arlington until after the fourth leg of the Pick Six, and then only the live tickets were sent through, so the track wouldn't be swamped with millions of losing wagers. Harn tapped into the system and altered Davis's electronic ticket so that his friend had the winner in the first four races and every horse in the last two. Davis couldn't lose. They'd already gotten away with this once, during a practice scam at Aqueduct. They would have gotten away with it again, had it not been for Volponi. Only the lucky and the mad had expected Volponi to win the Breeders' Cup Classic, the final race of the Pick Six. He was 43–1, and when he beat the favorite by six and a half lengths, he ruined every Pick Six ticket but one. Harn knew they were screwed even before the $3.1 million payoff hit the tote board. The FBI looked into the winning bet and thought it was suspicious that Davis had picked four straight winners, but then started hedging his bets. Within a week, Davis and Harn were in handcuffs.

I thought the scandal was great for horse racing. It put the sport on the front page of the *New York Times*, scored a feature in *Vanity Fair* magazine, and reinforced its image as a raffish sport out of *Guys and Dolls* or *The Killers*. The Breeders' Cup got the willies, though. It worried about alienating bettors—which is nonsense, because most bettors are hooked like marlin on thirty-pound test. Figuring it couldn't restore faith in the Pick Six after only one year, the Breeders' Cup appealed to a more basic impulse: greed. It guaranteed the Pick Six would pay at least $2 million. That worked on me. I wanted $2 million. It would be a nice surprise for Kate. We still hadn't furnished our apartment, and I wanted to replace the living room futon with a couch.

A month earlier, I had sold my old condominium for $36,000 profit. Now, that money was just wasting away in my bank account.

I had never played the Pick Six, but I knew you had to spend a lot of money to cover all the likely winners of six straight races. The bet was madly popular in New York, Miami, and Los Angeles, where the "carryovers"—the money that accrued when no one hit the Pick Six for several days—sometimes mounted to $5 million. In Chicago the carryover might reach $20,000 for an entire meet. Nobody played the Pick Six, so nobody played the Pick Six—it wasn't worth buying a big ticket to capture a pot so paltry. There was a mystique to the bet, though. It was the biggest prize in horseplaying—in 1999 a ticket at Gulfstream Park paid $3.5 million—and I had been captivated by Steven Crist's tales of his years as "King of the Pick Six," a title he earned by winning $162,000 one afternoon at Belmont Park. Crist devised a strategy that involved separating his contenders into "main horses" and "backup horses." He then plotted a complicated series of wagers, putting all his main horses on one ticket, then buying tickets on which he substituted his backup horses in the most difficult-to-handicap races. It allowed him to be wrong a few times a day, and it was cheaper than putting every contender on a single ticket, since the price of a Pick Six ticket increases exponentially as you add horses. Using two horses in every race costs $128. Using four costs $8,192. Because of the expense, Crist formed a syndicate, pooling his money with fellow gamblers. In his biography, *Betting on Myself,* he compared his system to "an old-style Chinese restaurant menu": "we were allowed either six selections from Column A or five from Column A and one from Column B."

There was only way to play the Pick Six: you had to go all in, using every horse you could afford. A two-dollar ticket, with a single horse in each race, was a minnow in the mutuel pool, destined to be swallowed by whales like Crist and his pals, who bet $2,000 a day. On the morning of the Breeders' Cup, I sat down with a *Racing Form,* a copy of Crist's book, a calculator, and a sheet of scratch paper. My Pick Six bet came to $1,780. (It didn't cost me quite that much, because I sold my father a ten-dollar share.) I figured I could afford it. The year was almost over, and I still dreamed of cashing a bet that would make me the peer of my gambling idols: Andrew Beyer, Steven Crist, Scott McMannis, Walter Matthau, and Pittsburgh Phil. What's the purpose of money, if not to enjoy life? And what's the purpose of life, if not to leave a story worth singing about?

The first leg of the Pick Six was the Mile. It was a turf race, and I loved Six Perfections. She was a filly competing against colts, but she'd been running in France, where she'd beaten Domedriver, who'd won the Mile at Arlington the year before. I bought a five-dollar win ticket on Six Perfections—so I'd have a consolation prize if the rest of my Pick Six tanked—and sat down under a television in the grandstand. Watching fourteen Thoroughbreds galloping across a nineteen-inch screen suspended at the height of a basketball hoop is like staring at a race through the wide end of a pair of binoculars; I didn't spot my black filly until she slipped out of the cluster of stallions in the final fifty yards.

"That was my top horse in the Pick Six!" I shouted to a pair of frat boys in front of me. I'd played her on every ticket. I was alive. Alive! I fanned the air with my jittering hands, then sat back in my chair and fidgeted through the twenty-five minutes separating me from the Sprint, a six-furlong race. I'd used three horses: Shake You Down, Aldebaran, and Valid Video. After half a mile, Shake You Down was second and chasing Cajun Beat. The timer froze at forty-three and one-fifth seconds, the fastest fraction I'd ever seen. Santa Anita is renowned for its drag strip racing surface—the difference between the soft eastern surfaces and the hard Southern California dirt is like the difference between cinders and asphalt—but there was no way Cajun Beat could run that hard for another 440 yards. Every day, 22–1 long shots sprinted to the lead, got their moment on television, and faded as the favorites ran past. But Cajun Beat kept it up. The cheap son-of-a-race-mare dragged his forty-three seconds of fame into a minute seven—and knocked me out of the Pick Six.

The moment the race was official, I pitched my tickets into a garbage can. It's bad luck to carry losing tickets, and it's really bad luck to carry $1,800 worth of losing tickets. I stalked off to the vending machine to console myself with a bag of animal crackers. On the way there, I realized I'd just been the kind of chump who keeps stoopers in beer, weed, and two-dollar show tickets. There was always a consolation payoff to bettors who picked five out of six races—and I only had one loser on my tickets! I sprinted back to the garbage can, hoping I wouldn't see a guy in filthy sneakers and a Sportsman's Park T-shirt rooting through it. The tickets were still there, nesting in a cardboard french fry tray. I tucked them into my jacket. A few minutes later, Islington, my number-one horse in the Filly and Mare turf, emerged from the herd to prevail by a neck. Three to go.

Had Minister Eric or Chapel Royal won the Juvenile, the race for hot two-year-old comers, they just would have set me up for a bigger heartbreak down the line. If you're gonna get dumped, get dumped after the third date, not during the rehearsal dinner. Action This Day busted me out of the consolation round by taking the Juvenile. At 26–1, he busted a lot of guys out. It was a day for long shots, evidently. That night, the Florida Marlins beat the New York Yankees to win the World Series.

The Pick Six paid $2,687,611.60. It all went to a jeweler from Rapid City, South Dakota, who'd bought his ticket in a local tavern. He spent eight dollars. Syndicates in New York and Las Vegas had pooled their money to crush the Pick Six with $5,000 and $10,000 bets, but a minnow from the Black Hills ate them all. The man planned to use the money to visit a racetrack.

"I've never actually been to a race live," he told the press. "I'd love to, but I'm stuck here. One of my dreams has always been to go to the Saratoga meet, so hopefully, now I'll be able to do that."

Good for him, I thought, but why couldn't I have thought, "Good for me"? That Pick Six would have paid a lot more than $21.40 for every week I'd spent in the bowels of a grandstand, soaking up enough cigarette smoke to put me in the lung cancer ward next to Marlboro addicts and mutuel clerks, suffering an upset stomach over dollar hot dogs and $100 bets. It even would have paid for all those nights handicapping, when I could have been playing bon vivant at a French-Vietnamese restaurant. I could have dedicated my victory to my mother, my late grandmother, and everyone else who thought I was wasting my life at the track. But my $1,800 had bought me three winners. You don't even get a consolation prize for that.

I didn't let the Pick Six get me down. For two months, I'd been winning consistently. It was time for me to step out as a gambler.

"I think you're three times better than you were this spring," Rob told me, after watching me bet on Pennington Gap, an all-out sprinter who held on by a diminishing inch to win at 5–1.

So why was I feeding chump change into the mutuel machines? Shouldn't a man with my talent for predicting equine behavior be betting at least $100 a race? He should. The Monday after my Breeders' Cup hosing, I returned to the bank and culled another three large from my real estate jackpot.

That Friday was Halloween. Even more frightening, it was the day my boss had summoned me to the office for a sit-down. The meeting was scheduled for three o'clock, which was also post time for the fifth at Hawthorne, a race that featured a full-nelson lock named Prairie

King. I'm not the type of guy who lets his work interfere with his gambling. People like that are workaholics, and they need twelve-step. I called Rob and asked him to run my bets that day.

"Gimme $100 to win on Dixie Whistler at 2–1 or more, and $100 to win on Ovo at 9–5 or more," I said. "I'll take care of Prairie King myself."

I took the El downtown early, so I could camp out in an OTB to play the first half of the card and sweat out my performance-review anxiety. With ten minutes to go 'til the fifth, Prairie King was 3–5. I gave up on him and hustled up State Street for my head-chomping. The meeting didn't go as badly as I'd feared. My boss didn't order me to stay away from the track. After we were done, I called Rob from the hallway outside the boss's office.

"I made the bet on Dixie Whistler," he said. "She finished second."

Damn.

"Did Prairie King win?"

"Yeah, he won."

Ordinarily, this wouldn't have been dismaying news, but Prairie King had come in at 2–1. While I'd been squirming on the carpet, the horseplayers at Hawthorne had been forsaking Prairie King's overloaded bandwagon to hitch rides in carts drawn by nags . . . and I hadn't been on the scene to scoop up their misguided dollars.

On my way home that night, a Halloween celebrant—OK, a preteen gangsta wannabe—hit me in the neck with a raw egg. All the demons had risen up against me. I'd blown $100 on the Halloween card. Had I been at the track to bet on Prairie King, I would have won $120 for the day. My head was so heavy with self-pity, aggravation, and woe that I lost $400 at the track the next day.

U

The best personal finance tip I ever received didn't come from a horseplayer. (Duh.) It came from my old friend Jim. We were standing in front of an ATM in the middle of a weekend bender involving beer, hotels, ice hockey, and free jazz. As I was debating how much to take out, he told me, "Whatever you get, you'll spend."

The same was true at the track. Now that I had a fresh three grand, I threw it around like a cokehead with a Christmas bonus. That Saturday, I bet $100 on Red River Aggie. Not only did I lose the money, I lost the esteem of Rob, whom I swayed to sacrifice the same amount through my four-star review of the filly's record. He glared at me for days afterward. Later in the afternoon, I attempted to recoup with a $200 show bet on a horse whose name is a middle-aged trauma I've suppressed to spare my psyche. I'm proud to say I didn't cry out when the horse developed rubber legs and vanished into the herd, but I immediately dropped the ticket on the floor, so not even I would ever know how much I'd lost.

Rob and Steve were burning up their bankrolls, too. Like the Internet bubble, the Hawthorne bubble had to burst as well, and when it did, it soaked its investors. In early November, when the cold began to petrify the ground, the best horses were vanned south to Turfway Park in Kentucky and the Fair Grounds in New Orleans. Left to run through the autumn were the plugs—the state-breds, the cheap claimers, the 0-for-23 maidens. Hawthorne became a bargain bin, a bazaar of $5,000 claiming races for horses who had never won three times in their lives and allowances for "Ill.-breds," an apt abbreviation for state-bred horses who had won only once. These animals made careers out of losing. It was impossible to guess which one was about to change its ways, but if you could, by some synthesis of numerology, astrology, biorhythms, and interspecies communication, the payoffs were stratospheric. Exactas and Pick Threes paid $2,000. Superfectas paid $30,000, a number that blinked on the monitors like a slot machine jackpot, showing everyone that Hawthorne was just as generous as the riverboats.

For the serious handicapper whose game was singling out the best horse and betting it to win, November was a miserable month. One Saturday, I found Rob slumped forward over his table in the Handicapping Center, shaking his head. He'd dropped a dime that day—$1,000.

"I don't understand," he said, "how you can be on top of the world one week, then feel like a complete idiot a week later."

"That's how this game is," I said, trying to console him. "You just have to win enough during the hot streaks to get you through the cold streaks."

"I guess."

"I think we need a new strategy."

I told Rob about a man I'd met in the clubhouse. He'd hit an enormous Pick Three by playing "All"—every horse—in the middle leg. The ticket cost him $180, but when a long shot won the second race, he collected ten times his investment.

"When the races are this unpredictable, betting strategy is as important as handicapping," I argued. "You're willing to spend $100 or $200 on a race, so you can just buy up all the possible winners and take money from people who can only spend two bucks or five bucks on a race. That's why they call big bettors whales—'cause they eat up all the little fish."

"Is that your new strategy?" he challenged me.

The next day, I sequestered myself in the clubhouse, where I didn't know anyone. I didn't want anyone watching me, in case this failed. The second race was for $4,000 claimers, just the sort of unhandicappable hoo flung that was producing those Vegas payouts. The night before, I'd written out a string of trifecta tickets, focusing on three of the twelve horses in the field. One of them had to win, but I used seven horses in the second spot and everybody in the third spot—you never knew what was going to happen back there, because some jockeys stopped whipping their mounts when they realized a win was impossible, just in the interest of animal welfare. My play covered 180 combinations out of a possible 1,220. At one dollar per ticket, plus a two-dollar trifecta box on my three "key" horses and twenty-five-dollar win bets on the favorites, it was a $242 wager, the most money I'd ever spent on a single horse race.

I wasn't even nervous. Part of my calm was due to the unreal enormity of the bet, which was so far outside my comfort envelope that I hadn't developed the emotional grammar to regret it. A $100 loss would have stung me worse. But a bigger part was the feeling that I'd covered every likely outcome. I thought I had the race wired. And I did. As I watched on a big-screen television (I was feeling too cool to step outside and watch the race live), Ragin' Raven, one of my key horses, slipped away in the stretch. A backup horse finished second, and an 18–1 shot came in third, validating my decision to hit "All." The only suspenseful moment was waiting for the payoff. When "$1,420" unspooled on the tote board, I had a signer, my first of the year. As I went to the window, I felt like I was cashing a stock dividend, not a lottery ticket. I hadn't scored a great handicapping coup. I'd used cash to buy myself a position that most other bettors couldn't afford. I filled out the tax form, tipped the clerk ten bucks, then carried the carbon to the Handicapping Center and slapped it down in front of Rob.

"My new strategy," I said.

That was my only signer. The following weekend, I tried another big trifecta—and then watched $120 flee to more fortunate wallets when the apprentice jockey on my key horse stood up on his mount after allowing a rival to cut him off on the backstretch. I wrote "BRING ME THE HEAD OF IRAM DIEGO" on my *Form* and stopped betting on trifectas, or on horses ridden by Iram Diego. My big shooter act only worked once. My bankroll just wasn't big enough to suck up the losses.

Rob dealt with the chaos on the track by wisely cutting his maximum bets down to $100 or $150, and—unwisely, so Scott believed—betting on out-of-town tracks. Scott never bet on a race unless he himself had made speed figures on the horses, so he ignored the action from Golden Gate Fields and the Fair Grounds playing on the televisions above his head. Not all the gamblers in the center were so disciplined. Big Steve was a tall, bearded fifty-year-old celebrating his layoff from a glass factory by spending his unemployment check on every race in Chicago, San Francisco, and New Orleans.

Frustrated with Hawthorne, Rob started betting as prolifically as Big Steve. He didn't use a program. He watched the post parade, picked the friskiest-looking horse, and bet five or ten bucks on it.

"Body language," he explained. "I just bet on the horse with the best body language."

Although Rob hit an $800 trifecta this way, Scott didn't approve. Big Steve was undoing everything he'd taught his star pupil.

"I'm worried that Steve's starting to influence him," Scott confided to me. "He's making a lot of bets he shouldn't be making."

Finally, Scott tried to reclaim his role as mentor by showing up Big Steve during one of the Saturday handicapping classes. In front of a crowded room, he zinged Steve for wasting his money on dumb bets.

"I'm a winner the last two days," Steve defended himself.

"Well, great," Scott shot back. "That makes up for the last thirty years."

# 19

## Bob the Brain's Big Score

fter Thanksgiving, Hawthorne gave us a chance to get our money
back. The track held another handicapping contest, the fall edition
of the tournament they'd sponsored on Derby weekend. Once again,
there was $5,000 for the winner, and for the top four finishers, a trip to
the $100,000 Daily Racing Form National Handicapping Champi-
onships in Las Vegas. For weeks, it was the talk of the track. Whenever
I ran into a regular, he asked me the same question: "You playin' in the
contest?" I'd sat out the spring contest, but I put down $100 to enter
this one, because everyone I knew was playing: Creighton, Terry, the
Stat Man, Bob the Brain, Primus Anthony, Blond Jimmy. Scott was
running it. Rob couldn't enter because he was a track employee, but he
was acting as private counsel to his friend Ed, a construction worker
from the East Side of Chicago.

The three-day contest started the Friday after Thanksgiving, so
Kate and I drove directly to the track from my father's house in Michi-
gan, where I'd spent the entire holiday evening handicapping, while
Kate and everyone else watched movies.

When I got to Hawthorne, my name was inked on a wipe-away
scoreboard, along with 150 others. Primus Anthony was sitting by the
window, right behind the buffet, with ten pastries stacked on his plate.

Bob the Brain seemed nomadic, like a deer. He roamed the room with a stack of papers balanced in the crook of his arm, always tilting his head back to gaze at a monitor through his slipping glasses. Creighton was hunched over a long-reserved table inside the Handicapping Center.

The contest went like this: every day, we bet an imaginary two dollars to win and place on a horse in races two, three, four, five, six, and seven. Eighteen races in all. Whoever accumulated the most money was the winner. There was one catch: you couldn't collect more than forty dollars to win or twenty dollars to place on a single horse. This was to prevent anyone from winning the contest with a single lucky long shot, which happened in one of the very first handicapping contests, the 1997 Sports Haven Challenge, in New Haven, Connecticut. On the final race, the Hutcheson Stakes from Gulfstream Park, nineteen desperate contestants played Frisk Me Now at 105–1. When Frisk Me Now swooped past two exhausted speedballs in the stretch, programs flew through the air, while men getting their first fix of religion that Sunday cried, "Hallelujah! There is a God!" Those nineteen guys ended up filling the top nineteen spots, changing the rules of contests forever, because if they'd been playing competently all weekend, they wouldn't have needed a 105–1 shot to get ahead. Of course, it's possible to beat the races with one huge payout a year, and some guys do. But, "These are handicapping contests, not betting contests," said Noel Michaels, the *Daily Racing Form* reporter who wrote the *Handicapping Contest Handbook*. "To me, every day you go to the track is a betting contest."

I'd brought a copy of Michaels's book with me, and I planned to follow his advice from the "Strategy" section: "Generally speaking, you can't win tournaments by betting horses in the odds range below 5–1."

On that Friday, though, favorites won the first five races: Biangood was 9–5, Timely Ending was 3–5, Majesty's Lass was 2–5, Tis Me was 4–5, and Jimmy's Saber was 6–5. It was a great day, if you liked the taste of chalk. The track was making this too easy. Playing the horses wasn't supposed to be one of those self-esteem boosting "new games" where everyone's a winner. It was supposed to be about screwing your neighbor. After every race, the crowd migrated to the scoreboard to see girls in green sport shirts ink in the new standings. It reminded me of election night at a county courthouse, with serious faces watching the clerk post results from every precinct. Going into the seventh race, I was 0-for-5, but I wasn't worried. The leader, who'd played every favorite, had only $35.80. A single long shot could bump anyone from serf to monarch.

In the seventh, I played Low Flyin' Jones, a 7–1 first-time starter. He never got out of tenth place. At the front of the pack, the race looked to be as worthless as all the rest. Luga, a deserving 4–5 favorite, dueled for the lead down the stretch and seemed ready to take over, but his determination failed, as so often happens with maidens, and his challenger, the 25–1 shot Quick to Fight, was suddenly alone in front.

"There's the bomber!" someone shouted, hailing the triumph of a long shot as Quick to Fight's payoffs—$53 to win, $13.40 to place— lit up on the tote board. "Who had that one?"

Bob the Brain had that one.

"I got it!" he shouted, scurrying across the room toward the tote board to see if anyone else had caught the long shot. I chased after him.

"How'd you get that horse?" I demanded.

Bob whipped open his *Form* to race seven. Quick to Fight's record—every horse's record—was grafittied over with Bob's personal runes: numbers, circles, lines, and arrows.

"The horse had three lifetime races and had improved in each race," Bob blurted, in his usual math-speak. "That's never a bad thing. He comes from a nondescript stable, but he was 5–1 in his debut, so he must have shown some promise. He finished ninth in that race, then sixth in a maiden claimer. After that, he was sold privately. His new trainer entered him in a maiden special weight race, where his speed figure improved from a 38 to a 48, according to my calculations, so he was getting better with each race. In the race where he ran the 48, he had trouble on the turn, dropping from seven lengths to thirteen lengths behind. Then he made a very sharp move gaining nine lengths into the wind. He also had a change to a better jockey for this race."

I hadn't noticed any of this. That's why my score was still zero dollars.

"I thought there were four good horses in the race: Quick to Fight, Air Academy, Lunar Power, and Luga. Quick to Fight was actually my third choice, but at 25–1, he was the best price in the race."

Bob had purchased two $100 entries (players were allowed up to three), so he put Luga on his favorite card, where he was playing all the short-priced horses, and Quick to Fight on his long-shot card. Quick to Fight made the long-shot card worth sixty-three dollars, putting Bob in ninth place. He would have made the favorite card worth $82.40, good enough for the lead.

"I should have put him on my favorite card," Bob moaned. "It was a tactical error, out of arrogance. I thought, 'Nobody wants to bet this horse.'"

Actually, nearly a dozen people had bet him. Quick to Fight was worth more than the first five winners combined, so all his backers went to the top of the standings. Bob was alarmed when he saw the name of the new leader: Steven Walker.

U

Every serious horseplayer in America knew the name Steven Walker. In 2000 Walker won the first DRF National Handicapping Championships at the MGM Grand in Las Vegas. His picture was in the *Handicapping Contest Handbook* and in ads for Bloodstock Research Information Services, the company that produced the racing programs Walker used in his victory. Walker was the only man who qualified for all four finals in Las Vegas, and now he flew around the country on his $100,000 winnings, trying to get into a fifth. Hawthorne was his tenth qualifier; he'd used up all his vacation time and more than all of his wife's patience, and the year was nearly over. He had to win.

Walker, an environmental engineer from Lincoln, Nebraska, was Bob's opposite in almost every way. Towheaded, rural, reserved, a man with a job and a family (although he would file for divorce almost immediately after the Hawthorne contest, explaining, "My wife can't stand horse racing . . . and this is just something I love to do"), Walker had the smooth-faced, well-groomed look of the weekend player, which was what he was, most of the time. Bob, on the other hand, was a voluble urban Jewish bachelor who drove a cab when the long shots weren't coming in and was at the track every afternoon when they were. A racetrack lifer who resented this I'll-just-bet-twenty-dollars-to-win-because-I-can't-gamble-the-college-fund dilettante invading his turf. Bob had given his entire existence to the track. Steven Walker had only given it his Saturday afternoons.

$$\cup$$

That night, Bob handicapped until four thirty in the morning. He'd noticed that horses with inside trips were winning, so he scoured the *Form* for speedy horses in the one, two, or three posts. The next day, in the Handicapping Center, he slammed his papers onto a table and let loose with a cry of injustice.

"Of all the people to be in this tournament, Steven Walker has to be here!" he shouted at the room. "My luck that Steven Walker has to come qualify!"

Scott McMannis's wife, Wendy, turned around when she heard that.

"Do you know who Steven Walker is?" Wendy asked.

Bob had never seen his picture.

"Who?"

Wendy pointed at the blond man in the seat next to Bob's. Bob shook hands with Steven Walker. They shared a table for the rest of the afternoon, but they never discussed the races. This was poker.

For Bob, Saturday was just as good as Friday. In the fourth race, he hit a 5–1 shot, Go Jesse Tyler. In the sixth, he loved Glint Eastward. Glint Eastward was coming off a bad trip (he'd been pulled up by the trifecta-destroying Iram Diego) and figured to run better if he didn't get into a traffic jam. But the horse was only 4–1, so

Bob went with his second choice, Stolen Honor, a 20–1 shot who'd run impressive speed figures in months past and seemed to be approaching his peak again.

In his essay "Self-Reliance," Ralph Waldo Emerson wrote, "Whoso would be a man must also be a non-conformist." Emerson didn't know it, but he had discovered the secret of beating the races. Glint Eastward got his usual lousy ride to finish fifth. Stolen Honor, breaking from the one post, ran the entire race on the rail and steamed through the pack to win by three lengths. Bob the Brain added $59.20 to his card. His fists did a jig as watched the clerk add the numbers to his total. But his mouth gaped as though he'd been punched when she carried the betting slips to the end of the scoreboard and wrote in $59.20 next to the name Steven Walker. Walker had also noticed that horses on the rail were running well. "How can I win against this guy?" Bob thought. Bob needed the money so badly, too. He had had a horrible year at the track, and he was hacking that cab every weekend just to scrape together enough money for small bets. With the $5,000 first prize, he could pay back rent to his roommate and still have the seed of a bankroll.

Again, Bob handicapped until the wee hours and showed up at Hawthorne unshaven, uncombed, and untucked. A second straight all-nighter would have left anyone looking disheveled. But Bob usually looked disheveled, so it was hard to tell how much ten hours of hand-icapping had taken out of him.

It didn't blur his betting skills. In the second race, Bob liked the 1 horse, Chile' File', who was 8–5, and the 2 horse, Robins Wish, who was 7–1. It was an easy choice. When Robins Wish won by five, Bob was within a few dollars of Walker.

Now that he was near the top of the board, Bob's strategy changed. He no longer had to stab at long shots to vault past the other contestants. He needed to play conservatively, to protect his position. With five races left, he couldn't pass up a good chalk, because if it won, and the other leaders had it, he might slip out of contention. So in race three, he went with Spectaculareleganz, at 2–1. She finished second, giving him $4.20.

"I knew if the right long shot came in, I'd play him," he said afterward. "I was concentrating on the best horse, hoping to shut everybody out."

In the fourth race, Bob played another favorite, Spirited Maiden. Walker took Curious Conundrum. Spirited Maiden stalked the leader all the way around the track, then galloped away to win. Curious Conundrum was forced wide on the first turn, crowded on the backstretch, and couldn't rally. For the first time in three days, Bob was alone with the lead.

It didn't last. Walker picked the winner of race five, putting Bob three dollars behind, "going into the race I liked least on the card," he said. As the tote board ticked down the minutes until the sixth race, Bob analyzed the odds. He calculated. Somers Tour was the best horse, but he was only 4–5. Still, if he passed up Somers Tour and Walker used him, he might end up ten dollars behind going into the final race, which would have been like trailing four lengths with fifty yards to the wire. Bob took Somers Tour "as a defensive move." The filly placed, paying $2.80, but Bob slid back into the third place, by twenty cents, because a third contender, Gloria Slivensky, had taken the 4–1 winner.

With five minutes to race seven, the horses were on the track, and Bob was standing in front of a monitor in a slumping posture that made him look as though he were sitting on the edge of a barstool. He stared at the sheaf of papers balanced on his arm. Then he stared at the odds. The superior horse was Ft. Mann. But Ft. Mann was the 2–1 favorite. If I like Ft. Mann, Bob thought, then Walker probably likes him, too.

"For me to win the tournament, I would have had to come up with a horse other than the horse the people ahead of me picked," he recalled. "Since Steven Walker is a good handicapper, I assume he took the best horse, Ft. Mann. I couldn't take Ft. Mann. That would be a terrible situation if we both took the same horse. The positions wouldn't change."

So Bob took the second-best horse and hoped that, on that Sunday afternoon, she would run the race of her life.

"I put Glittering Racket on my ticket," he said, "and I prayed."

Let Bob narrate the race:

"Glittering Racket battled hard to get the lead. She took a slight lead. Then who should come up the rail but Ft. Mann! Then Glittering Racket's jockey, Liz Morris, as if I was talking to her, the horse drifted in and cut off Ft. Mann. Ft. Mann went around and wore down Glittering Racket."

Glittering Racket finished second. But her $5.40 to place wasn't nearly as much as Ft. Mann paid to win and place. Dejected, Bob went to the washroom. Then, as he walked back toward the scoreboard to wait for the final totals, he spotted Walker standing in the doorway of the Handicapping Center.

"Who'd you have?" Bob asked.

"I took the entry," Walker said.

The entry—Rathleen and Di's Delight, running as a single betting interest—had finished third and fifth. Walker had been shut out. So had Gloria Slivensky.

Bob took a victory lap around the Handicapping Center, stopping at every table by someone who wanted to shake his hand. The room was full of his people: guys in baseball caps and slouchy jeans, guys who scribbled notes on *Racing Forms* with stubby pencils, guys who stretched their unemployment checks to cover food, rent, and gambling money. They knew Bob had devoted himself to the horses, and they were proud to see one of their own win.

Bob ended the weekend up eight grand—$5,000 for winning the contest and $3,000 for betting on his horses.

"It's not the kind of money I need to do what I want to do," he said. "I'm not going to increase my bets a lot, but it's a nice way to give myself a boost after a horrible year."

Steven Walker got his trip to the National Handicapping Championships at Bally's Las Vegas, where he once again faced Bob the Brain, along with 250 other qualifiers from all over North America. Bob considered himself a 40–1 shot to win the January tournament. Since Chicago has no winter racing, he'd have to handicap unfamiliar tracks. And indeed, he finished in the middle of the pack, about the same place as Steven Walker.

# 20

# The One-Eyed Man Is King

Just as at Arlington, I didn't start winning again until I was so close to the bone I had no other choice. "Sometimes," a man once told me, "you've got to go all the way to the bottom before you can start going back up."

You have to go to jail to find Jesus. You have to wake up behind the bus station with a fresh wound on your scalp before you stop drinking. You have to host *GE Theater* before you realize that maybe your future is in politics, not show business. The two-ton clock struck my hour of desperation on the same day Bob the Brain won the handicapping contest. If VH1 did a series on gamblers called *Behind the Money*, this would have been the moment when the narrator intoned, "After throwing away thousands of dollars on trifectas, Daily Doubles, Pick Sixes, Pick Threes, and horses so lame and sweaty they would be rejected for a petting zoo, our hero finally hit rock bottom . . . with a show bet."

Most cruelly of all, I was let down by my old friend Pennington Gap, my 5–1, my Mr. October. Pennington Gap was the most free-wheeling speedball in the Midwest. At Churchill Downs, at Turfway Park, at Arlington, he bolted from the gate like a greyhound chasing a squirrel off the track. Always the rabbit, Pennington Gap dashed two or three lengths ahead of the field, reducing every race to a contest between the limits of his stamina and the finish wire. Which would arrive first? In his last race, the finish wire. More often, his legs turned to fire hoses in the stretch, but he sometimes hung on for second or third.

In the ninth race, on the last day of November, Pennington Gap was the 9–5 chalk, but he wasn't taking a lot of action in the show pool. I decided to throw $120 into that wishing well. Rob followed my lead, laying down $200. He had forgiven me for Red River Aggie, plus he liked big show bets, because they racked up points on his Hawthorne Rewards Club card. Every dollar was worth two points, and every 10,000 points was worth a $200 rebate. Rob had already collected several rebate vouchers, which he'd stashed in a drawer as a hedge against bankruptcy.

Check your almanac, and you'll see that the ninth race at Hawthorne always falls after sundown on November 30. Rob and I watched it from the chilly gloaming of the deserted third deck. From that vantage, the track looked like a slot car diorama. Pennington Gap cut a perfect curve, running a lonely breakaway ten yards ahead of a rabble of pursuers. Dust puffed from his hooves in the cold, dry air. "We got this one," I thought, as he turned the corner into the stretch.

Then Pennington Gap hit the wall. His forelegs swam through unseen waters, and his stride clipped from a gallop to a canter. When he faded to third, I thought our money was still safe, but then two more jockeys whipped their mounts past his gasping carcass. Rob scowled. He never let me tout him again. But that bad tip on Pennington Gap seemed an appropriate bookend to November. It had been a gloomy month—a gray curtain had been drawn across the sun, the night was rising higher and higher against both ends of the day, the city was a gray stone, too cold to touch without gloves. And I had lost all the money left over from Arlington, all the money I'd won in October, and most of my last bank withdrawal. I'd flicked away $120 on Pennington Gap because I was desperate and frustrated, as promiscuous as a tavern floozy who's been let down so many times she no longer expects a thing from the losers she takes home.

I had to do something different. I couldn't afford to keep losing. Over the Monday and Tuesday break, I decided to revive a strategy I'd tried a few winters before: bet only when there's a false favorite in the race, a horse who can't win, but is sucking up so much money that it creates monster overlays on the rest of the field. From a mathematical standpoint, it made a lot of sense. The takeout is 17 percent. Suppose you're convinced that Guysnamedfrank, an even-money shot, has no chance to win. He's an eternal second-place maiden or he's dropping from $20,000 to $5,000, which suggests he's a lame-o the trainer is trying to pawn off on some chump. At 1–1, Guysnamedfrank is soaking up 41.5 percent of the betting money. Remove him from contention, and you've beaten the takeout. The odds are in your favor. The Pro had told me that a race with a false favorite is the best time to bet a lot of money. If it's the best time, why not make it the *only* time? Maybe it would work. Nothing else had.

That Wednesday, I secreted myself on the second floor of the grandstand, the most deserted quarter of the track, with sloping rows of brown stadium seats as empty as an upper deck overlooking a last-place baseball team. I sat behind a wood-paneled pillar, so no one would spot me and stop to chat. I wanted to commune with the tote board in perfect solitude, watching for false favorites as patiently as a hunter watches for deer.

The first day, I didn't spot one, so I bet a few small exactas to pass the time. But on Thursday, before the eighth race, the tote board called out to me. Remember the movie *L.A. Story*, where Steve Martin is a loser weatherman who gets messages from a freeway sign? I was getting a message from the Hawthorne tote board. It was telling me, "Go get it, kid."

The favorite, Lady Dealer, was 6–5, but to me, she was equine trash. The eighth was an allowance contest for horses who had never won a race other than a maiden or a claimer. Lady Dealer had run more than forty times, so you'd think she might have accomplished more than that. Betting on her would have been like betting on a twenty-one-year-old in a high school quiz bowl match. You'd think the lunkhead would have graduated already. But Lady Dealer always came close, so my generous fellow citizens of the Hawthorne Nation decided she was due. I turned, instead, to Rocket Royale. Rocket Royale had run only three times. In his last start, he'd broken his maiden in a $10,000 claiming race, but he was much classier than he appeared on paper: the horse he'd beaten, Charming Bid, had returned to win a maiden special weight race. That wasn't mentioned in the *Form*, though, so Rocket Royale was 8–1. I bet forty dollars, plus twenty dollars on a lesser contender named Miss Zebulon, just in case, and sat down to watch a race that was more thrilling than the Indy 500, the Tour de France, and the America's Cup, all wrapped up into one big blur of speed.

Rocket Royale sprinted to the front of the herd on his fresh young legs, taunting the field with the sight of his tail. Coming into the homestretch, he led by two lengths. Then a plugger named Bailar rushed forward from last place to investigate what was going on at the front of the pack. She drew alongside Rocket Royale in front of the tote board and, for a moment, their heads seesawed back and forth in what track announcer Peter Galassi liked to call "a ding-dong battle for the lead." I clutched my binoculars and clenched my teeth. Bailar must have been exhausted by her rally. Either that, or she was a hangin' pig (a horse who challenges the leader but never passes him). Rocket Royale suddenly sling-shotted forward along the rail. Only the bravest horses fight back—Cigar did it at the Dubai World Cup, Beamer'n Glick did it at Arlington, and now Rocket Royale was doing it at Hawthorne. As he dug in, his lungs were bellows, his hooves dug divots, and he surged to win by over a length, putting $380 on my voucher.

Every afternoon, on my way into the track, I stopped to review the day's card with Dino, the parking attendant who often took tips from the owners he waved through to the exclusive Lexus/SUV Lot. Usually I was just another benighted money-sieve begging for a winner, but that Friday, I finally had some bragging rights.

"Dino!" I told him. "You see that horse in the eighth yesterday? Eight-to-one! And I had him for forty bucks!"

"Yeah?" Dino stashed a stack of bills in the pocket of his bib and held out his fingerless glove. We clasped hands.

"Who you like today?" he asked.

It wasn't always a matter of spotting a comer like Rocket Royale. In most cases, it was enough to identify a bad horse and bet around him. I knew, even before I went to the track on the lucky thirteenth of December, that Starship Garnet would be the favorite in the ninth. I also knew she would lose. She had been the favorite in her last four races, and she had lost every one. I didn't know who was going to win, but if Starship Garnet sucked up all the cash, I wouldn't need to know. The prices on her rivals would be so fat I could lay bets all over the board and still make a profit.

I hid in my seat all afternoon, waiting for the ninth. As secretive as I was, Creighton managed to find me. When we ran into each other, in front of a bank of betting machines, he confessed that he had been feeling ill. Doctors had found a spot on his lung, and he was going in for tests.

"If it's cancer, I don't want 'em to do nothing for me," he insisted. "I'm just going to ask 'em to make me comfortable."

I thought about a day we'd spent together back in the spring. We'd been leaning over the balcony on the first warm, bright day of the year, watching the horses plod by in post parade.

"I wish I could have a hundred years of this game," Creighton had said then. Now he told me, "I'll be able to go with no regrets. I got to do what I wanted with my life, which was play the horses. I found out I couldn't make a living at it, but still, I got to be here every day."

(Creighton's lung turned out to be healthy, and the only medical crisis he suffered all winter was the loss of his eleven remaining teeth.)

When the ninth race finally arrived, Starship Garnet opened at 9–5. For twenty minutes, I hawkeyed the tote board, charting the odds on the three horses likely to beat her. With five minutes to go in the betting, Starship Garnet was 7–5. That was worth getting up for. I lingered in the wide concourse between the seats and the betting machines, my voucher clenched between my fingers. The odds were always volatile in the last five minutes, so I wanted to bet at the last second. As the horses jogged toward the starting gate, Fashionable Caton was 3–1, Flower Cart was 9–2, and Jewelia was 8–1. Those prices were good enough, so I struck: thirty dollars on Fashionable Caton, twenty dollars on Flower Cart, fifteen dollars on Jewelia. They ran 1-2-3. As the *Racing Form* would later report, "Starship Garnet was not a factor." I won $126. A sixty-one-dollar profit wasn't much, and yeah, I could have made more by betting the exacta and the trifecta, but I never complained about a winning day.

U

Over the next week, I bet five races and I won them all. Often, I had to wait until the last race and had to play two or three horses, but I waited, and I won. Then, that Saturday, I didn't bet at all. I sat quietly in my seat, because the tote board didn't move me. After a frantic, frustrating year, I had finally arrived at a state of tranquility. I had to take back what I'd told Scott about Beamer'n Glick. That fifty-dollar bet hadn't made me a horseplayer. The day I *didn't* bet was the day I truly stopped being a gambler, and became a horseplayer. There it was: learning the game had nothing to do with handicapping insights. It was all about licking the Fear of Regret, after you'd been beaten up and cleaned out by the pari-mutuel machine so many times that you finally arrived at an emotional place that allowed you to tell the track, "I don't need to bet. I've lost hundreds of races. I'm jaded. Give me a race I can get excited about, a race where the odds favor *me*, or the wallet stays shut."

Now, at last, I'd discovered the dark heart and soul of the game: it wasn't about predicting the behavior of the horses. It was about predicting the behavior of the other gamblers and exploiting their mistakes. As a sixty-five-year veteran of pari-mutuel combat once put it, "You're not playing horses, you're playing *people*. When was the last time you went to cash a ticket and saw a *horse* behind the window?" It was true. I was no longer looking for good horses. I was looking for good betting situations. And when I was only betting against false favorites, I didn't have to be smart—the rest of the crowd had to be dumb. And that happened a lot more often.

It was all about taking money from the dumb and the desperate, in all their weakness and ignorance. It was no different from any other business, where the goal was to sell an $18,000 car for $20,000, or to pay a worker twelve dollars an hour when he was worth fourteen dollars. No wonder a business professor was the best horseplayer I knew. Scott had once told me, "Whenever I'm losing confidence, I walk around on the first floor and ask myself, 'You can't beat these people?'"

When I told Scott what I'd learned, he said he'd been trying to teach me that for months, but I hadn't listened.

"If you'd come to all the classes, you would have figured that out a long time ago. But I always knew you were stubborn."

"I am stubborn," I said. "But I had to find out for myself that everything you were trying to tell me was right."

I could not have learned to play the horses by sitting in a handicapping class any more than I could have learned to hit a baseball by reading a book about Ted Williams. I had to whiff a thousand pitches before I found my stroke.

Gambling was the best self-improvement project I'd ever undertaken. I had met Andrew Beyer's challenge. I had made a serious attempt to beat the races, and I had learned that yes, it could be done, but only with the kind of single-minded devotion that one would apply to training for the Mr. Universe competition or memorizing the New Testament in ancient Greek. I had never in my life applied so much focus, so much self-discipline to any endeavor. If you're looking to spend a year of your life and several thousand dollars on a personal-growth experience, going to the track is every bit as worthwhile as a hiking expedition in Peru.

Even so, I hadn't learned perfectly. One frantic day, I threw away $200. On some races, I correctly deduced that the favorite was a pig, a chronic loser, but I couldn't pick the winner. At the end of that month, I had a profit of thirty dollars. But I guarantee you, that's more than most horseplayers won that December. And it sure as hell beat losing.

U

I stopped going to the track regularly around Christmas. How could a man focus on gambling when there were distractions like shopping for gifts and spending time with his family? But I showed up on the final day of the meet, the fourth of January. As I hunched through the owners and trainers lot, the stainless-steel wind slipped between my baseball cap and my upturned collar, chilling my ears to a bright scarlet. I looked up, past the concrete barrier, and saw a pixel of red against the bricks at the bottom of the grandstand ramp. My pace quickened until my line of sight cleared the barrier, and I saw that I was looking at a red cap, snug on the head of a man. The blind man.

"Lewis!" I shouted, once I was within earshot. "Lewis, it's Ted. Remember me?"

"Taaid . . . you're the one who took my picture."

"I didn't take your picture," I said. "I wrote about you. Where have you been all year?"

"I was in the hospital. They put a pacemaker in my heart."

I sorted through my wallet for a fin. When I found one, I stuffed it in his cup.

"I thought you got banned," I said.

"No. I was in the hospital. It's good to hear your voice again, Taaid."

"It's good to see you, Lewis."

I started up the ramp, but then I caught myself. "What's the Daily Double today?" I asked.

"Daily Double's 1-3," he said.

"1-3?"

"I b'lieve that's it."

"Thanks," I said, and then I jogged toward the gate. I didn't want to miss the first race.

# A Racetrack Glossary

**across the board:** to win, place, and show ("Gimme 5 across on the 8" means betting the 8 to win, place, and show)

**action:** the amount of betting money laid on a horse (as in, "This horse is 8–5—he's getting a ton of action")

**action bet:** a bet on a horse who doesn't have a strong chance of winning, but whose odds make him worth a small investment

**allowance race:** a race in which horses are not for sale. Usually it is restricted to horses who have not won a certain number of races in their lifetimes.

**apron:** the area between the grandstand and the track

**baby race:** a race for two-year-olds

**betting line:** a handicapper's estimation of each horse's fair odds

**bias:** a track condition favoring a particular post position or running style

**bomber:** a long shot

**bounce:** to run a poor race immediately after a taxing win

**box:** to bet on two or more horses to finish in any order in the exacta or trifecta

**bridge jumper:** a gambler who places a five- or six-figure show bet. Some people suspect bridge jumpers are laundering drug money. When a bridge jumper's horse runs out, the show prices on the winners are usually in double figures.

**broke his maiden:** won his first race

**bubble-gum ass:** a bettor who can remain seated all day without getting up to bet

**bucket shop:** a bookie joint

**bug:** an apprentice jockey's weight allowance, so called because there's an asterisk next to his horse's assigned weight in the *Form*

**bullet workout:** the fastest workout of the day at a particular distance (as in, "Golden Palm worked a bullet on Thursday—three furlongs in thirty-five and three")

**card:** a day's races

**chalk:** the betting favorite

**chalk-eater:** a bettor who plays favorites

**chalky:** a day when a lot of favorites are winning

**cheap:** a slow horse, or a race full of slow horses

**choking point:** a betting level beyond which a gambler's judgment is impaired

**claimer:** a horse who runs in claiming races

**claiming race:** a race in which every horse is on sale for a specified price

**closer:** a horse who comes from far behind

**"Come on with the 2":** the proper form of encouragement for a horse you've got money on. Horses are referred to by program number, never by name.

**dead on the board:** when a horse isn't being bet

**Daily Double:** or the Double, a wager requiring a bettor to pick the winners of the first two races

**The *Daily Racing Form*:** or the *Form*, a publication that lists the records of every horse running on a particular day

**dime:** a thousand dollars

**dutch:** to bet on two or more horses to win

**dope out:** identify the likely winner

**exotic wagering:** any multiple-horse bet, including the Daily Double, Pick Three, Pick Four, Pick Six, exacta, trifecta, or superfecta

**fin:** a five-dollar bill

**flat board:** when the odds of the betting favorites are close together

**fraction:** a horse's quarter mile and half mile split time

**gapper:** a gift from a winning gambler to a loser

**gate to wire:** all the way around the track (as in, "That horse led from gate to wire")

**get a price:** to get good odds on a horse

**gimmicks:** see *exotic wagering*

**hammer:** to place a big bet (as in, "The 8 just went from 3–1 to 9–5—somebody musta' hammered that horse")

**handicap:** to attempt to dope out (identify) the winner of a race

**hangin' pig:** a horse who challenges the leader but never passes him

**hole:** a horse's post position (as in, "Tricky Clearance is starting from the twelve hole")

**in the money:** a horse who comes in first, second, or third

**infield:** the area within the racetrack

**inside:** the part of the track closest to the rail

**key:** to bet a horse on top of two or more horses in the trifecta

**maiden:** a horse who has never won

**morning line:** the track handicapper's assessment of how the public will bet, it is printed in the program (as in, "He's 5–2 on the morning line")

**nickel:** a $5,000 claiming tag

**numbers players:** gamblers who bet the same numbers, race after race

**OTB:** an offtrack betting parlor, where gamblers can wager on televised races

**odds drops:** when a horse's odds shorten dramatically after the race begins, as the tote calculates last-second bets

**out of the clouds:** far back in the field (as in, "That horse came from out of the clouds to win")

**overlay:** an underbet horse

**pace:** the quarter-mile and half-mile times (as in, "Twenty-one and four— that's a hot pace")

**paddock:** the area where the horses are saddled before a race

**pari-mutuel:** a wagering system in which the odds are determined by the money bet on each horse. This term comes from a French phrase meaning "among ourselves" and is used in all American racing.

**past performance:** a set of statistics showing the records of the horses running that day. It is found in the track program or the *Daily Racing Form*.

**past-posting:** placing a bet after the gate opens

**pig:** see *cheap*

**play:** to bet. Don't say, "I'm going to bet on Danger Crocodile." Say, "I'm gonna play the 7."

**popped:** out of money

**post:** the gate from which a horse starts (as in, "He's got the one post today, so he'll get an inside trip")

**post parade:** when the horses march before the grandstand before a race

**price:** the odds

**prime bet:** a large bet on a horse with good odds and a strong chance of winning

**quinella:** a bet requiring a gambler to pick the top two finishers, in either order

**rail:** the inside part of the track

**route:** a race one mile or longer

**run out:** to fail to finish in the top three

**saver:** an exacta bet with your win horse in second place, so you can get your money back if he loses

**schneid:** a losing streak (as in, "This is the horse who'll get me off the schneid")

**scratch:** cash

**seconditis:** a condition afflicting slow horses who challenge for the lead but never win

**short form:** an edition of the *Daily Racing Form* that features past performances for the home track and two other high-profile tracks. It sells for $3.50, as opposed to five dollars for the regular edition.

**shut out:** to arrive at the window too late to place a bet

**signer:** a win so large it has to be reported to the IRS

**simulcast:** a race broadcast from an out-of-town track

**single:** to use only one horse in a leg of the Daily Double, Pick Three, Pick Four, or Pick Six

**sitting chilly:** to pass a race when you're ahead for the day

**speed:** a horse who sets the pace

**speed figures:** statistical ratings of a horse's races that take into account whether the track was faster or slower than normal on that particular day

**sprint:** a race under a mile

**stakes race:** the most prestigious type of race, with the biggest purse. The most lucrative are graded stakes races, classified as Grade I, Grade II, or Grade III.

**stalker:** a horse who runs just behind the leaders

**stooper:** someone who searches the floor of a racetrack, looking for winning tickets thrown out by mistake

**sucker horse:** a horse who repeatedly finishes second, leading bettors to believe it's set for a winning effort

**superfecta:** or the super, a wager requiring bettors to pick the top four finishers in a race

**tapped:** out of money

**tip sheet:** a publication offering selections for each race

**tote board:** an electronic scoreboard on which the odds are displayed

**trifecta:** or the tri, a wager requiring a bettor to pick the top three finishers in a race

**trip notes:** a narrative of how a horse ran his race, usually focusing on whether he ran into difficulties

**turf race:** a race run on grass

**two and two:** two dollars to win, two dollars to place

**undercard:** the races preceding the feature

**underlay:** an overbet horse

**whale:** a big bettor

**wheel:** to bet a horse on top of two or more horses in the exacta or Daily Double

**wire** (n.): the finish line

**wire** (v.): to lead all the way